# Praise
## Every

"Read this first sentence carefully: It's rare that the event that catalyzes an author to write a book occurs after the book is written, but that's the unlikely case with "Every Day (I Thank You)."

Do I have your attention? Good.

This is author Renato Wakim's second book, and as with his first work, "Why Not? A Memoir - Migration Journeys, Melodic Strides, and Quests for Meaning," he has a message for his readers. The world isn't a good place or a bad place; it's just a place. The goodness (or badness) comes from how we show up and choose to engage with it.

Entire cities could be built on the foundation stones of books that fall into the categories of self-help, self-actualization, individual leadership, and other prescriptive themes. Been there, read that, bought the t-shirt. But this book? It isn't prescriptive at all—it's *descriptive*, and that carries with it a world of difference.

Renato's book relies on his gifted skill as a storyteller and his personal life stories, which play out on the global stage, to show his readers why the points he makes in the book are worth thinking about. It most definitely is NOT yet another book about the ten things the reader can do to be healthier, happier, wealthier, more muscular, better looking, energetic, or competitive. It is none of those. In fact, it's interesting that those are all adjectives, and books that rely on that particular part-of-speech are legion. This book, on the other hand, is about adverbs. The author does not spend countless pages telling the reader what she or he should do to improve various aspects of their life; instead, he tells them *why*. The difference is profound.

The chapter titles alone are good giveaways: *For Harnessing the Higher Spheres of Music, Art, Science and Knowledge. For Choosing Your Leaders Wisely. For Adopting a Mindset of Patience and No Harm.* Those three, chosen at random, demonstrate the breadth, depth and richness of this work.

We are all members of a community, which means that our lives are interwoven with the lives of others. As a community, we care for each other, because that is the essence of what a community is, and why it forms the basis of civil society. So: Who should read "Every Day (I Thank You)"? Business leaders. Community leaders. Parents. Spouses. Honestly, anyone who cares about others—or wants to.

As for the catalytic event that caused Mr. Wakim to write the book, but that occurred after the book was written? You'll just have to read it, won't you?" — Steven Shepard

Professional author, photographer, audio producer and educator, Steven Shepard, PhD has written extensively throughout his life. He is the author, among several books and articles on a wide variety of topics, of the award winning "the Nation We Knew - How an Extraordinary Geophysical Event Reinvented America—and the World" as well as the creator of "The Natural Curiosity Project", a Podcast that is devoted to the idea that Curiosity leads to discovery, discovery leads to knowledge, knowledge leads to insight, and insight leads to understanding.

"Gratitude, the sheer theme of this book, is the return to the origin. It calls us to remember where we come from, to recognize the forces that sustain us, and to acknowledge our place within the broader network of life. It becomes a transformative force, guiding us back to our most fundamental connections with ourselves, each other, and the universe at large. Gratitude closes the loop in the cycle of giving and receiving, creating a continuous flow that strengthens relationships, builds communities, and fosters a sense of belonging and unity".
~ Every Day (I Thank You)

# Every Day (I Thank You)

Tales of Appreciation
for Hands,
Hearts, and
Minds

# Renato Wakim

ONION RIVER PRESS

Burlington, VT

Copyright © 2024 by Renato Wakim

All rights reserved. No part of this publication may be reproduced, distributed, or transmitted in any form or by any means, including photocopying, recording, or other electronic or mechanical methods, without the prior written permission of the publisher, except in the case of brief quotations embodied in critical reviews and certain other noncommercial uses permitted by copyright law.

Onion River Press
Burlington, VT 05401
info@onionriverpress.com
www.onionriverpress.com

ISBN: 978-1-957184-73-9

Library of Congress Control Number: 2024918041

Cover and book design: Process Process Process LLC

Book Editor: Rose Winters

With my love

for Jeritza,
who gave me my life

for Silvia,
who gave me
Catherine Bianca, Giana and Eric,
and my life back

# Contents

A Reflective Note on Rock Cairns and Their Symbolism vii

Prologue xi

Every Day (I Thank You)

1. For Cultivating Your Life with Kindness, Purpose and Joy 33
2. For Adopting a Mindset of Patience and No Harm 61
3. For Making the Extra Effort to Understand and Support Your Fellow Human Being 99
4. For Taking Care Of Yourself and for Caring For Those Next to You ~ And Beyond 119
5. For Harnessing the Higher Spheres of Music, Art, Science and Knowledge 151
6. For Choosing Your Leaders Wisely 177
7. For Embracing Your Planet the Same Way You Embrace Your Nation 207
8. For Going the Extra Mile Attempting to Capture What True Love Is 247
9. For Navigating the Nuances of Life and Death, War and Peace, Old and New, Rich and Poor, Black and White, Male and Female, Yin and Yang, and Everything in Between 275

Epilogue

Afterword

Acknowledgements—I

Acknowledgements—II

Bibliography

# A Reflective Note on Rock Cairns and Their Symbolism

OVERLAPPING EACH OTHER, CAIRNS, those deliberate stacks of stones found in various cultures around the world, serve as powerful symbols and have a multitude of meanings and purposes that transcend time and geography. From the ancient Mongolians to the mountain dwellers of South America, the practice of erecting cairns demonstrates a universal human inclination to mark our presence, memorialize our journeys, and communicate with both our contemporaries and future generations.

The symbolic richness of cairns is profound. They stand as beacons of guidance, helping travelers navigate through barren or complex landscapes, leading them to safety or towards significant locations. This practical application has spiritual undertones, as the path they mark is not only physical but can also represent the journey of life, guiding us through its complexities and challenges.

The use of cairns as a form of meditation or prayer altar adds another layer to their significance. Analogous to the writing of this book, each stone, as each chapter, can represent an intention, a thanksgiving, or a prayer for others, creating a tangible manifestation of human hopes, gratitude, and interconnectedness—the ultimate goal of this literary work. The act of stacking stones, with each addition mindful of balance and harmony, mirrors the human desire for stability and equilibrium in life.

Moreover, as memorials or burial monuments, cairns connect us with the past, serving as a physical reminder of those who have come before us. They honor the dead and ensure that their presence is felt long after they have departed this world, grounding us in our history and heritage.

The duality of strength and fragility inherent in cairns reflects the human condition. The strength lies in their endurance and the solidity of stone, while their fragility is evident in the balance of each stone upon the other, a metaphor for the delicate balance of life itself. This balance requires attention and care, much like the relationships and values we hold dear.

Cairns as landmarks, especially on mountain summits, symbolize achievement and the human spirit's resilience and desire to reach new heights. They mark a point of accomplishment, a moment of pause to reflect on the journey, celebrate the present, and anticipate the future.

In recent years, the indiscriminate building of cairns has brought some controversy to the initiative. While some areas such as national parks use rock cairns effectively, other parks don't build or maintain rock cairns and warn visitors to not rely on these rock piles to guide their hike. However, they all have the same rule: when coming across a cairn, it is suggested not to disturb it or tamper with it. If an intentional cairn is tampered with, then future visitors may become disoriented or even lost. The same works for building unauthorized cairns. Moving and disturbing rocks disturb the soil and make the area more prone to erosion while affecting fragile vegetation and micro ecosystems.

In their simplicity, cairns carry profound meanings—stability, creativity, self-worth, simplicity, strength, fragility, and peace. They remind us of our connection to the earth, to each other, and to the generations that will come after us. Like the chapters we write everyday to our life journey, as symbols of navigation, memory, and spiritual intent, cairns embody the complexity and beauty of the human experience, standing as silent witnesses to our passage through this world.

There are
two sides
to every story


And then
there is
the truth.

~ Anonymous


∞

# Prologue
## Why This Book

LET ME TELL YOU WHY I wrote this literary work. Like many, I like to think that I am a curious observer of the world around me and beyond. With an ever constant attempt to draw inspiration from the known—and the unknown—I group up compelling ideas and images of gratitude associated, like a prism, with stories of varied people who contribute genuinely to the world. By weaving together tales of both well-known figures and everyday heroes, I wanted to create a tapestry of human experience and engagement around the proposed themes throughout the chapters. Using an encompassing perspective to learning and change, I highlight the need for wonder and involvement that may resonate in meaningful initiatives. With that in mind, it is my goal that this perspective may inspire readers to recognize and appreciate the contributions of those around and beyond them, encouraging a sense of community and interconnectedness.

## What This Book is Not About

Zillions of things are there to be thankful for. Just think about that for a moment. It is not too difficult to find them if we dig a little deeper into our lives.

Consider the countless blessings that surround us. With a moment of reflection, we can uncover a plenitude of reasons to be grateful. Delving into our lives with a bit of introspection reveals a treasure trove of things to appreciate. In that sense, taking a moment to acknowledge gratitude, even in times of difficulty, allows us to embrace our humanity fully.

Gratitude is a powerful tool. Besides being thankful for everything we experience as value in our lives, it is an effective medium. It enables us to confront pain and adversity head-on when needed. By shifting our focus toward the blessings and gifts in our existence, we cultivate resilience and abundance amid the inevitable challenges. It is a mindset of gratitude that empowers us to navigate through moments of pain and scarcity with strength and perspective.

While manifesting gratitude in this book, it is important to highlight that this non-fiction work is not necessarily about being thankful to an abstract or divine entity for anything done or undone.

It is also not about being grateful for my existence nor for yours. Nor for my country or your country; nor for our planet or the stars. It is not about any kind of religious connection that prompts me to be thankful for the person that I am or for the person that I am not; nor for being thankful for the things that I have or for the things that I do not have. Nor does it relate to a metaphysical belief that some sort of Supreme Being guards us from evil and is merciful regarding our misdeeds.

No.

Although honestly considerate for all of the above, this book is an invitation to look around all things human; then, taking nothing for granted, recognize the effort of myriads of individuals. It starts with our own selves and those next to us.

A number of those mortals perceive that the Almighty, the Creator, the Eternal—God, Allah, Yahweh—or whichever entity we choose to name or represent our sentiments, dreams, and convictions—is not inescapably involved in our actions and obligations as creatures. If nothing else, to my view, this entity has already done its part of the task.

I will explain what I mean.

Many ordinary humans are doing extraordinary things and actions, individually and/or collectively, to make this world a better and more livable place. As if attempting to overcome a permeated force field, betterment is happening despite all kinds of obstacles. I'll name a few of the stumbling blocks, not exclusive to this or that part of the planet: persistent inequality, the dilemmas of education, (un)employment and immigration; environmental despair with biodiversity loss, species in extinction and water scarcity at center stage; destructive and senseless politics, rampant corruption; inexplicable violence, hunger, and meaningless wars; freedom and voting rights threatened; mental health crisis, healthcare and social security uncertainty. And on and on and on. So many, countless issues. It is not arduous to admit that the challenges we face during our present times are beyond significance. We all know that. It is a heavy task to describe where to begin.

My objective is to focus on a few but compelling actions that are contributing to make an impact and thus instrumental to help change and improve the world we live in—countries, communities and consequently our individual lives: in positive and meaningful ways.

*"So long as man remains free, he strives for nothing so incessantly and so painfully as to find someone to worship."*
~ F. Dostoevsky, novelist—*The Brothers Karamazov*

A word on the divine. With my pursuit for a grasp on spirituality, or call it curiosity and wonder, or yet transformation-manifestation, I have profound respect for its genuine representation and historical attempts for characterization.

Just as I have regard for the honest men and women who have been attempting to break ground and make inroads to portray the importance of deity and its relevance to our existence throughout the realms of time. However, no offense to anyone, and rather deferential, I will leave it alone. It is just a monumental effort to broach it in this literary work and one that I know I am not qualified for and have no intent to explain. But there is one thing I must say. I take issue and have an unsparing time understanding—and accepting—the misuse of all heavenly-related things.

Whether or not for opportunistic reasons and the ways we earthborn souls have been exploiting, manipulating, and abusing nature, especially, our very own species, the idea of humans hoisted as gods or demigods—public figures or not—does not appeal to my senses. Enough of that. We know better.

With a nod to my soliloquy days, I pose a question: how to separate out my life, our lives, from the world we live in? Is it worth trying to detach ourselves from reality for the pursuit of safeguarding our own integrity and developing awareness? Is it even possible? There are good reasons to engage in such a reflection. The world in the 21st Century is a complicated one. And yet, it has been like this, to a great extent, for as long as history and imagination can reach.

*"Each generation doubtless feels called upon to reform the world. Mine knows that it will not reform*

> *it, but its task is perhaps even greater. It consists in preventing the world from destroying itself".*
> ~ Albert Camus, philosopher, author, dramatist, journalist, world federalist, and political activist

From every possible angle, our nature is entrenched in innumerable variables. Starting with the complexity and distinctive characteristics of our own bodies, minds and personalities summed up in our own minuscule constellations—our own DNA. With reference to that, it is worth mentioning the nature of our dependency on those compassionate beings—parents, adopters, educators, caregivers, mentors, coaches, you name them—who devote their lives to help raise us and provide care to the best of their abilities and intentions. And that goes from day one of our existence throughout a good enough level of autonomy as adults—and many times, beyond that.

The aforementioned may be perceived as truisms that dwell in us, whether or not we consciously choose to dedicate much thinking and time to them. The fact is, as we embark on the daily trials, travels, troubles, and tribulations of our times, we find ourselves in the middle of a struggle: constantly striving to achieve something. Pushed and pulled from one end to another. Perplexed and bewildered. Shocked and awed, to quote a certain part of our recent history.

# So Then, What is This Book About?

*"Is anyone working on a bomb that makes people love each other? We already have it. It's called Music."* ~ Michael, a Teacher

Getting to the core of the above tantalizing question and answer, let's divert for a moment from the foundational aspect of how this book was conceived.

Virtuoso bassist, innovator, composer, arranger, producer, author, teacher, and multi-instrumentalist five-time Grammy award winner Victor L. Wooten is a co-founding member of the supergroup Béla Fleck and the Flecktones, a unique band that combines jazz and bluegrass music. He opens the acknowledgements of his inspiring book *The Spirit of Music* with the following words:

"The biggest Thanks, Gratitude, and Love to GOD and Her staff for allowing Life and Music to flow through me." And elaborates further on an unusual reflection: "Could Music as a whole ever be threatened? Could Music get sick, die, or even worse, be killed? Could we wake one morning to find Music removed entirely from our existence? Is any of this possible? If so, would you do anything to stop this tragedy from happening? It sounds crazy, like a conspiracy theory, right?"

It is intriguing the way Victor L. Wooten approaches the ultra-reality of Music in our lives. And also, the way he is grateful by referring to Music as an essence that's been allowed to stream through his life system. And most interestingly, a blessing graciously provided by a superior feminine manifestation in assistance alongside the Unfathomable.

# Gratus Animus

*"Gratitude unlocks the fullness of life. It turns what we have into enough, and more. It turns denial into acceptance, chaos to order, confusion to clarity. It can turn a meal into a feast, a house into a home, a stranger into a friend. Gratitude makes sense of our past, brings peace for today and creates a vision for tomorrow."*
~ Melody Beattie, author, journalist

It is a fact that I traverse most of my days with some kind of tune playing and humming in my mind and on my lips. It's one of the ways I find to keep my marbles together. In my debut book, *Why Not? A Memoir – Migration Journeys, Melodic Strides, and Quests for Meaning* I write a lot about music and its meaning. Why? Because music, good music, is motivational, it is restorative, and moving. As a symbolic as well as a practical value, it transcends. Besides being one of the highest manifestations of art that can inspire people, give them hope, make them believe in something greater, or even let them escape for a moment, there is more to it. When language fails, music's purpose is to express and modulate emotions, our natural instinctive state of mind deriving from circumstances, mood, or relationships with others. Music in its sublime manifestation often helps healing because it is something that can promote human well-being by facilitating human contact and entry points of connection; it gives human meaning, and imagination of possibilities, tying it to our natural social aptitudes.

*"Music can help maintain a balance between matter and spirit, both of which are essential to life,*

*and can also help awaken a new consciousness."*
~ Edgar Willems, artist,
musician and music educator

Music and imagination. The latter is described as the faculty or action of forming new ideas, or images or concepts of external objects not yet manifest to the senses. It is at one of those moments, while tracking new and old music tunes, while driving and casually choosing my music accompaniment of a given moment, that I slip through a very special piece from my depository: "Every Day (I Thank You)". Like every great tune which we listen to a thousand times and always find something new about it, I find myself asking, not for the first time, how and why the composer of this exquisite jazz piece came up with its title and what message one is trying to convey. Without an immediate answer, I spontaneously realize that I can draw insight from its 'language' resonating inside me. From then on, putting pieces together and fostering my imagination around the theme 'gratitude' or to the things that I am thankful for every day.

*"Music expresses that which cannot be put into
words and that which cannot remain silent."*
~ Victor Hugo, author

Combining my instincts with the subject of my curiosity, here is the probable story behind this special tune. It took me years to chase and learn about the title's meaning, which I recently twigged from "The Music Aficionado". This is a blog that publishes quality articles about Jazz, Rock, Prog, Folk, Film Scores, Psychedelia, and Pop from the golden age of music, covering artists, albums, songs, album covers and more. The article dates to September 19, 2017, the album's title is *80/81*.

"Five jazz musicians convene at Talent Studio in Oslo, Norway. The date is May 26, 1980. They were jet-lagged from red-eye flights and had a full day of recording ahead of them. The session was the brainchild of the youngest among them, a 26-year-old guitarist whose dream was to bring some of his most admired musicians to play together for the first time as a group. What ensued was one of the most productive and inspiring recording sessions in modern jazz. After just over one day of recording, the session yielded a double LP album for the ages."

The story of *80/81* is thorough and fascinating, but I will extract only the glimpses of Pat Metheny's album as it relates to the title of this book.

Metheny, a prodigy but still a young musician compared to the others, had the greatest appreciation for all four instrumentalists he assembled to join him in the recording— starting with bassist Charlie Haden and drummer Jack DeJohnette, "who between the two of them played with most anybody in jazz who is worth listening"—plus the pairing of two tenor sax musicians, Dewey Redman, and Michael Brecker, two already acclaimed musicians on their own rights. "Metheny did not just ask four great players to come over for a session. He had a clear vision for how they will sound together and wrote new music with their individual style and personality in mind".

One of the highlights on *80/81*, the focus of my inspiration, is a piece Metheny wrote for Mike Brecker. The tune, title of this book, was written in a hotel room in

Bremen, Germany late one night after a gig. "In the rich catalog of Metheny's well-crafted melodies, this is one of the most memorable and a special one due to Brecker's soulful playing." As a composition, it is certainly the most interesting and complex on the album: "I have done a lot of work to create a tune with different sections and tempos. It has a development and a form that is not a straight song. But all of that is nothing compared to the emotional depth that Mike played in the melody."

# The Human Factor

For Michael Brecker, who was in the process of kicking a drug habit at the time, the whole session was a life altering event, and this tune in particular affected him deeply. Says Metheny: "When I was writing the tune, I was hearing how Mike would play this, and the tune is very strongly associated with Mike now. He was going through a difficult time then. He was cleaning up his life and was not there yet. He was suffering a lot."

It is just amazing what individuals can do 'when life gives them lemons...', to quote a proverbial phrase. Metheny had the deepest account for the saxophonist as he could see his fellow musician—later to become one of two of his best friends, along with Charlie Haden—encouraged by optimism and positive can-do attitude in the face of adversity.

Decades later, after uncountable days and hours of intricate, extraordinary artful collaboration between the two musicians, at the memorial service held for Mike Brecker—gone too soon!—in New York's Town Hall on February 20, 2007, Metheny articulated in his eulogy to his friend: "The real thing that made Mike so special as a musician, as a player, was his incredible ability to communicate what it is to be human. The complications of it. The struggle of it. The joy of it. To manifest a sound that could describe things about what it is to be here on earth that everyone, musician or not, could feel and recognize as being true."

*"What we love about music is not that it sounds good. What we love about music is that it sounds inevitable. It's claimed the thing that we all know is unfolding. Whether we want to accept it or not. And it's there,*

*always. We just need to harness it. Be open to it."*
~ Jon Batiste, singer, songwriter, multi-instrumentalist, bandleader, composer

"Every Day (I Thank You)"— https://youtu.be/CoVIhmMAkbc?si=8R-e7bQgfIBCgIzb —the tune— is capstone and stimulating music. The title of this book and inspired by its melody, architecture and musicianship, it is with that in mind that I have associated its significance to me to a sequence of nine broad themes which, one fine day and out of the blue, slipped through my system, one by one.

Brought up by my perception of being some of the meaningful topics of our present times, perhaps of all times, before you get to that, I must disclose that this book has plenty of symbols, quotes and citations—perhaps overflowing with them—that I intentionally use to provide evidence and a fresh voice to my narrative, sincerely and honestly. Especially those that bring real meaning to my existence.

Full circle, this book is about gathering thoughts and considerations of gratitude along with short stories of individuals and groups—past and present, from all over the place—making their mark on this world. It is an attempt to encapsulate a holistic approach to engagement, learning, and change, a concept suggesting that for any initiative or effort to be truly effective and transformative, it requires us to pitch in not just intellectually, but emotionally and practically as well. Tales of Appreciation, as the subtitle communicates, for Hands, Hearts and Minds. And, most importantly, appreciative to those that I behold as being agents of change. Good change. Sometimes known individuals, sometimes not well-known, other times anonymous to the public. But all of them are beyond the concept of relevance.

Aldous Huxley's controversial dystopian *Brave New World* warns, among other messages, of the dangers of giving the state and economic agents control over new and powerful technologies. It also tells us that it is possible to make people content with their servitude. Opposite to Huxley's most remarkable book in which many of his predictions came to fruition in years and decades after its release, the author's last work was a novel on a utopian fantasy—*Island*—about a society in which a serious effort is made to help its members realize their desirable potentialities. "This is an attempt to write a practical utopia," Huxley tells us. "Nothing is easier, of course, than to enunciate ideals and to say, well, wouldn't it be nice if everybody were good and kind and loving, etc., etc.? Of course, it would be very nice, but the point is, how do you implement these ideals? How do you fulfill your good social and psychological intentions? And when you come down to this problem, you see, it's a very complex problem of organizing family life, organizing education, organizing sexual life, organizing social and economic life. I mean, there are endless factors involved in this. And to try to work out what all these factors should be, is, I must say, I find it a very interesting job".

> *"Develop interest in life as you see it, in people, things, literature and music—the world is so rich, simply throbbing with rich treasures, beautiful souls and interesting people. Forget yourself"*. ~ Henry Miller, novelist

Glancing over and beyond our radiant and incredible Gaia, in our smallness, fragile, on this temporal but staggering voyage, contemplating the unbound existence of an estimated 100 billion galaxies in the universe—home to an unimaginable cornucopia of planets—it is fair to look for intelligent life out there. I'm fine with that, without a doubt. But we've got plenty of brainiacs down here we can count on, who are causing great and positive impact in other people's lives. Without much fanfare. As it ought to be.

# A Suggestion For Sailing Through This Book

Before you get started, you may ask if there's a sequence to be followed between one chapter to another. Yes and no. As it pleases the reader, you may shuffle around chapters and pick the ones that bring more resonance to your mood and curiosity. Then, move back and forth. For the most part, they are all interrelated and could have been written in a different order.

As you dive into this work, there's a page at the end of every chapter in which I invite you the reader to take notes and express yourself on what each topic means to you. Perhaps, this will inspire you and also become an opportunity for you to kick-start journaling, if you haven't done that yet, or even start developing your own writing experience. It'll be worth your while.

Thank you for joining me on this journey.

*For those who want to let go*
*I invent the wharf*

*I invent more than loneliness gives me*
*I invent a new moon to brighten*
*I invent love*
*And I know the pain of throwing myself*

*I wanted to be happy*
*I invent the sea*
*I invent in myself the dreamer*

*For those who want to follow me*
*I want more*
*I have the path of what I always wanted*
*And a sailboat ready to depart*

*I invent the wharf*
*And I know the time to throw myself*

~ "Cais" (Wharf), Milton Nascimento, songwriter

# Every Day (I Thank You)

### I

## For Cultivating Your Life with Kindness, Purpose, and Joy

*"If I could give you one thought, it would be to lift someone up. Lift a stranger up—lift her up. I would ask you, mother and father, brother and sister, lovers, mother and daughter, father and son, lift someone. The very idea of lifting someone up will lift you, as well."*
~ Maya Angelou, memoirist,
poet, and civil rights activist.

"KINDNESS ISN'T NORMAL." This may sound like a negative statement, but it's not. Quite the contrary if looked at from a different perspective. With these words, author Houston Kraft names the very first chapter of his valuable book, *Deep Kindness—A Revolutionary Guide for the Way We Think, Talk, and Act in Kindness*. "I spent a lot of time thinking about the importance of Kindness in a world seemingly too busy for it. Kindness is one of these essential things that we collectively say is good, but we collectively aren't good at it."

Indeed, an observer of human nature knows that experiencing frequent acts of kindness has become less spontaneous and a somewhat scarce pursuit. Yes, we are just too occupied 'living our lives.' Stirring up our time with stuff. Wildly getting from point A to point B. Mistaken by some as weakness, there was a time when even speaking about kindness could be embarrassing for some people and arouse suspicion on those who were not necessarily on the same frequency as the speaker. Especially in the workplace, where we spend a third of our existence. Not anymore. There are new winds bringing kindness to our lives. Why? Because it is intrinsic in us to crave it. To long for its manifestation. To wish for things to positively change at the expense of more of it.

No word was more relevant to the popular Confucius, one of the greatest Chinese philosophers, than the word *ren*. Its meaning revolves around five virtues: respect, magnanimity, sincerity, earnestness, and kindness. In an effort to find the proper meaning for the latter, it can be depicted as compassion, sympathy, altruism, benignity, true goodness, consummate action, love, human-heartedness.

Kindness was not invented by the philosopher, obviously, but he took it to the next level. Confucius was possibly the first thinker "to place kindness, and love, at the top of the pyramid", according to Eric Weiner, author of the delightful *The Socrates Express—In Search of Life Lessons from Dead Philosophers*. The cliché but relevant "Do not impose on others what you yourself do not desire" is a timeless teaching. For Confucius, kindness is not soft or squishy. It is not feeble or weak, not masculine or feminine. Kindness is practical. It is vital. Attainable. "Extend kindness to all and you can turn the whole world in the palm of your hand."

"The family is our ren gym," says Weiner as he deepens his understanding of the philosopher's teachings. "It is where we learn to love and be loved. Proximity matters. Start by treating those closest to you kindly and go from there. Like a stone tossed into a pond, kindness ripples outward in ever-widening circles, as we expand our sphere of concern from ourselves to our family to our neighborhood to our nation to all sentient beings. If we feel compassion for one creature, we can feel it for all of them."

Weiner acknowledges the need to go out of one's comfort zone when it comes to spreading the jewel that kindness can bring from inside out. "Too often, though, we fail to make the leap from familial kindness to a broader benevolence. Too often parenting remains 'an island of kindness in a sea of cruelty,' as two contemporary authors put it. We need to escape the island or, better yet, enlarge it and invite others to join us."

*"Kind hearts are the gardens. Kind thoughts are the roots. Kind words are the blossoms. Kind deeds are the fruits."* ~ Kirpal Singh, author

It is time we were a little kinder. Starting with ourselves, then to those around us and to the world itself. Like farmers setting out to plant a crop, we are concerned about the outcome of what they will cultivate. Those worries and struggles dissipate once the seeds are well positioned in the previously prepared soil, and the proper watering is provided. Cultivating here has a much broader sense than the simple act of preparing and raising a given crop. Rather, it elevates to nurturing and encouragement.

"Our capacity for kindness", Weiner continues, "is like our capacity for language. We are all born with an innate ability to speak a language. But it must be activated, either by our parents or *Rosetta Stone*. Likewise, our inherent kindness must be mobilized, and the way to do that, Confucians believe, is through study. By "study" the philosopher does not mean rote memorization or even learning, per se. He has something deeper in mind: moral self-cultivation. What we are taught, we learn. What we cultivate, we absorb. There are no small acts of kindness. Each compassionate deed is like watering a redwood seed. You never know what heights it might reach."

# Kindness and Unconditional Courage

Houston Kraft has a clear intent when defining "a more thoughtful vocabulary for the critical important concept of Kindness", with capital K. Politeness and feel-good Kindness - he curiously calls them Common Kindness and Confetti Kindness—are desirable and not to be neglected in a world of shallow relationships and superficial interactions, not to mention the domain where a certain indifference dwells. Besides, the social media era has not helped mitigate much of that feeling—quite the contrary. Whilst it is "demonstrative of basic respect for others, these acts of Kindness aren't necessarily changing anyone's world". Kraft goes on to say that "almost always, they are rooted in good intentions and delivered in an earnest attempt to help". But he contemplates a third way, where a deeper kind of Kindness takes center stage as "a category of care that the world desperately needs."

> *"You may want to rethink being okay with things that you really are not okay with. You may want to reconsider associating being a good person with how much you're willing to suffer in silence. You can be a kind person and still say 'I'm not okay with this.' Being kind is not about being the human equivalent of a doormat."*
> ~ Unknown

Kindness is not a "soft skill" and it's not about being nice, although one can be both—nice and kind. Strong and bold, it is more like a superpower. Kindness in its deepest sense overcomes selfishness and fear and has nothing to do with one being submissive or permissive. It is, rather, "The sort of generosity that expects nothing in return. The commitment to consistent, thoughtful action that proves, over time, that your giving is not dependent on circumstance or convenience", Kraft says. He goes beyond the idea of the external act of Kindness suggesting that "it requires careful self-reflection, profound courage, a willingness to be humbled, and hard-earned social and emotional skills … if we are ever going to live in a world that is less divisive and more compassionate."

Philosopher and statesman, Seneca, is a major figure of the Roman Imperial Period. One of his widely known quotes, "Wherever there is a human being, there is an opportunity for kindness", and many more examples of impactful thinking and teaching around kindness can be drawn from scattered records in history. Maria Popova's writing on *The Marginalian*, "The Stoic Key to Kindness", is keen on the observation of another remarkable Roman figure: "Marcus Aurelius in his timeless *Meditations*—notes on life he had written largely to himself while learning how to live more nobly in an uncertain world that blindsides us as much with its beauty as with its brutality - returns again and again to kindness and the importance of extending it to everyone equally at all times, because even at their cruelest, which is their most irrational, human beings are endowed with reason and dignity they can live up to."

Popova adds to it: "Seventeen centuries before Tolstoy looked back on his long and contradictory life to make the bittersweet observation that 'nothing can make our life, or the lives of other people, more beautiful than perpetual kindness,' Marcus Aurelius draws on the other great refrain that carries his philosophy—the insistence that embracing our mortality is the key to living fully—and writes to himself:

"You should bear in mind constantly that death has come to men of all kinds, men with varied occupations and various ethnicities… We too will inevitably end up where so many [of our heroes] have gone… Heraclitus, Pythagoras, Socrates… brilliant intellectuals, high-minded men, hard workers, men of ingenuity, self-confident men, men… who mocked the very transience and impermanence of human life…. men… long dead and buried… Only one thing is important: to behave throughout your life toward the liars and crooks around you with kindness, honesty, and justice."

# The Pay It Forward Concept

Serendipity, that fortunate stroke that rarely but surely happens to all of us, for some more than others, is the occurrence and development of events by chance in a happy or beneficial way. But truly, is there such a thing?

Here's a heartwarming episode at a Starbucks Coffee in Bellevue, in bean land Washington State, that beautifully envelops the essence of cultivating life with a little kindness. Although not a new practice, fresh and similar stories happen across the country daily. This one, the simple act of one woman choosing to pay for the caramel macchiato of the driver behind her, set off a ripple effect that lasted for about seven hours, involving 234 people in an unbroken chain of generosity and goodwill.

This story is a vivid illustration of how a single, seemingly small act of kindness can inspire a collective movement, bringing a sense of community and happiness to many. It's a reminder that our actions, no matter how minor they may seem, have the potential to create significant positive impacts on the lives of others.

"I can't believe this is happening!" says Joyce, a new hire, astonished.

Her and her team's engagement in keeping a tally and encouraging the continuation of this chain underscores the joy and purpose found in participating in acts of kindness.

The curious takeaway here is how to interpret the experience. The conclusion of the chain with the 234th customer, who decided not to continue paying it forward, highlights an important aspect of the act of kindness—it's a choice. While the concept of paying it forward was joyfully embraced by many, it ultimately relies on the individual's willingness to participate. Therefore, this ending does not diminish the beauty and impact of the chain of kindness; instead, it serves as a fun reflection on the nature of each individual's generosity, which is voluntary and not obligatory, as they're not there to check for the results.

This narrative is not just a testament to the kindness of individuals but also an inspiring tale that showcases how purpose and joy as a by-product of a cordial act can be cultivated through simple acts of giving. It serves as a powerful example of how we can all contribute to a kinder, more joyful and interesting environment around us, one small gesture at a time.

# Purpose Revisited

Making our lives more interesting takes a great deal of effort. Setting goals with a clear vision of what we want to achieve is not only desirable but helps us order our minds, situating ourselves in time and space, thus allowing for potentially increasing our welfare. A few key variables give direction in helping us recognize our purpose in our lives. Before examining some of the variables, here is a valuable reflection on the topic:

"A sense of purpose can be a critical roadmap in your journey of life. It can help you determine when you're heading in the right direction and when you may be way off course. Science suggests that having a sense of purpose is vitally important to well-being—both for our physical health and our state of mind. There's growing research that shows a clear sense of purpose is one of the cornerstones of human flourishing." Richard Davidson, Founder and Director of the *Center for Healthy Minds*, further adds that "people with a strong sense of purpose tend to be more satisfied with their lives in general."

Whoa, it's that simple? The intent here is not to make this a trivial task and I often think that for many this seems to be beyond one's ability. It used to be for me and still is in some ways. But being aware of the need to have a purpose is half-way through the battle. It keeps the carrot ahead of us, especially when a pathway to growth is the reward. As Craig Childs, on *Lifehack*, examines the path to purpose, his thinking is profound and deserves attention:

"Everyone begins with a need to preserve self, keep the body and its basic goals from disintegrating (survival, comfort, pleasure). When bodily safety is no longer in doubt, one may expand one's horizons to include family, neighborhood, religious or ethnic groups leading to more complexity even though it usually implies conformity to conventional norms and standards. Many get 'stuck' in this mode, not desiring to go beyond."

Let us dive in even deeper: "The next step is reflective individualism, turning inward to find new grounds for authority and value. One no longer blindly conforms but develops an autonomous conscience. The main goal becomes the desire for growth, improvement, and actualization of potential."

Craig's opinion is that fewer reach this level of conscience. As a final step, he concludes that "building on all the others, is a final turning away from the self, back toward an integration with others and with universal values. This extremely individualized person willingly merges his interests with those of a larger whole—a cause, an idea, a transcendental entity."

Craig's perspective on the evolution of consciousness and personal development culminates in a profound realization: after a journey of introspective individualism and the quest for self-actualization, the ultimate step is a return to collective integration. This stage transcends the focus on self and embraces a broader connection with others and universal principles. Here, the highly individualized person chooses to align their personal goals and interests with the greater good, dedicating themselves to causes, ideas, or transcendental beliefs that extend beyond personal gain. This level of consciousness is marked by a deep sense of unity and purpose, where individual achievements are seen as part of a larger, interconnected whole. Craig suggests that this stage of development is rare, highlighting the challenge and depth of commitment required to reach such a level of moral and ethical integration.

# Pumping Joy

*Cultivating joy means developing emotional awareness and a mindset that focuses on joy and gratitude. It means taking actions that align with purpose."* ~ Anonymous

A quote from *Meddlers - Mind Your Own Business*, coaches, and consultants in the private sector - sheds a ray of simplicity to the concept: "Joy will sometimes find us on its own, but we're generally responsible for going out and finding it ourselves. It's an active search, not a passive waiting. In some ways, you can boil it down to two things—surrender and expression."

Again, cultivating here plays a crucial role in how we insert joy into our existence. And we all need to remind ourselves that this is a practice that requires action from time to time. Surrendering revolves around removing ourselves as passive spectators of our aspiring well-being to becoming the enablers, and consequently, the beneficiaries—and benefactors—of the experience of 'installing' joy in our lives. Not only do we act to improve our own immediate surroundings, but we provide influence to improve the lives of our loved ones—those known to us and those yet to be encountered. Simply put, getting ourselves out of the way by removing preoccupation and unnecessary concerns. Changing the things we can change and stepping out, far from neglecting or ignoring, but stirring clear from the things we cannot change or influence.

In retrospect, using our tools and expression to build our pathway to integrate joy into our system—and use it when we and the world around us need it.

Good music, good laughter, and smart movement are good starters to help expression and creativity. They stir up our senses. Epicurus, the great philosopher of pleasure, was the philosopher of the body as well as the mind. He believes that the body contains the greatest wisdom and "defined pleasure differently from the way most of us do", says Weiner on *The Socrates Express*. "We think of pleasure as a presence, what psychologists call a positive effect. Epicurus defined pleasure as a lack, an absence, of disturbance. It is the absence of anxiety rather than the presence of anything that leads to contentment. Pleasure is not the opposite of pain but its absence."

Brenda Han, writing on *Matter, Inc.*, another coaching, training, and consulting organization, demystifies joy in interesting ways:

"What is the meaning of joy? It's not something I have spent much time thinking about before, but when I stopped working a few months ago it was the first time I could stop and think." Brenda goes on and mentions that the fact of her taking a career break in the middle of a pandemic without the ability to travel created a "hotbed of introspection (and mild anxiety) for the mind", especially after having worked almost two decades in a high demanding industry without ever stopping. She states that there's a lot out there about the differences between happiness and joy: "In my view they can be used interchangeably, but there's definitely a difference between a euphoric high from say attending a live concert to a deep sense of well-being and contentment that is not dependent on an external factor. The latter to me is joy."

Joy, a much higher level of pleasure, like Kindness and Purpose, is indeed something else. It is beyond the emotional state of great delight or happiness caused by something exceptionally good or satisfying. Rather, it is peace of mind. The absence of fear or anxiety about the future. Acceptance of the things we cannot change. It is being present and finding comfort in solitude. The pure pleasure of existing, it is the essence of being.

# Green Buttons and Red Hearts

*"This is the true joy in life, being used for a purpose recognized by yourself as a mighty one. Being a force of nature instead of a feverish, selfish little clod of ailments and grievances, complaining that the world will not devote itself to making you happy. I am of the opinion that my life belongs to the whole community and as long as I live, it is my privilege to do for it what I can. I want to be thoroughly used up when I die, for the harder I work, the more I live. I rejoice in life for its own sake. Life is no brief candle to me. It is a sort of splendid torch which I have got hold of for the moment and I want to make it burn as brightly as possible before handing it on to future generations".*
~ George Bernard Shaw,
playwright, critic, polemicist

In late 2016, seeing a growing trend of unkindness in the world, Karyn Ross had an idea. That idea was to create small green buttons with red hearts on them and slips of paper with messages such as 'Plant Kindness and Grow Love', and 'Practice Kindness'. Karyn's idea was to anonymously leave buttons and slips wherever she was—airports, grocery stores, restaurants—for people to find! A small reminder that wherever we are, whoever we are, and whatever we believe in, as long as we treat each other kindly, the world will be a great place for all of us.

Sound quixotical? Let's reflect on it.

Three years later, in 2019, Karyn founded *The Love and Kindness Project Foundation*. It is dedicated to creating a world of love and kindness before money. The Foundation, a registered 501(c)(3) charity, focuses not on raising funds, like many public charities, but on "raising kindness."

*The Love and Kindness Project Foundation* does that by: "Giving out, at no cost (including shipping), Love and Kindness Buttons!; Providing materials and support for those who want to facilitate Kindness Activities; Hosting Kindness Events at schools and other locations around the world; Providing micro-grants, support and coaching to help people create their own love and kindness proposition."

That's great but, that's it? Karyn doesn't stop there. Among multiple publications, she is the author of *The Kind Leader: A Practical Guide to Eliminating Fear, Creating Trust, and Leading with Kindness*. Karyn's view of leadership is unique and deserves careful attention.

"Kindness and leadership aren't often synonymous. Ask someone to describe "good leadership" to you and you will hear many adjectives used. And though there are many more that come to mind, kindness isn't one of them. And here's the problem with that."

To summarize her thoughts, in a world where strength is perceived primarily as the capacity to use and/or dominate by force, there's a lot of confusion that requires dissecting understanding; especially, when it comes to one's attempt to live and advocate for kindness. Before getting to that, the notion of strength is widespread in our Western-focused culture. It is commonplace to hear one person described as "stronger" or "weaker" than another. And yet the concept of strength is a myth—detrimental at times—which reinforces many of our social ills. It is a concept that ought to be abandoned altogether.

Karyn articulates a straightforward stepping stone:

"Kindness takes strength to practice on an ongoing basis. Leadership takes strength to practice on an ongoing basis. Practiced together, they can change organizations, cultures, communities and countries for the better."

Which brings us to reflect on kindness and its hearth in the workplace. "What a leader models—how they think, speak, and act—influences the people they lead. Leaders who think, speak, and act unkindly give legitimacy and permission to those they lead to think, speak, and act in exactly the same unkind ways. In an increasingly fragmented, polarized, and divided world, we need leaders who will bring people together, not divide them. We need kindness to become synonymous with good leadership," ponders Karyn.

*The Kind Leader: A Practical Guide to Eliminating Fear, Creating Trust, and Leading with Kindness*, gives us five ways that one can start practicing Kind Leadership today in the workplace:

*Recognize unkindness is happening...and call it out!* Don't be silent. Standing up for your values is what strong leadership is all about.

*Call for a "Time Out" when you hear and see unkindness.* State the facts of what you see happening and explain how it is making you feel. It takes a huge amount of strength not to blame or belittle others!

*Speak up for others less privileged than yourself!* Kind Leaders have the strength to stand up for others, especially when they are in minority and/or marginalized communities.

*Walk Away! You don't have to "take it"!* When you feel that you aren't able to respond in a kind way, walk away until you are calmer. Holding your temper when you are emotional takes a huge amount of strength! Make time to deal with the issue when you are calmer!

*Write a letter of complaint,* call HR, sign a petition, raise a flag, take a stand, call and offer support. It's easy (weak) to let incidents pass by at work, in the community and the country. It takes strength to consistently stand up for what you believe in.

> *"A part of kindness consists in loving people more than they deserve."*
> ~ Joseph Joubert, Essayist

Caring for others and working to create positive effects and outcomes for them isn't weakness. Rather, it's strength.

Kind Leaders make difficult decisions all the time", says Karyn. "They have constructive conversations all the time. They 'get things done' and get results all while helping people learn and grow in safe, supportive environments and kind cultures all at the same time."

Karyn's purpose for *"The Kind Leader"* is to teach leaders how to lead with kindness so they can influence the people they lead to cultivate kinder workplaces, organizations, and the world. Again, this is not about being a nice leader. Rather, it's about being a kind and thoughtful individual who aims higher for their team as a whole. The book offers a deep theoretical understanding of the importance of leading with kindness and also provides practical exercises for the reader to use. Karyn aims high: "By the time you finish the book, you will feel confident in your ability to lead with kindness and also to address organizational problems at work, at home, and in the community with kindness."

# Living the Purpose

A starting point to address stages that go from an unkind environment or cultural system to one that becomes more prone to kindness should revolve around a simple observation: we are all leaders, in one way or another. At work, at home, in our communities, there's always someone following us and the other way around.

Katie Anderson, an internationally recognized leadership coach, consultant, and professional speaker, best known for inspiring individuals and organizations to lead with intention, has a keen perspective:

"At the essence, any cultural change starts with the individual. Human relationships and dynamics exist; if you change how you're showing up, you shift the dynamic already. So, if you show up with more respect, with more kindness, with more caring, with more curiosity, the dynamic changes, it gets amplified, thus, giving space to creating that culture."

During her interview with Karyn Ross on the launching of *The Kind Leader,* Katie Anderson poses a critical question:

"Are you kind all the time?"

Karyn's answer may come as a surprise:

"No way! Kindness and kind leadership is a practice that takes practice, the more we do the more comfortable we get. Therefore, more confidence is generated."

Being an advocate for one's belief requires manifestation and Karyn is resolute in what she propagates:

"I was out to dinner the other night and the discussion turned (as it often does) to all the problems we are experiencing in the world right now: school (and other) shootings in the United States, climate crisis and global warming, the mental health crisis causing so much harm to so many.

"'People certainly need to be a lot more resilient now than they used to be. We need more resilient training,' someone said.

"'What we need is more kindness, and kind leadership,' I said, "Because kindness reduces the need for resilience!'

"'That's true,' the person said. 'But what can I do? I don't have power. I'm not in a leadership position…I'm just a regular person?' As she was speaking, I saw her shoulders slump and the sad look of resignation on her face."

Karyn is not alone on her crusade for kindness in the workplace and in our day to day lives. In his piece *Why Kindness at Work Pays Off* for Harvard Business Review, Andrew Swinand outlines the myriad positive impacts of kindness at work for both business and human outcomes.

He shares simple routines for spreading kindness and for creating and sustaining an organizational culture of kindness:

1. Practice radical self-care. Being disciplined about your own well-being, managing your workload, and setting appropriate boundaries helps you sustain your own well-being and have the energy and bandwidth to practice sharing kindness with others.

2. Do your job. Hold yourself accountable, do what you say you will, and conduct self-reviews to support continual improvement. When your own job is in a relatively light period, be intentional about reaching out to support colleagues who are struggling.

3. Reach out with intention. Be intentional about establishing and nurturing social connections at work, especially in hybrid and remote settings.

4. Recognize and acknowledge people. Authentic, thoughtful recognition and acknowledgement helps people feel cared for and enables a culture of kindness.

5. Be conscientious with your feedback. Recognize the distinction between niceness (which can lead to be people-pleasing and be disingenuous) and kindness (which is honest yet sensitive). Practice kindness in offering feedback to build someone up and help them grow.

The genuine question to ask is: What strategies can we use to foster a culture of kindness at work? At home? In our community?

Like the many vocal and/or anonymous advocates for kindness in our present times, Karyn Ross has a unique way portraying her cause, which can become everyone's cause: "I'm not just working on making a kinder better world myself, I'm working on activating people to join me on working on it. I can't do it myself... and I don't have all the solutions. I do know that each of us can play a role! We can model kindness and lead others at work, at home and in the community, regardless of what formal role we have! And we can work together to come up with new and creative ways to combat the unkindness we are seeing and experiencing around us, each and every day. It will take a lot of strength, but there is strength in numbers!"

> *"People resist change because they focus on what they are going to lose instead of on what they are going to gain"* ~ Paulo Coelho, lyricist and novelist

"Change means doing things differently." Karyn does not have the answers for everything, nor does she claim kindness is a panacea. However, her team around the world and herself are not watching the skies. Hands on, they are on a sound mission to Help People Create a Better, Kinder World: https://loveandkindnessproject.org/ An internationally acclaimed speaker, Karyn is an artist, an award-winning author, consultant, coach and practitioner, and travels the globe teaching people her unique system of combining creativity, continuous improvement and kindness to make ours a better place to coexist. As well as being the owner of KRC (Karyn Ross Consulting) Karyn is one of the "Founding Mothers" of *Women in Lean - Our Table*, a global group of more than seven hundred and fifty women Lean practitioners! Karyn is also Founder and President of the *Love and Kindness Project Foundation*, a registered public charity and *The New School for Kind Leaders*. She has created both of these initiatives to help people around the world think, speak, act and lead more kindly. In her own words "Kindness—and kind leadership—is the solution…and the preventative!"

> *Broken windows and empty hallways*
> *A pale dead moon in the sky streaked with gray*

*Human kindness is overflowing*
*And I think it's going to rain today*
*Scarecrows dressed in the latest styles*
*With frozen smiles to chase love away*
*Human kindness is overflowing*
*And I think it's going to rain today*
*Lonely, lonely*
*Tin can at my feet*
*Think I'll kick it down the street*
*That's the way to treat a friend*
*Bright before me the signs implore me*
*To help the needy and show them the way*
*Human kindness is overflowing*
*And I think it's going to rain today*
"I Think It's Going to Rain Today"
~ Randy Newman, songwriter

Planting, tending, improving, then harvesting, the essence of cultivating. For some of us, kindness does not come as easy, and it seems like a personality trait destined for someone else. On the contrary, we can all learn to be kind. Kindness is not just a trait we either have or lack; it's a skill and a mindset we can all work to cultivate, we can all work to develop.

Some might argue that cultivating kindness may be a pivotal aspect upon which our very survival as a species depends. With the proper understanding of its relevance, this may lead us to the refinement of our soul, of our conscience, or whatever we want to call and give meaning to that deep inner voice above and beyond our obvious existence. As we consider the systematic, intentional, and concerted effort to develop the ingredients that gravitate around kindness—compassion, forgiveness, equanimity, generosity—if we want to impact ourselves, our families, our organizations, our communities, or our world for the better, we may gain ground by aiming at nurturing and growing our own selves, thus expanding our own inner beings.

What will it take?

# Your Thoughts
## On Cultivating Your Life
## with Kindness, Purpose, and Joy

# Every Day (I Thank You)

## 2

### For Adopting a Mindset of Patience and No Harm

*Little patience, need a little patience
Just a little patience, some more patience
I've been walking the streets at
night, just trying to get it right
It's hard to see so many around,
You know I don't like being stuck in the crowd
~ "Patience"- Guns N' Roses*

RECENT HISTORY HAS TAUGHT US a lot about life's unpredictability. The fresh memory of the entire planet going through the experience of COVID-19 will be in our hearts and minds for quite some time. Like many things that we should learn at school—and we don't—from basic skills such as cooking, how to handle money and personal credit cards, to rights, to learning from failure, as well as physical and mental survival skills,—if there's one aspect to be emphasized during that period, there's one that is essentially critical: the relevance and complexity of relationships.

Starting with the most meaningful one, the foundation of our existence, the relationship with our own self and how it shapes us to coexist with the world around us and beyond. "How you feel about yourself and your relationships with others colors your perspective on life." On a mission—from articles on their blog to videos, eBooks and emails—*Hack Spirit* shares the importance of creating positive relationships to live a fulfilling life. "We cut through the fluff and give you actionable and straightforward advice to improve your relationships with others and yourself."

We need a lot of that, don't we?

From a scientific and medical perspective, one doesn't have to be a keen observer to notice that COVID-19 did not create a new mental health crisis but expanded an existing tinderbox, highlighting that we simply do not have the resources and breadth of effective treatments to deal with it. The big question in many people's minds is: how can we as individuals contribute to making our lives more livable if the skills and tools are not readily available when we need them? Breakdown or breakthrough?

The stress that followed through the pandemic caused a plethora of feelings such as fear, anger, sadness, worry, numbness, and frustration; habit changes, such as diet, energy levels, mixed desires, and conflicting interests, culminating with difficulty concentrating and making decisions. To make things more challenging, although many actions were implemented to mitigate the effects—from the scientific community to government to local networks to family and friends circles—it seemed that the nightmare was here to stay. Just like the *"Groundhog Day"* film so well depicted decades ago. "Phil experiences the previous day's events repeating exactly and believes he is experiencing *déjà vu*. He unsuccessfully attempts to leave the town and retires to bed. When he awakes, it is again February 2. Phil gradually realizes that he is trapped in a time loop." Sound familiar?

> *"Patience is waiting. Not passively waiting. That is laziness. But to keep going when the going is hard and slow – that is patience. The two most powerful warriors are patience and time."*
> ~ Leo Tolstoy, author

What do patience, time, and relationships have to do with one another? And how does resilience factor into the equation?

It may not always seem obvious, but there is a link between patience, time, relationships and resilience. Patience can be defined as the capacity to accept or tolerate delay, trouble, or suffering without getting angry or upset. Or yet, of having the capacity to regulate reactions and emotions when results or gratitude is put off. On the other end, resilience is the ability to recover quickly from difficulties and challenges we encounter.

So what's the connection?

Patience is a hallmark of resilience as it travels from the time we allow ourselves to understand its process through the way we manage the quality of our relationships with the inner and outer world. *Flexicrew—Flexible Workforce Solutions,* consultants on careers and on the workplace, describe their perspective:

"The more they are able to tolerate and withstand circumstances in their lives without an angry response, the more indicative that is of their ability to endure tough circumstances and recover from them with speed and ease (*Sood*, 2019). Thus, taking the time to strengthen one's patience skills subsequently strengthens one's resilience."

# Mindset As a Key

*"Mindset is everything. Like the eye of a storm—find the sunshine and calm within you, even if there is chaos outside of you."*
~ Brittany Burgunder, author

Outlook. Perspective. Mindset. They all have a similar meaning. "A characteristic mental attitude that determines how to interpret and respond to situations—a complex mental state involving beliefs and feelings and values and dispositions to act in certain ways", according to *Thesaurus*. Why is mindset so important in our existence? Because in most cases it invariably determines the outcome of our lives. It is the lens through which we view the world, no matter the scale and magnitude. It shapes our perception, how we solve our problems and interact with each other. It is the software that runs our thinking and decision making.

According to Jonas Reseem on *How to Use Self-Talk to Build a Better Mindset*, "Your mindset largely depends on how you talk to yourself. And the reason it's so important is because your inner dialogue is the only conversation you can't walk away from. What's more, it affects everything you do".

Like most things of this nature, it works as an asset as well as a liability. Using the right key determines the success of every action when confronted with the need to apply the required mindset at a particular moment and circumstance. Beyond the common example of the glass "half empty" or "half full", our mindset can quickly change what we think, feel, and do. The paradox of a mindset is that sometimes we don't know that we're stuck in one until we step out or adopt a different mindset.

Embracing change with all its blessings and curses falls into place here. Developing an open mind to new ideas and to other ways to look at each episode of the day goes the extra mile to help us do things differently. Embracing change is to become adaptable. It implies that adversity becomes an element not to be feared but rather a champion, an opportunity to improve ourselves or try new experiences. It brings growth. And yes, looking at a glass half full is the positive starter needed. A good start.

# No Harm of Any Nature

*The most potent weapon in the hands of the oppressor is the mind of the oppressed.*
~ Steve Biko, anti-apartheid activist

In an extreme chapter of world history, there's a parallel to be drawn. The reason most of the West and the majority of democracies in the 21st century reject the idea of totalitarianism—or autocracy, to be more precise—is simple: a form of government in which the state has no limits in authority and does whatever it wants is, or should be, a thing of the past. It's not only anachronic and incongruous in the present but it hurts the most fundamental laws of the human condition: our ability to choose. Nazi Germany and Stalinist Russia offered a taste of what the end of humanity would look like. And history has recorded the terrifying experience. Hannah Arendt, political philosopher, author, and Holocaust survivor dissects, in the *Origins of Totalitarianism*, that absolutism didn't spring up out of a void. Rather, it is just one possibility along a path that most countries are on at one time or another. Which emphasizes the importance of understanding what it is.

The blog Fs, *Wisdom You Can Choose*, is keen in analyzing that historical moment:

"One of the most disturbing things about Nazism in Germany is how quickly the country changed. They went from democracy to concentration camps in fewer than ten years. Most of us assume that the Germans of the time were different from us—'we'd never fall for the kind of propaganda that Hitler spewed. And our democracy is too strong to be so easily dismantled.'"

Right?

Wrong.

Arendt writes that "the success of totalitarian movements ... meant the end of two illusions of democratically ruled countries...." One illusion was that most citizens were politically active and were part of a political party. In many modern democracies, we can see evidence of indifference and pervasive feelings of helplessness. There is low voter turnout and an assumption that things will be the way they are no matter what an individual does. There is pent-up energy in apathy. Arendt suggests that the desire to be more than indifferent is what totalitarian movements initially manipulate until the individual is totally subsumed."

The aforementioned is the point and focus of this reflection: Adopting a mindset of no harm, or its personal practice, is the individual and conscious decision of not causing damage, physically or mentally, to others under any circumstance. Starting with ourselves, it comes from the certainty that hurting people, animals and/or the environment is unnecessary to achieve an outcome and refers to a general philosophy of abstention from violence. Whatever the reasons on which we may base these assumptions, be them moral, religious or spiritual principles, a pragmatic one resonates as being just enough and justifiable. Why? Because no harm has a powerful "active" and "activist" element. Gandhi and Martin Luther King Jr. offered the world the principles for *nonviolence* as a means to achieve political and social change. Pragmatic and strategic, they both saw nonviolent action or civil resistance or yet civil disobedience as an alternative to passive acceptance of oppression or armed struggle against it.

Important examples in history attest to the effectiveness of no harm as a choice and as an agent for change. Indian Independence from Great Britain, Civil Rights for African Americans, the 1989 "Velvet Revolution" in the former Czechoslovakia, and most recently the nonviolent campaigns of Leymah Gbowee and the women in Liberia achieving peace after a fourteen-year civil war. Where does it start? It starts with a unique resolve. It begins with the understanding of the chain of thought that leads to implications that unfailingly result in the escalation of violence if patience, or the lack of it, as a precursor to a cascade of afflictions, is not seen as a priority in our lives.

# Windfall or Torment

Recent years of political upheaval depicted the effectiveness of mass manipulation, which almost resulted in disastrous consequences to this country and to world democracy. And we're not out of the woods yet as our flawed democratic system may allow for unpredictable outcomes. When insidious actors demonize others, when they take their humanity away, they make violence not only possible but likely. Aggravated by lies spread around cable news, the Internet and social media, which run faster than truth, that's how violence is normalized, that's how democracies are lost. "It is critical to understand that it is simple to isolate people who already feel isolated. When you feel disconnected from the system around you and the leaders it has, when you believe that neither your vote nor your opinion matters, it's not a huge leap to feel that your very self has no importance. This feeling is what totalitarianism figured out how to manipulate by random terror that severed any form of connection with other human beings." This is the world during and after WWII. Its resemblance to occurrences in recent times—and still very much alive—is not a coincidence.

In today's world, the same people who feel isolated bring along the sentiment of being victims of the system. Whether that sentiment of anger and victimhood will be vectored toward the ballot box remains to be seen. Luke Mogelson, in his book, *The Storm is Here: An American Crucible,* goes inside the mindset of the January 6 insurrectionists: "Victimhood is essential to their identity and their world view. And it's really the emotional experience that animates and pushes them to take extreme action." From Mogelson's perspective, for the insurrectionists, victimhood is a real experience—at least in their minds. "The fact that they are not (victims) means that they have to invent or accept fabricated adversaries and antagonists to rationalize that emotional experience of victimhood. That's where the conspiracy theorists come in, that's when purveyors of propaganda come in, that's when (certain) politicians come in, because they're constantly providing these phantom menaces in order for their followers to feel constantly under threat."

Yet, during and post-WWII, Arendt accurately points out that "totalitarianism demands total, unrestricted, unconditional, and unalterable loyalty of the individual member. Such loyalty can be expected only from the isolated human beings who, without strong social ties to family, friends, comrades, or even mere acquaintances, derive their sense of having a place in the world only from their belonging to a movement." Dire and consequential times, then and now.

Our actions around the way we handle ourselves in relation to the outer world can make the act of converging the two ideas of 'patience' and 'no harm' less than spontaneous. On the other hand, there's a difference between impatience and sense of urgency. Joe Broadmeadow in his article *American Impatience: Blessing and Curse*, on "JEBWizard Publishing", surgically explains in glimpses two sides of America's personality. Whether or not controversial, "history tells the story of who we are, where we come from, and can potentially reveal where we are headed:

"Americans are an impatient people. It seems it is a characteristic we've borne since the very founding of this nation. When the Europeans first set foot upon the land, driven here by several factors, impatience for change played a major part. The original colonists sought tolerance for their differences in religious tenets. They were impatient with a government unwilling to change and accommodate them. Their impatience with conditions in Europe took hold in America. They grew impatient with Native American resistance to their usurping of traditional tribal lands. This impatience grew under the boot heel of English domination, erupting in open rebellion to the crown. It led to the creation of a new experiment in self-governing, disdain of royalty, and loathing the concept of divine ascension to the throne. Our impatience drove us to ignore many of the founding principles—life, liberty, and the pursuit of happiness—as we exterminated Native Americans in a quest to seize their land to satisfy our impatience with the status quo."

Broadmeadow goes beyond observing that "Yet, over time, despite sometimes violent changes, we came to tame our impatience and learn to direct it toward the common good. When our impatience clashed with the resistance to abolishing slavery and the secession of those who refused to release their fellow humans from bondage, we went to war. Our impatience with the continuous bloodshed faced an ever more powerful force in the commitment and dedication of one of the greatest Presidents we have ever had, Abraham Lincoln. Lincoln understood our impatience and turned it to accomplish the goal. It was our most costly war, yet we survived."

The author also looks at the preceding of WWII for answers to his call: "In 1939, the world plunged into a global conflagration. Our impatience with the last vestiges of the depression caused us to turn away from the battle as something outside our concern. Roosevelt understood this and sought to help those affected European nations without coming up against our intransigence to get involved. When the Japanese attacked Pearl Harbor, and the Axis powers declared war on the United States, Americans put aside their impatience. For four long years, we fought and died to save the world. Yet, an element of our impatience drove us to victory—and set the stage for our potential destruction. Seeking an end to the war ignited an effort to develop a weapon so terrible no one would want to use it."

"And we succeeded and failed. We built the weapon and, in our impatience with waiting for the inevitable fall of Japan, became the only nation to use atomic weapons. By July 1945, the defeat of the Axis powers was inevitable. Germany had surrendered, the Japanese were starving, surrounded, and running out of oil. When the Japanese refused to believe we had such a devastating weapon, despite efforts to convince them, our impatience compelled us to grant them a view of Armageddon. Thus came the destruction of Hiroshima, followed by the obliteration of Nagasaki. Our impatience had ended the war and opened a new chapter in world history. Soon, the atomic bomb gave way to ICBMs—missiles equipped with thermonuclear warheads. The dawn of MAD—Mutually Assured Destruction—was upon us.

The dual nature of impatience, often seen as a flaw, has paradoxically been a catalyst for some of humanity's most remarkable achievements. Broadmeadow highlights the drive to put a man on the moon as it exemplifies how impatience, when harnessed with a clear vision and purpose, can push the boundaries of human potential and accomplishment. This impetus to be the pioneers in space exploration, to be the first to step beyond our earthly confines into the cosmos, underscores the profound impact of directing our restlessness toward a monumental goal. It illustrates the immense power of human ambition and determination, revealing that within our impatient nature lies the potential for groundbreaking discoveries and advancements. This perspective invites a reevaluation of impatience, not merely as a vice to be tempered but as a force that, when aligned with purposeful objectives, can lead us to achieve the extraordinary and propel us into new frontiers of exploration and understanding.

"Youth have always been impatient, wanting each day to come sooner, to flyby, and then move on to the future they view as both destiny and a better place. Impatience fueled by the mistaken belief they have all the time in the world. With age comes the desire to slow down time, savor the moment, fend off the rapidity with which it passes. Yet when confronted with a challenge, we've forgotten all the lessons of history. We ignore the benefit of tempering impatience despite the hard lessons of our history", Broadmeadow concludes.

# 'Terpeniye'

However much goodness it may bring, patience alone is not a panacea and ought to be carefully practiced. It pays off when properly applied but it requires attention in order not to become complacence. The other side of the coin is that too much patience may lead to combustion and the result could yield explosive circumstances. An article from the Foreign Policy Rising, posted on March 29, 2017, is emblematic of the perils of excessive patience. If Americans are historically impatient, like the previous article portrays, Russians are clearly on the opposite spectrum. Glimmers of *The Russians' 'Endless Patience' and Why it Matters When it Breaks* craft a view through a different cortex:

"There is a word in Russian that has no equivalent in the English language: *terpeniye*. Something like patience and grit, *terpeniye* is the endurance of daily, mundane misfortunes, annoying relatives or a faltering career. It's also the bearing of suffering from melancholy, poverty and true hardship." As George Friedman said, the "Russian' strength is that they can endure things that would break other nations."

At the time this article was released in 2017, with Russia going through one of those self-discovery moments revealed by the government's opposition on how corruption had been tearing the social fabric of the nation, "*Forbes* was already asking if Russia was on the brink of a new Bolshevik Revolution."

Author Alexandra V explains: "While the West may have a romantic fascination with democratic upheavals, Russians do not. The Russians' fear of chaos and destabilization during 'democratization' is prominent in the living memory of the 'Wild 90s.'" Here the author refers to arguably this being the reason for the rising to power of a certain erratic leader in the first place, to this day. "And this lies in the dual side of the protest coin: Russian civil society is notoriously weak. Russians do not organize protests, are difficult to mobilize and don't tend to join civil movements … If Russians are protesting, something must be truly wrong." Russians are navigating through uncharted waters and may be bringing the world to a stalemate since the Ukrainian invasion in February, 2022. Reflections on the subject will be mentioned again later in another chapter where leadership and its implications are front stage.

"There is another phrase in Russian—*terpeniye lopnulo*—used when the patient, suffering-bearing *terpeniye* has burst. As historian Dmitri Trenin argues, "Russian people do not change their leaders every four to six years through the ballot box, but they bring down the entire state…on average every fifty years." It's not clear whether the Russian state is in danger yet. But what is clear is that Russians' patience is wearing dangerously thin."

The observation about Russian political dynamics reflects a pattern of profound and turbulent change rather than regular, incremental shifts in leadership through democratic elections. This perspective suggests that when change occurs in Russia, it's often not through the routine mechanism of voting but through more dramatic, systemic upheavals that can reshape the entire state structure. The historical context supports this view, with significant transformations happening approximately every half-century, including revolutions, the fall of the Soviet Union, and other major political shifts.

The current sentiment indicating that Russians' patience may be "wearing dangerously thin" hints at underlying social, economic, and political tensions and international isolation that could potentially lead to significant changes. This situation underscores a critical point in Russian history where the accumulation of dissatisfaction among the populace could reach a tipping point, leading to another major transformation. The precise outcome or when it might occur remains uncertain, but the statement captures a sense of brewing unrest and the possibility of a pivotal shift in Russia's political landscape.

Simultaneously, so is most of the world's patience around Russia's actions, in and on Ukraine; and in Russia itself and elsewhere where the crackdown on freedom of speech, crushing, imprisonment, surgical assassinations of opponents to the current regime, and the passage of increasingly draconian laws aimed at stamping out any dissent grows to critical levels. It gets old by the day and remains to be seen.

> *"So, the word is more sincere than concrete. So, the word is not a trifle. Then, may noble people begin to grow. And their words will break cement."* ~ Nadya Toloknnikova, Russian musician, conceptual artist, and political activist, founding member of the feminist group Pussy Riot, at her speech following the funeral of Alexei Navalny, at the opening of the FEAR NOT exhibition, quoting the words of Aleksandr Solzhenitsyn, Russian writer and Soviet dissident

# Cultivating Patience in an Impatient World

As we dreadfully breathed through a pandemic of biblical consequences, the whole planet waited for a coronavirus vaccine so that life could get back to normal. It felt like all of us were characters in *Waiting for Godot*. But unlike Samuel Beckett's play, where the protagonists are waiting for something that probably will never happen, we did expect that an all-encompassing cure would be found. We like to think that the results seem encouraging thus far, though much patience was needed and it is still required as we navigate the aftermath of a rough ride.

Manfred F. R. Kets de Vries, from INSEAD Knowledge, portrayed the momentum: "For many of us, 'cabin fever' has raised its ugly head, contributing to various mental health problems. Some of us may even have been quite sick, had a brush with death or had someone close to us die. It has been difficult to remain calm, cool and collected. In our world of overnight delivery, fast food and overall instant gratification, many of us don't even give ourselves the time to read a novel. Instead, we prefer to read short articles or watch YouTube clips. When our needs aren't met immediately, we become frustrated. Stress elevates our cortisol levels and triggers our flight or fight response. Impatience can transform leaders into agitated, poor decision makers. It can harm our reputation, damage our relationships and escalate already difficult situations. In sum, impatience is a root cause of much unhappiness in the world today."

Whether we recognize the moment and seize it, is up to each individual to decide. Deep breathing and consciously pausing can go a long way; and finding that equilibrium is what makes the difference. De Vries proposes that we discover our patience triggers (people, situations or even certain words), reframe the situation (use our conscious thought processes), fantasize (daydreaming or using other forms of visualization), practice empathy (put aside a self-centered view of the world), practice gratitude (to help build new relationships and boost current ones), use humor (to help defuse a situation that could otherwise spiral down), be realistic (by accepting situations beyond our control), practice mindfulness (to bring awareness of our experiences via our senses, thoughts or emotions), and ask others for help (to discover our trigger points and guide us into the proper ways of channeling them).

> *Two things define you: Your patience when you have nothing and your attitude when you have everything.*
> ~ Imam Ali, thinker, teacher

The pursuit of intelligence when seeking harmony, by adopting patience and no harm in our lives, is the real equation to be solved and requires a lifetime of dedication to the cause. De Vries helps us understand that the notion of practicing patience as an art form involving concealing impatience offers a nuanced understanding of how patience can influence one's life.

Patience is not merely about waiting passively; it's an active process of managing emotions and reactions in situations that test our endurance and tolerance. By viewing patience as an art, it implies that there is skill, practice, and intentionality involved in cultivating this trait, rather than it being an innate quality that one either possesses or lacks.

The approach to patience—as something to be practiced and refined—suggests that the benefits of patience extend beyond immediate peace of mind. By learning to manage impatience and navigate through frustrations with grace, individuals can create a more pleasant environment for themselves and those around them. This, in turn, can lead to better decision-making, as patience allows for thoughtful consideration and avoidance of rash actions that might lead to regret.

Moreover, the practice of patience is linked to long-term satisfaction and success. In various aspects of life, including careers, relationships, and personal goals, patience enables individuals to persevere through challenges, work steadily toward objectives, and wait for the right opportunities without succumbing to despair or frustration. This persistence and ability to delay gratification are often key components of achieving lasting success and fulfillment.

In essence, practicing patience by learning to conceal impatience is not about denying one's feelings but about channeling them in a constructive way. It's about building resilience, fostering a positive outlook, and laying the groundwork for a future that is both satisfying and successful.

To be hopeful in bad times is not just foolishly romantic. It is based on the fact that human history is a history not only of cruelty, but also of compassion, sacrifice, courage, kindness. What we choose to emphasize in this complex history will determine our lives. If we only see the worst, it destroys our capacity to do something. If we remember those times and places — and there are so many—where people have behaved magnificently, this gives us the energy to act, and at least the possibility of sending this spinning top of the world in a different direction.

> *And if we do act, in however small a way, we don't have to wait for some grand utopian future. The future is an infinite succession of presents, and to live now as we think human beings should live, in defiance of all that is bad around us, is itself a marvelous victory"*
> ~ Howard Zinn, historian, playright, philosopher

# Patience and Its Virtue

"Just a minute," Sarah's frail voice travels through from behind the door.

This story beautifully illustrates the profound impact that patience and a small act of kindness can have on both the giver and the receiver. It serves as a powerful reminder that behind every interaction, there's a human story and a chance to make a positive difference in someone's life, even in the most fleeting moments.

"Could you drive through downtown? I'm in no hurry," she said. "I'm on my way to hospice…I don't have any family left. The doctor says I don't have very long."

Breaking his near muted silence, the driver quietly reached over and shut off the meter then asked, "What route would you like me to take?"

The New York City taxi driver's decision to go beyond the call of duty—to step out of his car, to patiently wait and then to offer a ride without charge—transformed an ordinary fare into a final, cherished journey for the elderly Holocaust survivor. Jack's actions reflect a deep sense of empathy and compassion, recognizing that sometimes, the best thing we can offer is our time and presence.

This story also underscores the importance of viewing every encounter as an opportunity to extend kindness. The driver's willingness to drive through downtown, to listen to the woman's stories, and to simply be there for her. Acts that don't always require grand gestures; often, it's the willingness to listen and to be present that counts the most.

"I'm tired. Let's go now." As they arrive at her final stop, she asks, "How much do I owe you?"

"You don't owe me anything," Jack replies.

"But you have to make a living," Sarah insists.

"I'm sure there will be other passengers," the driver responds.

Two orderlies came out as if they had been expecting her.

Without thinking, the driver bends and gives the lady a hug. She holds on tightly.

The driver's experience illuminates how simple acts can be as rewarding for the benefactor as they are for the beneficiary. Jack's reflective silence, gratitude, and decision not to take any more passengers that night attests to the deep emotional impact the experience had on him, possibly reshaping his perspective on life and the importance of compassion.

A call to all of us to practice patience and understanding, the story tells us to not underestimate the strength of our actions, and to remember that behind every service, there is a human being with their own story, fears, and hopes. It's a lesson in humanity, teaching us that the moments we create for others can resonate in our own lives, reminding us of the beauty and depth of human connection.

# 'Please be Patient. Student Driver'

In the universe of bumper stickers and rear windshields, some signs proclaim "Caution: Student Driver" or "New Driver, Be Kind" or "Please Be Patient. Student Driver." All designed to remind other motorists that this driver doesn't have many miles beneath his or her wheels—and to use good judgment.

Looking closely, there is so much content on the quoted words. Skipping the semantics, and jokes apart, the sign we all see at least once a week—if not once a day—deserves attention if not reverence. *Washington Post* columnist John Kelly writes a sensible article on the subject and the title itself has a powerful message: "On the highway of life, maybe we should all be student drivers." Here's an excerpt:

"The roads would be a lot safer if we all were a little more understanding of our fellow drivers—more polite, more accommodating. Imagine if we all gave the car in front of us plenty of room, used our turn signals, let vehicles merge in front of us, passed on the left, used our headlights in the rain, cleared the snow from the roofs of our cars ... In other words, if we did the things they teach us to do in driving school."

Perpetual student drivers, perpetual students. This is what we are. We are perpetual learners. Preferably, not for the sake of knowledge but for the sake of learning. If given the right push from the very start, we may learn to learn and make it a lasting experience. And most importantly, by choice.

*People fly, people flee*
*People clam and say, "It wasn't me"*
*People fish, people beef*

*People arm to teeth*
*Yes, you've got people on the tube*
*Walking on the moon*
*People at the bottom of the sea*
*People in tombs*
*And People in igloos*
*Even a tribe of pygmies*
*People are the mainspring*
*Turning the world around*
*People, they're the mainspring*
*Spinning this world upside down*
"People" ~ King Crimson, prog-rock band

# Let's Grow Kids

*"I believe that if you want to have a deep, positive impact on our world, you have to start with children."*—Aly Richards, CEO, Let's Grow Kids

Virtues don't always need to be taught to the little ones. Nonetheless, proper guidance and role models go a long way. The Montessori method is one of a significant number of examples of child-centered methods of education. This one in particular involves specific child-led activities (referred to as "work"), classrooms with children of varying ages and teachers who encourage independence among their pupils. Like many other thoughtful methods, it sees virtue as a universal behavior that is recognized by people of many different cultures and necessary for every child's happiness and well-being. Once they are learned, or let be manifest, a child will follow them for life.

Kindness, patience, hard work, confidence, independence, honesty, responsibility, creativity, wisdom, perseverance, compassion, respectfulness, self-sufficiency, courage, helpfulness, grace, courtesy, joyfulness, sociability, humility, curiosity, and gratitude and service, are some of the virtues to be encouraged and fostered. Virtues such as these help to build a child's character and inspire those around them to become better people as well.

Shooting for the stars and getting to the moon, isn't that worth the trouble?

Every effort to get kids in school may make a difference not only to a child's life but to an entire community.

Let's Grow Kids values are transparent:

"We are change makers for children. Known for our transformational social mission and family-friendly policies, Let's Grow Kids staff, board of directors, and volunteers include state government leaders, national nonprofit directors, business executives, marketers, grassroots organizers, and early childhood educators and administrators with proven successes creating social transformation, advocating for policy change, and upgrading Vermont's child care system." Let's Grow Kids' commitment to creating and fostering a smart and healthy child care system revolves around providing Vermont's children the certainty that investing in their well-being, birth through five, is a catalyst for positive social change. "We are all about our community relationships. We support each other, our campaign partners, and advocates to realize shared success." By engaging and listening to the communities, a mindset of inclusion is intrinsic within the organization and campaign, therefore dedicated to building a system that promotes equity and diversity.

With a steadfast and yet agile mentality, "we pay attention to and adapt readily to our ever-changing environment in order to achieve our campaign goals." Let's Grow Kids's strategy is clearly defined: "In addition to our focused, coordinated, data-driven approach to our work, we are always collaborating and communicating with those around us—we go further by working together!" Intentional about sharing clear and timely information about their work, priorities, mission, and values, Let's Grow Kids seek to build trust—the foundation of a better future for all.

Vermont's child care system has accomplished a lot but it is far from perfect. Speaking of perfection, is there such a thing? Higher-quality child care in any environment is essential to the healthy development of youngest children, and it affects the State's ability to thrive, to broaden the tax base, to maintain the stable workforce businesses need, and to support economic stability and growth. Vermont is not always an affordable place to live, work, and raise a family, and its economy requires great attention, in part due to better access to affordable child care.

What makes the work of Let's Grow Kids so relevant and dependable is the 'birth through five' focus of their action. How important is it to support boys and girls at that tender age? It's HUGELY important. It does seem obvious, doesn't it? Well, if it really were that obvious why would a work like that be necessary? Let's examine that a little closer.

> *"We define learning as the transformative process of taking in information that—when internalized and mixed with what we have experienced—changes what we know and builds on what we do. It's based on input, process, and reflection. It is what changes us."*
> –From *The New Social Learning* by
> Tony Bingham and Marcia Conner

Parenting and/or caregiving is no joke and the first five years of life are critical. On the upside, one of the topics that becomes so important in raising a child are physical and cognitive development. While no two children develop on the exact same timeline, there are sensitive time periods in which major developmental milestones are reached, and one of the most critical stages of development and learning is from birth to five years old. The first five years of child development are essential to their health, wellbeing, and the overall trajectory of their lives in a variety of ways.

We all know that children need to be nurtured, talked to, and supported by their parents or caregivers, especially during their first five years of life. Patience and dedication are crucial and there's no other way around it. But what if this doesn't happen? What if a child's caregiver is negligent of, or unable to fulfill, their parental/caregiving duties?

When parents or caregivers fail to meet the emotional, physical, and mental needs of their child during these growth stages, for whatever reason, that's when potential future mental problems begin to germinate. That's when harmful and undesirable paths develop for all involved. Studies show when a child experiences neglect at a young age, it often manifests into deep-rooted issues that stay with them throughout the child's life, especially making an impact on the child's emotional intelligence, emotional development, and social skills and ability to play and socialize with other children.

The outcome is sometimes grim: by not receiving proper treatment from their caregivers during these child development stages, children are inevitably more prone to behavioral issues, low self-esteem, and/or lacking a sense of belonging, which may evolve into depression, mental health issues, and addictions. Unfortunately, these are the preceding steps to creating dysfunctional individuals.

*"We don't teach understanding the other, which is fundamental in our days; we don't teach uncertainty, what a human being is, as if our human*

*identity were of no interest. The most important things to know are not taught."* ~ Edgar Morin, Philosopher

What is the fundamental role of an entity like Let's Grow Kids?

Longtime friend Theresa A. Wood is a Child Care Champion at the Let's Grow Kids Action Network. Her words during a visit to a child-care unit:

"I had the great opportunity to visit a first-class, high quality childcare / pre-K this morning. The commitment, love and dedication that the folks at Apple Tree Learning Center provide to the children and families they serve is inspiring. We need more affordable, high quality child-care centers in Vermont, and we need to recognize the value that the people working in these centers bring to the education of young children and pay them accordingly."

Theresa Wood's appointment to the Vermont Legislature in the fall of 2015 marked the beginning of a significant legislative career that would soon intersect with the goals and efforts of Let's Grow Kids (LGK), the prominent organization focused on improving early childhood education in Vermont. Early in her tenure, Wood's introduction to LGK came through a senior field organizer from the organization, setting the stage for a deep and informative relationship that would markedly influence her understanding and legislative priorities regarding early childhood care and education.

"After an hour getting the sense of the organization, I learned about its essence and the need to identify the people that needed to connect with LGK. And

I knew that if they were going to make a difference, they would have to be persistent, it was going to take time and that they needed to lay the groundwork; it needed to be researched, informed, and that everybody counted, no matter the party lines," reveals Theresa on the efforts to push the project forward.

The information and perspective Wood gained from LGK highlighted several critical elements necessary for making substantial progress in the realm of early care and learning. First, she recognized the importance of being resolute; understanding that meaningful change in policy and public awareness around early childhood education would not happen overnight. This long-term vision underscored the need for strategic planning and consistent effort.

Secondly, Wood learned that any successful initiative would require intelligence and knowledge. LGK emphasized laying a solid foundation of information and evidence to support their advocacy for early care and learning. This approach ensures that efforts are not only well-intentioned but are also effective and targeted to address the specific needs and challenges faced by families and caregivers in Vermont.

Another key lesson was the importance of inclusivity and bipartisan support. Wood and her legislative team understood that advancing early childhood education initiatives would require collaboration and the engagement of a diverse range of stakeholders.

Aren't the well-being and development of children, after all, universal concerns that transcend political affiliations?

LGK's strategic approach also involved identifying

and connecting with key individuals and legislators who could help drive their mission forward. This network-building was essential for creating a broad base of support and ensuring that early care and learning were recognized as critical issues deserving of public and legislative attention.

Moreover, Wood's learning journey with LGK not only emphasized the significance of early care and learning for the future of Vermont, but the benefits for the broader societal and economic well-being. "Based on research," as expressed by Theresa, "we needed to lay out the reality of what we had as a State and what was lacking in regards to accessibility, affordability, and quality," the challenges in early childhood education that are not just state-level issues but part of a national and global conversation about the value of investing in the earliest years of a child's life.

The discussions around the needs in childcare, highlighted by reports and the work of the Blue Ribbon Commission prior to Wood's legislative start, served as a preamble for advocating for improved childcare services in Vermont. These efforts aimed to lay out the stark realities faced by families across the state—underscoring the gaps for access, as well as economic and qualitative aspects, to plant the seeds for systemic change in how early childhood care and education were valued and supported.

Theresa Wood's early experiences and interactions with LGK framed her approach to her legislative work, emphasizing even more the importance of knowledgeable, determined, and bipartisan hands-on efforts to enhance early childhood education. Through collaboration with organizations like LGK and by drawing on comprehensive research and community engagement,

Wood and her colleagues aimed to address the critical needs in early care and learning, recognizing its profound impact on the future of Vermont and beyond.

> *"No one has yet fully realized the wealth of sympathy, kindness, and generosity hidden in the soul of a child. The effort of every true education should be to unlock that treasure."*
> ~ Emma Goldman, writer, political activist

Indeed, Vermont has a history of being at the forefront of various social causes, and its approach to childcare is no exception. The state's progressive stance on issues ranging from environmental conservation to healthcare reform showcases its commitment to pioneering policies that aim to improve the quality of life for its residents. This dedication extends to the realm of childcare and early childhood education, where Vermont seeks to lead by example through comprehensive legislation and initiatives designed to support families, children, and educators.

# Patience, Focus and, Above All, Purpose

The passage of Act 76 represents a significant milestone in Vermont's efforts to enhance childcare and early childhood education, reflecting a concerted effort by legislators to address a critical issue that affects many families across the state. However, the challenges facing Vermont's childcare sector mirror a broader, national issue within early childhood education and care. Despite Vermont's proactive stance on childcare through legislation like Act 76, several critical issues persist, highlighting the complex nature of reforming childcare systems:

- Difficulty Attracting and Retaining Teachers: The early childhood education field often struggles with attracting and retaining qualified teachers due to low wages, limited career advancement opportunities, and demanding work conditions.
- High Tuition Costs: For families, the cost of childcare can be prohibitively high, rivaling and sometimes exceeding the cost of college tuition. This financial burden places significant stress on families, especially those with multiple children or those living on a single income.
- Long Waiting Lists for Few Slots: The demand for childcare often surpasses the supply, leading to long waiting lists for available slots. This issue is particularly acute for infants and toddlers, where the staff-to-child ratios are lower, and the care requirements are more intensive.

Signs of a failing system or a work in progress?

The culmination of these challenges fosters a sense of a

systemic breakdown among all stakeholders—families, educators, and childcare providers. Families struggle to afford and access quality child care, educators grapple with low wages and burnout, and providers face operational and financial hurdles in delivering their services. Undoubtedly, all stakeholders truly love what they do. But love alone won't do the job.

Addressing these challenges requires a multifaceted approach that goes beyond legislative reform. It involves increasing investment in the childcare workforce through higher wages and professional development opportunities, expanding subsidies to make childcare more affordable for families, and increasing the supply of quality child care slots through incentives for providers and support for new program development. Moreover, there's a need for broader societal recognition of the value of early childhood education and care, not only as a support system for working families but as a critical foundation for children's development and future success.

Theresa Wood, alongside her diligent, thoughtful colleagues in both the House and Senate, are playing a pivotal role in spearheading the initiative, demonstrating the importance of childcare and early education as a legislative priority. The journey to the enactment of Act 76, despite the initial veto, showcases the complex process of lawmaking and the determination of Vermont's legislators to support families and children. Act 76 stands as a testament to the collective efforts of lawmakers, advocates, and communities to prioritize the needs of young children and their families, setting a precedent for other states to follow in the pursuit of comprehensive childcare reform. A worthwhile work in progress.

Patience pays off. In October 2023, the news of $125 million as a substantial investment by Vermont lawmakers significantly helped address what is widely recognized as a child care crisis and marked a significant effort to ease the financial burden on parents seeking quality care for their children. When a state approves such a considerable amount in subsidies or financial assistance, the primary goal is to make childcare more affordable and accessible for families. By reducing the direct cost of child care for parents, these subsidies can significantly contribute to easing the financial pinch many families experience.

While the immediate impact of such an investment may be felt by the families who benefit from reduced child-care costs, the long-term effects can include a stronger, more resilient economy and improved educational outcomes for the next generation. Given that these subsidies are a recent development, continuous monitoring and evaluation will be essential to assess their effectiveness and to make adjustments as necessary.

Advocates pointing out that the investment is paying off is a positive early indicator. Success stories from parents who have benefited from the subsidies, along with reports of improved quality and accessibility of childcare, would further validate the effectiveness of this substantial financial commitment. However, the true measure of success will be seen in the sustainability of these improvements and their impact on the broader societal level, including workforce participation rates, economic growth, and long-term educational achievements.

*For some people, it's very difficult to
believe in politics. And, if you don't believe
in politics, democracy tends to wither.*
~ Martin Wolf, journalist

# Your Thoughts Here On Adopting a Mindset of Patience and No Harm

# Every Day (I Thank You)

### 3

## For Making the Extra Effort to Understand and Support Your Fellow Human Being

*So we're different colors and we're*
*different creeds*
*And different people have different needs*
"People are People"
~ Depeche Mode, electronic music band

"ONE OF THE VERY FIRST BATHROOMS that I pumped in seven years ago was at O'Hare International Airport (ORD). I was running in between flights and my boss had to hold my pumped milk while I ran back to the bathroom because I forgot my blazer hanging on the back of the bathroom stall. I was thankful for an amazing boss like him but imagine if I had an app that helped me find and access a dedicated space for me instead of a dirty bathroom?"
~ Nikkie Kent, a Working Mama

Our lives improve dramatically when we find nimble, creative and sensitive ways to circumvent inhospitable as well as inappropriate environments. Better yet, when ingenuity and hard work combined with a deep sense of humanity generate the substitute for unsuitable settings. This is the story of our lives. Stay on.

Each individual should have the right to make decisions and have choices about how they live their life. Each person has different ideas about what is important and what makes them feel best. Making our own choices about the things we do is fundamental because it gives our lives meaning. Family relationships, romantic relationships, friendships and acquaintanceships are the determinant factors for bringing meaning to our natural order.

Relationships are the fuel for learning. It truly surpasses the basic but highly important meaning of a connection between persons of blood and marriage, or emotional connections between people. If true learning is the ultimate goal of our existence through growing and transcendental experiences, it is without question that it starts with the very first relationship, that is, with the committed guardian(s) that give(s) us the support to flourish in the hopefully most welcoming environment.

What are the first and most significant events in a newborn's life?

Besides the immediate care at birth—delayed cord clamping, thorough drying, assessment of breathing, skin-to-skin contact, and thermal care, the early initiation of breastfeeding is the doorway to a baby's successful survival. The very first moments of breastfeeding, within one hour of birth, not only protects the newborn from acquiring infection but reduces newborn mortality. It facilitates emotional bonding of the mother and the baby providing a positive impact on duration of exclusive breastfeeding.

Breastfeeding, as one of the deepest acts of love between two beings, giver and receiver, is proof of the significance of such a glowing reality. But it's important that no extra pressure is dumped on a mother, as a precaution for her to not experience a sentiment of failure in case there are difficulties in the process of breastfeeding. It is what it is and every good intention should be rewarded. In her article, *Breastfeeding as a Spiritual Practice. Restoration Earth: An Interdisciplinary Journal for the Study of Nature & Civilization*, Molly Remer has a profound vision and understanding of the importance of the initial relationship of a child, enriched by the mother's embracing of the act of breastfeeding as an uncanny encounter for both beings:

"I have learned a lot about the fundamental truth of relatedness through my own experiences as a mother. Relationship is our first and deepest urge. The infant's first instinct is to connect with others. Before an infant can verbalize or mobilize, she reaches out a hand to her mother. I have seen this with my own babies.

Mothering is a profoundly physical experience. The mother's body is the baby's "habitat" in pregnancy and for many months following birth. Through the mother's body the baby learns to interpret and to relate to the rest of the world and it is to the mother's body that she returns for safety, nurturance, and peace. Birth and breastfeeding exist on a continuum as well, with the mother's chest becoming the baby's new 'home' after having lived in her womb for nine months. These thoroughly embodied experiences of the act of giving life and in creating someone else's life and relationship to the world are profoundly meaningful."

# A Glance Beyond Borders

As we broaden our perception and understanding on the theme, reflecting on the topic of breastfeeding would be incomplete without taking into consideration the cultural aspects of this important bonding experience.

Lana Hallowes, on *Babyology*, writes an interesting article about breastfeeding in multiple cultures. *From Mongolia to Italy: How breastfeeding differs around the world*, brings excerpts on the theme in eleven countries. Below, a sampling of what happens out there in six of them:

Mongolia
"In Mongolia, breastfeeding is celebrated and public breastfeeding encouraged with 65 percent of babies being exclusively breastfed for the first six months of life. Breastfeeding also tends to continue until after the second birthday. It isn't unheard of either for 'mother's milk' to be enjoyed by dads, chugging down a glass with their breakfast that their partner has expressed for them. In poor neighborhoods, breast milk is considered valuable and is traded for necessities like bread and eggs."

Kenya
"Up until recently, Kenyan mothers have not been supported in their right to breastfeed their babies. In 2003 only 13 percent of mothers were breastfeeding exclusively for the first six months. Nowadays, thanks to a strong public health campaign, 61 percent of mums with bubs this age are breastfeeding exclusively. The expectation to return to work straight after having a baby (what maternity leave?), poverty and poor knowledge about the benefits of breastfeeding are all cited as

obstacles to breastfeeding."

Australia
"In Australia, 96 percent of mothers initiate breastfeeding, according to a National Infant Feeding Survey. However, less than half (39 percent) of babies are still being exclusively breastfed by three months and about 15 percent by five months, according to the Australian Breastfeeding Association. This puts us quite low on the list of countries who breastfeed their babies beyond the newborn stage, which is quite sad."

India
"In parts of India, colostrum used to be discarded and viewed as a sign of infected breast milk —mothers would actually express this milk and throw it away! Thankfully, this doesn't happen so much anymore, according to one study. That said, India ranks poorly in regards to breastfeeding practices overall. Public breastfeeding is still frowned upon and only 44 percent of women are able to breastfeed their infants within an hour after delivery."

Brazil
"Brazil used to have a high infant mortality rate (63.2 deaths per 1,000 babies in 1985) and low breastfeeding numbers. Thanks to a strong public health campaign promoting the benefits of breastfeeding, this shocking statistic has been drastically reduced to 16 deaths per 1,000 babies.

"If you visit Brazil today, you'll likely see women breastfeeding their babies and children in public and without shame. Brazil has also banned advertisements that promote formula feeding, and businesses that are rude to women trying to feed their children typically face fines.

"All this work has made Brazil a leader in welcoming and inclusive views on breastfeeding. In 2018, there were only 292 human milk banks in the world – where women can donate their unused breast milk to help hungry orphans, the poor, or other mums who can't produce milk – and Brazil ran and operated 220 of them. Thankfully, that number has risen across the world – we now have 750!"

Italy
"In Italian hospitals, dummies [pacifiers], formula and glucose are encouraged right from the get-go. According to La Leche League International, a nonprofit advocacy group that aims to raise awareness and acceptance of breastfeeding, the introduction of bottles in the 1970s changed the Italian parenting culture dramatically. Although breastfeeding isn't shunned in Italy (the Catholic church even promotes it), only 19 percent of women continue to breastfeed past four to six months, despite 85 percent being breastfed at birth." It is refreshing and encouraging to perceive that people and impressions evolve in regards to breastfeeding. As much as it takes time and incredible effort to educate individuals and communities, gaining awareness spontaneously tends to be a slow process and requires support beyond the family cell. Governmental initiatives, nonprofit organizations, and the private sector may play a critical role here.

# Nothing Is Easy

Much to people's disappointment, controversies galore and are not exclusive to this or that particular culture.
In her book *Inventing Baby Food: Taste, Health, and the Industrialization of the American Diet*, Amy Bentley argues that distaste for public breastfeeding in the US began with the sexualization of female breasts in the 19th century and was accelerated by the rise in processed baby food occurring around the same time.

Maureen Shaw on the *Shame No More* series, has a similar take here: "A quick Google search on breastfeeding in public returns numerous reports of women being bullied while breastfeeding, asked to retreat into bathroom stalls to feed their babies, or worse, asked to leave the premises altogether. This harassment is by no means a new phenomenon. Breastfeeding moms have dealt with shaming long before social media and citizen journalism helped bring it to light."

In a perfect world—is there such a thing?—with the exception of health conditions that may simply impede the initiation and duration of breastfeeding, it would be substantial to see the great majority of mamas—with the no less consequential support of papas—putting their best foot forward around breastfeeding their child for at least the first year. Studies have revealed that the babies who breastfeed for a longer period of time grow a more steady and matured mind, not to mention the physical benefits created by a consistent development of a better immune system. Besides, mothers who breastfeed have higher levels of satisfaction and are said to be happier.

Breastfeeding brings a lot more than just physical benefits. Breastfeeding is considered by many to be a spiritual exercise. The act of nurturing another life through your own body is a powerful activity and goes beyond the visible boon. Babies who have been breastfed beyond the age of one, grow up to be more emotionally mature and stable adults as compared to the babies who have not been breastfed. There is plenty of medical and scientific evidence to back up this statement.

# Changing the Landscape

"Congratulations mama, you birthed a tiny human! Soon, if not already, you'll become an expert on the basics of napping, spit up, and diaper rash. But new moms also need to learn how to return to work empowered. Employers, coworkers, friends—even family—aren't always supportive when it comes to breastfeeding and pumping in the workplace."

*Pump or Bust*, by author Karlee Vincent, "is a great resource for any new parent navigating the workplace while nourishing their baby, a must-read for the breastfeeding parent and the community that needs to support them," attests Sascha Mayer, from Mamava. Karlee Vincent is a parenting advocate who has lived through the trifecta: traveling, working, and pumping. This new and fresh perspective on breastfeeding in the workplace and beyond offers a rich, candid and captivating outlook on the journey of new motherhood. Karlee's own and investigative experiences resonate deeply, reminding us that "as new parents, we navigate not only the arrival of a precious baby but also a transformative evolution of ourselves."

# The Mamava Experiment

"Moms have been breastfeeding babies for...well, since the dawn of time. Yet there's still stigma around breastfeeding in public and moms still lack the support they need to pump at work. Why is a natural human function—that literally sustains life—so controversial? Why is breastfeeding support for working mothers so slow? The history of breastfeeding has been shaped by shifting cultural norms and it reflects the quest for substitutes—for breast milk and for breasts. Enjoy this condensed history of human infant feeding—breast, bottles, and formula—through the ages." [1]

Sascha Mayer and Christine Dodson took the bull by the horns. Literally fed up with pumping in bathrooms and borrowed spaces, these visionary women and thoughtful leaders applied their decades of expertise in design and brand strategy with a clear sight of this modern day human dilemma to solve a problem that was largely invisible: the lack of lactation spaces in workplaces and public spaces. The result, the creation of Mamava.

*"We'd pumped breast milk in closets, bathrooms, and cars. We'd had enough."*

Mamava—it is spoken like "Mama-va", as the Spaniards would say "Mama-go"—is a company born in the Queen City, moniker for Burlington, VT in 2013 to address the cultural issue of breastfeeding by "increasing equitable access to the structural support that breastfeeding parents need at work and on the go."

---

1 The aforementioned quote is an excerpt from a session of Mamava's web page, The History of Breastfeeding, portraying quite an interesting chronology. The link: https://www.mamava.com/mamava-blog/history-of-breastfeeding

But it's more than that: "Mamava is dedicated to transforming the culture of breastfeeding. The category creator of freestanding lactation pods, Mamava provides breastfeeding parents with private, dignified, and comfortable spaces to pump or nurse."

Mamava's Chief Revenue Officer, Nikkie Kent—then Hessney when we first met in the same office building complex in 2010—was already a brilliant and successful young professional running the Vermont office of a major worldwide printer manufacturer and digital solutions provider:

"I started off my career in sales as my first job out of college working for IKON Office Solutions. What a fun company with an amazing group of mentors and people. I walked in the door for my interview and told my future boss and mentor Sharyn "I am just looking for someone to give me a chance, I promise I will work harder than anyone and not let you down."

A few years later and with a meaningful sales managerial and leadership experience on her belt, Nikkie left to become the Director, then the Vice-President, Retail and Account Management of a promising local online ecommerce, marketing and data platform service for grocery chains. From day one, I knew Nikkie was well on her way to becoming a quintessential professional. Smart, energetic and incredibly personable, her constructive and foundational mindset was evident:

"Two major influencers in my life... My family and 'The beautiful game.' My family gave me unconditional love and support to believe that I could do and accomplish anything. My dad showed me through example the importance of work ethic. These fundamental values set me up to spend my childhood working towards a Division I soccer scholarship. Being a part of a team felt like I was a part of something so much bigger than myself. This set me up for a lifetime professional pursuit of being on and building winning teams."

We kept sporadic contact over time until reconnecting five years later. By then, Nikkie had just had her first child—little baby boy Asher, Nikkie's first exceptional fulfillment in the realm of parenthood:

"It was like playing (10) 90-minute soccer games back to back with no water break and then winning the best championship prize of my life." Nikkie's life had understandably moved from being a high-octane professional to being a high-octane professional first time mama! Truly accomplished, personally and professionally, Nikkie had great hopes to continue to balance out her life now that her family had grown in meaningful ways.

# No Picnic

*"Women, like men, should try to do the impossible. And when they fail, their failure should be a challenge to others."* ~ Amelia Earhart, aviation pioneer, writer

Life is great, right? Not so fast. Frustrated by not having a reciprocate and more forward thinking positioning from her employer when it came to supporting the sought-after balancing life she had aimed for, Nikkie looked out for her professional soul mates. And found them.

"Mamava is changing the world and being a part of that feels like I'm not "working" at all, says Nikkie in one of her statements around this great company. And adds:

"Mamava has designed the first free-standing lactation suite which provides a clean, comfortable and dignified place for a mother to pump or nurse wherever she might need it. Mamava's mission is to create a healthier society through a changed cultural perception of breastfeeding that affords every woman the opportunity to nurse her child regardless of her circumstances." Nikkie's experience is genuine: "I lived with the problem for a whole year, it was the hardest marathon I've ever run, with little to no support or resources to get me through it. I pumped four times a day for a year in airport bathrooms, restaurant bathrooms, cars, offices with windows and I was one of the 'privileged' pumpers. I'd imagine that the barista at Starbucks doesn't have an office with a lock on it or more than a 30-minute break. I strongly believe it is every woman's right to nurse her child and for the 47% of women who go back into the workforce after having children, they need to be supported and have accommodations to support their breastfeeding goals. Mamava provides the solution for businesses to be in compliance with the Affordable Care Act, while also serving as an excellent advertising platform for brands eager to connect with a highly targeted, engaged and high-value mama audience. Businesses and brands alike have been benefiting from the earned media generated by taking a progressive stance to support moms and families. In the end, we have built a community by providing support and resources to both of our customers: the world who needs to buy our pods and our mamas who need to use them."

Mamava has hit multiple goals and accolades—and is poised to great heights and meaningful growth: "Our Lactation Suites can be found in Airports, Hospitals, Sports Stadiums (Fenway!), Convention Centers, Public Schools and Universities, Private Businesses, Government and the Military and even Museums and Zoos."

Nikkie's inspiration and pride? "People who are passionate and want to change the world to be a better, more inclusive, more supportive and loving place. I am motivated by their energy and pursuit of excellence to move communities, countries and culture forward." What makes her proud? "Being a working mom. It's the hardest thing I have ever done, to choose to spend 40 hours a week away from the most important thing in my life. At the end of the day I know that in order to be the best mom I can be, I must be my best self and that self is building off of the person I have become for the first 31 years before I became a mom. I am very proud that my boy has an example in his mama for a strong sense of self."

Nikkie now is mama not only to Asher, but Addison and Penelope joined the fam in recent years. She lives in Vermont where she loves to grow, make, and eat good food. Her partner Jeremy is also a working papa and a true embracer of the cause of parenthood.

# Intentional Design: Problem and Purpose

The importance of understanding the needs of the users, the business and merchants, then focusing on the problem and purpose of the design is what makes the effort worthwhile. Intentionality here is key because when it's ignored, the design becomes irrelevant. Good design is that which is intentional and therefore considers its long-term impact on both direct and indirect users. Co-founder Sascha Mayer's thinking, as the business evolved and became more mature, as follows:

"Just like a mother raising a child, the goal was to create a healthy and self-sustaining business that could thrive without me."

Mamava's Sascha Mayer, the co-creator of a new market segment, the freestanding lactation pods, in 2013, spent ten years as CEO "shepherding it from a concept (born at my kitchen table) to a profitable business." And then, in June 2022, she found a new CEO to run the company.

As a CEO, Sascha pitched to investors, developed products, hired vendors, designed office spaces, and wrote Mamava's employee manual. "We built a team, sold thousands of pods, bought a factory, and weathered the COVID-19 pandemic. But I realized that in building the business, I had moved further away from the reason I started it in the first place—to create a better experience for breastfeeding parents. Now, experience is my primary focus, and I also get to use the coolest acronym in business: CXO, or chief experience officer."

# CXO?

In a nutshell, a C-level, more engaged and conscientious leader. As objective kindness and thoughtfulness play out in the equation, the new role is tuned into the human experience. Rather than a singular focus on either customer experience, employee experience, or user experience, the CXO attends to the full breadth of audience experiences, both inside and outside the company. Sascha's job is to ensure that "every interaction audiences have with Mamava is excellent and aligns with our brand mission and values."

This is not always easy and it takes an army of equally principled collaborators to make Mamava stand out:

"Many of my colleagues joined the company because of our mission to support breastfeeding. Often they have a personal connection to the challenges of breastfeeding, and they want to make it easier for other parents. Whether it's with customer service or working with supply chain partners, when my colleagues can make that mission connection, they become the most powerful brand ambassadors we have—and they can only do this if they are feeling engaged and respected at work."

Nikkie Kent's decision to create room and navigate new waters in her personal and professional life brings her tenure at Mamava to a bittersweet but incredible outcome:

"2024: The end of my Mamava era and the start of a new chapter. In December, I made the hardest and bravest professional decision of my career. To find the courage to move on from the company I've spent the past eight years loving and building, in search of a different kind of growth.

"I have been so proud to push for progress in breastfeeding equity, creating infrastructure where it did not exist before. I've had the privilege of working with the most amazing clients and partners and together with a hardworking team we moved the needle and changed the world for new parents. What a lucky life experience to start something from scratch, build and evolve a business strategy, successfully commercialize a product, humanize the pumping experience in the workplace and grow the company enough to create jobs and recruit amazing people to work there. The purpose, the progress and the people worth every high and every low.

"Sascha Mayer and Christine Dodson I have unwavering appreciation for you, the brand that you created, the visionary founders that you are and the grind of the startup journey that we went through together. Thank you for supporting me and giving me the opportunity to make a difference.

"For now, I'm taking a much needed professional pause to create space for something new. I'm looking forward to spending time with my three little kids who have all been born and raised right alongside Mamava. I'll be cheering her on from the sidelines, dreaming up what's next!"

Mamava has shown many the way. Where do we go from here when it comes to making inclusion an equitable and readily available developmental resource?

# Your Thoughts Here
# On Making the Extra Effort to Understand and Support Your Fellow Human Being

# Every Day (I Thank You)

## 4

### For Taking Care Of Yourself and for Caring For Those Next to You ~ And Beyond

*If the sky that we look upon should tumble and fall
Or the mountains should crumble to the sea
I won't cry, I won't cry
No, I won't shed a tear
Just as long as you stand, stand by me*
"Stand By Me" ~ Ben. E. King, songwriter

**HAVING ONE'S HEART IN THE RIGHT PLACE** seems to be a good way to define caring, doesn't it?

Jean Watson is an American nurse theorist and nursing professor who is best known for her theory of human caring. Jean Watson's Nursing: *The Philosophy and Science of Caring*, considered a classic, is one of the pioneers in introducing the science of human caring and rapidly became one of the most widely used and respected sources of conceptual models for nursing. It offers a contemporary update and the most current perspectives on the evolution of the original philosophy and science of caring, from the field's founding scholar.

Caring is essential in the nursing profession—and beyond—because it helps in the healing process. For nurses, it is a way to show empathy, compassion and emotional support toward their patients. Caring can be done in many different ways, including talking to an individual or supporting them physically. We know it is not circumscribed to the profession of nursing as it goes way farther than the realm of caring in exchange of material benefits, e.g., in hospitals or nursing homes.

According to Watson's vision, "a core concept for nurses and the professional and non-professional people they interact with, 'care' is one of the field's least understood terms, enshrouded in conflicting expectations and meanings. Although its usages vary among cultures, caring is universal and timeless at the human level, transcending societies, religions, belief systems, and geographic boundaries, moving from Self to Other to community and beyond, affecting all of life".

# Skin In The Game

"I don't care." "Who cares?" "I couldn't care less." "Why should I care?"

We all know the multiple meanings of the above statements and probably say them or think about them every now and then. The fact is, every time we talk or think that way, it typically is not true. Why? Because these are phrases that stand in for a range of ideas and emotions. Among their many meanings, they go from expressing confusion, disinterest, 'open-mindedness,' awkward admiration, and even malicious intent. It is not necessarily 'polite' to say "I don't care," we really mean something else. It may also mean exactly the opposite. Or, that we are too lazy to think about an answer. Or even the classic "I don't know."

For better or worse, we are not always aware that words have meaning and that they may impact relationships in meaningful ways. Food for thought, abandoning the casual "not caring" is not a bad idea altogether. The majority of us not being nurse practitioners, it is worth drawing some inspiration from these usually compassionate individuals. Caring, literally or metaphorically, helps bring our hearts to where they need to be while the subject of our interaction remains in a neutral place, unaffected, undamaged and perhaps, prone to be helped. And hopefully healed. Even if it is only for a fraction of time.

# A Brave Lady in Crimea, the 'Avenging Angel'

Wars invariably show the most despicable and darkest sides of human nature. Inevitable acts of cruelty degrade the spirit, brutalize our souls and, for periods of time, shut down the avenues of connection and understanding between human beings, so critical for our existence and survival. But wars can also bring out the best in people.

There's no better reference for caring than the creator of Modern Scientific Nursing. It started with the crusading endeavors of Florence Nightingale during and after the Crimean War, between 1854 and 1856. "The Lady with the Lamp" blended Christian ideals, strict discipline, and a sense of mission to open the door for what is known today as the nursing profession.

Florence was born in Tuscany, Italy in the same city of her name, from an affluent British family. She earned the nickname 'the Lady with the Lamp' during her work at night when she would ambulate among the beds, checking the wounded men, holding a light in her hand.

A figure larger than life, Florence was by no means a conventional individual during her time. She was well-acquainted with challenging working conditions, and nursing was not a common practice at the time, especially for a woman. Well educated, she also loved writing and traveling, spoke multiple languages and had a natural skill for analyzing data.

The groundwork of nursing practiced across the world were pioneered by this greatest character in nursing history.

She helped to define nursing practice by suggesting that nurses did not need to know all about the disease process like the medical field.

In October of 1853, the Crimean War broke out. The British Empire along with allies were at war against the Russian Empire for control of the Ottoman Empire. Just as it is role-playing in present days with the Ukrainian assault, a century and a half ago Crimea had become a geopolitical hotbed, pitting an expansionist Russia against much of the world. Thousands of British soldiers were sent to the Black Sea, where supplies quickly dwindled. By 1854, no fewer than 18,000 soldiers had been admitted into military hospitals.

From the *History Channel*, here's a picture of the British experience: "At the time, there were no female nurses stationed at hospitals in Crimea. The poor reputation of past female nurses had led the war office to avoid hiring more. But, after the Battle of Alma, England was in an uproar about the neglect of their ill and injured soldiers, who not only lacked sufficient medical attention due to hospitals being horribly understaffed but also languished in appallingly unsanitary and inhumane conditions."

Florence's work brought the field of public health to national attention. She was one of the first in Europe to grasp the principles of the new science of statistics and to apply them to military—and later civilian—hospitals. Florence forever changed the face of the nursing profession, as she not only created sanitary conditions so that patients could receive the best care, but elevated the quality of caring, bringing more dignity to its realm.

# Lili's Precious Guide

Lili's story resonates deeply with the universal challenges of caregiving, the complexity of family dynamics, and the inevitability of facing mortality. It captures the essence of a journey many find themselves on—navigating the turbulent waters of caring for aging or ailing loved ones while managing the demands of their own lives. The scenario is well known for many. It is one where the personal meets the universal; caregiving is a role that many will take on, yet each experience is profoundly unique.

Friend and neighbor for almost two decades, Lili Udell Fiore's decision to write a book on this topic addresses a significant gap in resources for caregivers and those grappling with how to provide a dignified and peaceful end of life for their loved ones. *Lili's Caregiver's Guide* serves as a beacon for those in the throes of caregiving, offering solace, guidance, and true practical advice. It acknowledges the weight of the caregiver's role and the often overlooked emotional and physical toll it takes.

"What started as a few short pieces on important information for Caregivers, and how to prepare and create your Loved One's best possible passing, has turned into a full manual with forms and lots of personal history from my life and some from my friends," reveals the author.

The inclusion of lessons and wisdom garnered through both personal experience and formal education enriches Lili's narrative, making it not just her story compilation, but a guide for others. Her certification as an End-of-Life Doula, underpinned by the teachings of her father, Reverend Lee Udell, lends a depth of understanding and compassion to the difficult conversations and decisions surrounding death and dying.

Moreover, the book underscores the importance of preparing for the end of life, not just in practical terms but as a profound aspect of living fully. Through her father's teachings and her own experiences, Lili emphasizes the value of understanding death as a part of life, encouraging conversations that many shy away from.

"The hardest thing about aging and illness" says Lili, "is we feel that we have lost control of our lives, and in many ways that is true. We don't know what we can count on to stay the same because so much of what our life looks like has changed so drastically."

School, in general, as previously mentioned in this book, does teach us a lot of essential things—but some fundamentals tend to be undervalued. Lili's guidebook addresses a gap in our societal education, providing crucial knowledge and resources that many of us are unprepared for until we face these challenges head-on. It's not just a handbook for the present moment of caregiving or grieving but a preemptive measure for understanding and navigating the inevitable experiences of aging that touch every life. By offering practical advice, emotional support, and a comprehensive approach to the multifaceted journey of aging and loss, Lili's work becomes an indispensable companion through some of life's most challenging yet universal experiences.

Incorporating Dr. Gary Chapman's concept of *The Five Love Languages* into caregiving, as Lili has done, is a profound approach that enriches the caregiving experience for both the caregiver and the care receiver. This framework, which identifies five primary ways people express and experience love—Words of Affirmation, Acts of Service, Receiving Gifts, Quality Time, and Physical Touch—offers a lens through which to understand and travel through the emotional landscape of caregiving relationships.

By identifying and understanding the primary Love Language of a loved one in need of care, caregivers can tailor their support and communication in a way that deeply resonates with the care receiver. This personalized approach can be particularly meaningful when caring for someone who may not be able to communicate their needs and feelings in traditional ways, such as those with advanced dementia or terminal illness. Lili's own experience is as emblematic as it is transcendental:

"My mother and I fought for years. I never understood what I was doing wrong and why we couldn't communicate better. Well, I discovered that my love language was Words of Affirmation—so I thought that if I was verbal and loving and supportive with her she would know how much I loved her. Well, guess what? My mom's Love Language was Acts of Service—so she needed me to 'do' things for her versus use words... BIG miss! As soon as I read the book, I talked to her, and we were both so relieved and happy to know why we were having so much trouble. Two lives changed in a matter of a few hours. It took me to read the book and call her up! It was seriously life-changing, and when she was ill and dying, it gave me the insight I needed to make sure that I showed her that I loved her in a way that she could easily receive it, which made all the difference in the world to us both."

Lili's practical and keen observations teach us that applying the Love Languages in a caregiving context does more than just facilitate effective communication; it fosters a deeper emotional connection and ensures that actions of care are perceived as expressions of love and support. In her own experience with her mother, if the care receiver's primary Love Language is Acts of Service, practical help around the house or assistance with personal care tasks may be experienced as deeply loving gestures. Conversely, if their love language is Quality Time, simply being present and engaging in shared activities can significantly enhance their sense of being loved and valued.

Understanding critical aspects of caring can illuminate past misunderstandings or conflicts within the family dynamics, offering a path to reconciliation and healing. Recognizing that miscommunications often stem from differences in expressing and interpreting love can alleviate guilt, frustration, and resentment, paving the way for more harmonious relationships.

As one of the most important highlights of Lili's book, her guide offers a deeply compassionate and practical approach to one of the most challenging aspects of caregiving for someone with cognitive decline. Walking the journey alongside a loved one experiencing symptoms of Alzheimer's, Lewy Body Dementia, or other forms of dementia requires immense emotional resilience and flexibility. As Lili suggests, adapting to the ever-changing landscape of dementia with love, understanding, and humor can significantly impact the well-being of both the caregiver and the loved one.

Here are some key takeaways from Lili's approach:

1. *Embrace Loving Kindness and Understanding*
Dementia fundamentally alters the way individuals perceive and interact with the world around them.

Approaching these changes with a heart full of love and understanding helps maintain a connection that transcends cognitive decline. Recognizing that behaviors like paranoia, agitation, or confusion are symptoms of the disease, not personal choices, can help caregivers respond with empathy rather than frustration.

## 2. *Infuse Situations with Humor*

Humor is a powerful tool for coping with stress and can lighten moments that might otherwise be fraught with tension and sadness. Laughter can provide a temporary escape for both the caregiver and their loved one, creating moments of joy amidst the challenges. It's important, however, to ensure that the humor is not at their loved one's expense but rather a shared experience that brings them closer.

## 3. *Be Present in Their Reality*

Attempting to correct or argue with a loved one's altered perception of reality often leads to further distress. Instead, Lili advises "dancing with their reality" by entering their world and engaging with them on their terms. This approach can reduce frustration for both parties and promote more harmonious interactions.

## 4. *Utilize Distractions*

Distractions can be an effective way of shifting focus from distressing thoughts or behaviors to more positive activities. Whether it's through engaging in a favorite hobby, looking through photo albums, or simple tasks, these distractions can provide a sense of normalcy and pleasure.

## 5. *Incorporate Music*

Music has a unique ability to soothe, uplift, and reach

parts of the brain that remain intact far into the disease process. Playing beloved songs or melodies can awaken memories, stimulate emotional connections, and even prompt sing-alongs or movement.

Caring for someone with cognitive decline is an emotional rollercoaster, but by adopting Lili's recommendations, caregivers can create a nurturing environment that respects their loved one's dignity and enriches their quality of life. It's about finding balance, seizing moments of happiness, and cherishing the time spent together, even as challenges arise.

Lili's recommendations to both the caregiver and the care receiver (when possible) bring precious and practical steps that can significantly impact the caregiving experience. It equips caregivers with the knowledge needed to express love in the most impactful way, ensuring that their efforts to support and comfort are aligned with the care receiver's emotional needs.

Widely encompassing and deeply engaging, from legal, medical and personal care perspectives, to special caregiving circumstances, *Lili's Caregiver Guide* is a lighthouse. Through its highly practical narrative, it is a vital contribution to the discourse on caregiving, death, and dying, providing much-needed insight and support. It's a testament to the strength found in vulnerability, the wisdom in experience, and the power of shared knowledge. For readers, whether they are currently caregivers or simply wish to understand more about creating a compassionate end-of-life experience, Lili's book carries the promise of being an invaluable resource.

# A Way Forward

Looking for and finding lighthouses that illuminate the way forward for our humanity through caring for each other as individuals—and uniting our cultures in love and compassion as a whole—is practical and objective. It is food and remedy at the same time. Yes, it takes a lot of effort. Carefulness. Circumspection. Prudence. Concern. The list is long. But it's not only beneficial to the receiver—it reduces stress, increases happiness, and brings a sense of social connectedness. It is also beneficial to the giver's well-being. Especially in difficult times, it helps develop empathy. No wonder true caregivers feel valued and experience personal growth in significant ways. These individuals gain a variety of skills from their experiences and gain intangible benefits that last a lifetime.

The article on "The Conversation" in *Asian countries do Aged Care differently. Here's what we can learn from them*, from Angelique Chan, University of Singapore, enlightens our understanding on the dilemma of caring:

"Unlike in Western countries like Australia, traditional Asian cultures place a heavy emphasis on filial piety—the expectation children will support their parents in old age. Historically, filial piety played an important role when families were large, pension schemes unavailable and life expectancy was around 50 years old. Today, however, families in east and southeast Asia are much smaller, divorce rates and rates of non-marriage are increasing, and fewer adult children are living with their parents. These demographic shifts are nowhere more apparent than in China, Hong Kong, Japan, Singapore, South Korea and Taiwan."

To make things more interesting, almost everywhere in the developed world, people are living much longer. "By 2030, the UN estimates 60% of the world's older population (60+) will reside in Asia." It is worth highlighting that Asian governments continue to promote the idea that "families should be primarily responsible for the care of older family members, amidst these demographic and cultural changes."

Modern life and constant economic and social pressure push families, especially many adult children, to encounter immense obstacles when fulfilling the demands of filial dedication. "Those who are unable to provide care because of work demands or their own family responsibilities often find it emotionally difficult to put their parents or grandparents in institutional care."

Because of these challenges—as well as the rapidly aging populations in many Asian countries—societies are being forced to think creatively about how to improve community care for the elderly who don't have around-the-clock family support. A holistic focus? Not quite, yet. In many developed economies, aged care has become increasingly fragmented. In the traditional model, an older person typically has specialists for each organ and may visit a general practitioner, a doctor in a polyclinic, a hospital, and/or a traditional healer over the course of a year.

The irony is that none of these health records are integrated.

# Integrated Care Means Caring

"The idea is to provide older and 'undeserved' people with medical and social support when they need it, but not to take them out of their communities," says Angelique Chan. Research in these communities has shown older adults who "age in place" are happier and have a higher quality of life than those in institutions. It sounds great and it is. In this model, a registered nurse and health care assistants are situated in communities and provide health and social care to residents living in their own areas. The goal of this system is to manage people's health and social care needs at home to reduce frequent hospitalisations and entry into nursing homes.

"China, for example, is currently experimenting with different models of community health services to achieve an integrated care system. Japan has invested heavily in the training of geriatricians and the development of community care services."

In the next decade, the models of health and social care for older adults must be re-imagined like this to support aging populations.

Integrated care seems to be the way forward, not only for the rapidly aging populations in the richer Asian countries but also in the West. "This is the best solution for maintaining a high quality of life among older adults where it is no longer possible to rely on the family as the primary support system for older adults."

# China Rises

Navigating history can be fascinating, especially when we have the ability to detach ourselves from current-day events and focus on the subject of our discovery journey. Given its historic longevity and relevance, it is hard to think of a more profound and meaningful country and its denizens where historical facts are so abundant. China is one of these countries.

Let us take, for example, what is known as the Four Great Inventions. Those were inventions from ancient China that are celebrated in Chinese culture for their historical significance and as symbols of ancient China's advanced science and technology. They are the compass, gunpowder, papermaking, and printing, which truly altered the course of the world. China held the world's leading position in many fields in the study of nature from the 1st century BC to the 15th century AD, with the four great inventions having the greatest global significance. These four inventions had a profound impact on the development of civilization throughout world history. However, while the Four Great Inventions serve merely to highlight the technological interaction between East and West, some modern Chinese observers have noted that other Chinese inventions were perhaps more sophisticated and had a greater impact on Chinese civilization. Nevertheless, not everything is about inventions.

# The Caring Dragon

A mythical creature considered a member of the animal kingdom concept, like the Phoenix, the Kylin, and the Tortoise, the Dragon plays an important role in the imaginary conscience. Although there is an immediate tendency to associate the mythological Dragon to the Chinese and its multicolored festivals, we encounter records of its folkloric representation in multiple cultures such as the Egyptian, European—particularly the Greek, and also Middle Eastern mythologies, to name just a few. Beliefs about dragons vary considerably through regions. Dragons in Western cultures since the High Middle Ages have often been depicted as winged, horned, and capable of breathing fire. Dragons in eastern cultures are usually depicted as wingless, four-legged, serpentine creatures with above-average intelligence.

Dragons in Chinese culture, unlike the Western dragons, are not depicted as enemies to be defeated. They are considered wise and welcoming and a sign that good things will come. With ancient Chinese origins, dragon boat racing and its history has been traced back more than 2,000 years. It was created as a rite to awaken the hibernating Heavenly Dragon. The first participants were superstitious Chinese villagers who celebrated the 5th day of the 5th lunar month of the Chinese calendar (the summer solstice). Racing was held to avert misfortune and encourage the rains needed for prosperity - and the object of their worship was the dragon. The dragon of Asia has traditionally been a symbol of water. It is said to rule the rivers and seas and dominate the clouds and rains.

# Dragonheart

Trust makes our hearts beat as one. When two or more people work together on a task, caring for and trusting one another, their hearts beat faster and become synchronized.

"Dragonheart Vermont strives to strengthen and empower breast cancer survivors and supporters through the challenging sport of dragon boating, instilling in its members the values of teamwork, fitness and community giving." As a dynamic dragon boat organization located in Burlington, Vermont, Dragonheart Vermont has been ahead of the curve when it comes to bringing their members to the higher grounds of teamwork and collaboration.

Whereas dragon boating is a fast-growing team paddle sport that embraces athletes of all ages, gender, and abilities, Dragonheart today is so much more than that.

Starting as a breast cancer survivor team, Dragonheart Vermont presently has two hundred members that make up their ten different teams. "Our actions stand out both on and off the water. Our DHVT teams excel and have been named national and world champs. We are committed to our Vermont community and host the Lake Champlain Dragon Boat Festival where people in our community team up to race dragon boats for charity."

Born of a time-honored Chinese tradition, dragon boat racing today engages more than fifty million people worldwide every year. Dragon boats are about forty-one feet long. Twenty paddlers sitting two by two stroke in unison, guided by a drummer at the front and a steersperson either seating or standing at the back of the boat that keeps the boat on course. The boat glides when all twenty paddlers stroke in time.

As more than a sport, dragon boating has gained popularity because of its inclusive nature, embracing people of different ages, genders, and abilities. "It is the ultimate team sport!" In addition to youth, premier and senior teams, the sport includes teams of cancer survivors, paraplegics, and the visually impaired.

Dragon boating offers an equal playing field for all. From Dragon Boat Vermont's website:

"What other sport can match that? The key to success for a dragon boat team lies in the team members' ability to stroke together. It's teamwork at its best—twenty-two hearts beating as one!"

# It's Alright, Abby

"What inspires creativity? I've tried to figure out why sometimes I feel incredibly clear, tapped in and articulate, and other times distracted, lazy and muddled. Often inspiration comes to me when I'm massaging, and I think it may be linked to movement, the energy between me and the client, or the stillness and breath that come naturally with massage. I often wish I could pause the session to write as the ideas seem to flow in a magical way, only to disappear just as quickly. The 'daydreaming' often brings me to a place of awareness and revelation I find amazing, and it reminds me how slowing down itself can encourage self-reflection and inspiration. How do you do it, friends who create? Do you carve out intentional space-time or just grab a pen or guitar when the mood strikes?"

The words above reflect one person's profound aim at self-realization. Living ten-plus years in the iconic Colorado mountains of Avon/Edwards made my friend Abby Kenney an even more free-spirited individual than she had been as a native of Vermont. Not only did she expand her love of nature, and respect and appreciation for all things living as evident in her clear respectfulness for all creatures, but it was in Colorado that Abby truly flourished as an individual genuinely connected with her own and other people's wellbeing.

To illustrate where geography confluences with poetry and music, the song, "America the Beautiful" was based on a poem written by professor, poet, and writer, Katharine Lee Bates, during an 1893 trip to Colorado Springs, Colorado. When she got to the top of Pikes Peak, the view was so beautiful that it inspired her to write, "All the wonder of America seemed displayed there, with the sea-like expanse."

The same regard for generosity and giving was what prompted Abby to move from Colorado back to Vermont in 2014. Her focus now was to spend time with her father as his condition due to prostate cancer worsened, and to help support her mother in caring for him. A brave and resilient survivor, he would have a terrible decline over the next three years, which really took a toll on her. After his death in 2017, Abby and her Mom tried to adjust, supporting each other intensely.

> *"And the tears come streaming down your face*
> *When you lose something you can't replace*
> *When you love someone, but it goes to waste*
> *Could it be worse?"*
> "Fix You" (a) ~ Coldplay

Life manifests to each of us in strange ways. Diagnosed with breast cancer in August, 2018, Abby felt like she was in the prime of her life. "In 2018 I was slowly pulling away from my grief, and feeling joy and hope for the future. I had been working part-time for the airlines since 2015 but hadn't been able to travel much with Dad's worsening health. I had just started to travel again and was happily using my benefits. Earlier in the year I went to Chile and Peru and hiked Machu Picchu. I spent *Midsommar* at my friend's house in northern Sweden, and bopped around Finland a bit before meeting my friend in Mongolia. That summer I was in phenomenal shape and was taking steps to start IVF and hopefully get pregnant, when I found a lump in my breast."

Abby's love of the unknown, new places, and people, would give way to a new and unexpected journey: the battle of treatment and the pursuit of healing.

"I was not yet at the recommended age for a routine mammogram, so I asked for a referral. I wanted to get it checked out before I started all the hormones associated with pregnancy. My diagnosis was a shock I couldn't fathom. I was so healthy! I practiced massage therapy and was fortunate enough to love my work, did yoga, exercised regularly and had lots of time outdoors, avoided chemicals, ate organic foods, avoided stress, and all of the other preventative measures I had learned. It just didn't make sense. Everything turned upside down, and I had to embark on an overwhelming and terrifying journey. My body had always been my greatest ally, and suddenly I felt doubt at what it meant to be healthy. I wondered what could possibly have led me to develop breast cancer, and people offered me a lot of unsolicited advice, often contradictory. I didn't understand how to support my body while also trying to kill a part of it (with chemotherapy and radiation), that was also trying to kill me. The idea of a cancer 'battle' made no sense to me.

Fighting my own body? I had gone from caregiver to patient, and I wasn't familiar with this role; was this the lesson? Was my diagnosis trying to teach me to slow down, to receive?"

Coming from the holistic world of bodywork, Abby definitely leaned more toward less invasive and "alternative" methods of treatment: "I unconsciously assumed that I would take alternative routes if ever faced with a diagnosis like this. Once I dove into statistics, evidence, science, and exhaustive research, however, I changed my tune. I had a very aggressive and deadly type of breast cancer. Herbs, essential oils, colon cleanses, juices, and saunas were not going to save my life. Accepting that I had to submit to these harmful and damaging therapies to save my life was one of the hardest decisions I ever made. I faced resistance and judgment from all sides, mostly from my massage therapist friends. It was a lonely road. The nurses in the infusion center ended up being my biggest resources and cheerleaders, knowledgeable about the medication side effects and endlessly kind, caring and supportive. Some of them are my friends to this day."

*I moved to California in the summertime*
*I changed my name thinking that*
*it would change my mind*
*I thought that all my problems they would stay behind*
*I was a stick of dynamite and it was*
*just a matter of time, yeah*
*Oh dang, oh my, now I can't hide*
*Said I knew myself but I guess I lied*
*It's okay, it's okay, it's okay, it's okay*
*I wrote a hundred pages but I burned them all*
*(Yeah, I burned them all)*
*I drove through yellow lights and don't look back at all*
*I don't look back at all*
*Yeah, you can call me reckless, I'm a cannonball (uh, I'm a cannonball)*
*Don't know why I take the tightrope and cry when I fall*
*Oh dang, oh my, now I can't hide*
*Said I knew what I wanted but I guess I lied*
*It's okay, it's okay, it's okay, it's okay*
*If you're lost, we're all a little lost and it's alright*
"It's OK" ~ Nightbirde, singer-songwriter

# The Dragon Knocks On the Door

"I kept going to my weightlifting circuit classes at the gym, but things had changed. Now I'd go to lift weights on the way to the hospital to get chemo, knowing that I wouldn't be up for much for the following week. After a week's recovery from each chemo infusion, I'd get on the treadmill and struggle through a slow 5k jog, tears streaming down my face. One day, a friend commented that my 'aura seemed smaller,' and asked if I was okay. I was pushing and trying to maintain a sense of normalcy, but I was also shrinking, feeling increasingly alone and dark. For years I had seen a woman working out there and heard that she was a professional athlete, a dragon boat paddler on the National team. I didn't even know what a dragon boat was. Her name was Nikki, an incredibly fit and strong woman. One day she approached me and said that she'd heard that I had breast cancer, and asked if I'd heard of Dragonheart Vermont. She told me about the sport and its connection with breast cancer, and encouraged me to check it out and hopefully join. It was still winter, and in Vermont the paddling happens in the summer, but Nikki emphasized the powerful community, and that there was training all year round."

Abby was finishing chemo and still had surgery and radiation to go. The treatment would have to run its course:

"As soon as I recovered from my surgery enough to lift weights, I started going to DHVT's off-season training. I had never been in a dragonboat and knew nothing about the sport, but I loved to exercise, and fit right in during OST [on-site training]. People were so welcoming. Every time I went to train, people encouraged and supported me, and I learned that DHVT had many different teams, made up of different age groups, cancer 'status,' or gender-some competitive and some more recreational. Out of over 200 members, about 65 seemed to be breast cancer survivors, and we had our own boats: Sisters and Soul Sisters."

By summer, Abby was all in: "When the teams hit Lake Champlain in June, I attended a Sisters' training weekend and started to learn the fundamentals of paddling. As it turns out, DHVT has a very well-established and competitive program thanks to John and Linda Dyer starting it about 15 years ago (now 20!), and lots of enthusiastic athletes here in Burlington, VT who love to support the cancer community and try new things. I happened to join in 2019—the year that DHVT was sending multiple teams to Colorado in August for the National competition. The winners of these races won a bid to the World Championships in France the following year. So even though I felt pretty horrible, had a lot of lingering pain and tightness from the radiation, was on hormone modulators, and still receiving a monoclonal antibody infusion every 3 weeks, I was officially invited to join the competitive Sisters team and start training for Nationals."

Through the effort of this incredible group of individuals, the outcome could not be more auspicious: "We won!" Always a great sensation, though the real victory for Abby was the community and the constant support she received as a part of the DHVT club. "On the boat we shared and laughed, sang and cried, and gave it our all, trying to paddle in perfect time with speed, power and efficiency. Before and after training drills and races, we would put our hands on each other's backs, connecting as a boat, our energy becoming one. That summer I also experienced the power and beauty of my first flower ceremony. All of the breast cancer survivors drew our boats together on the water, floating as one, and we were all given flowers (hundreds of us). After honoring those we had lost, there was silence and singing, lots of tears and smiles, hugs between the boats, and then we all threw our flowers into the water–sunflowers from Eugenie's gardens. I've experienced many flower ceremonies since, and it's a memorable and moving experience for everyone involved, including those witnessing it." With tears of joy come the epiphany: "Is there a single person who hasn't had their lives touched by cancer, or witnessed the sickness or suffering of a loved one? Every time we were on the water, or fundraising in the community, or training together, was a celebration of life."

*When you try your best, but you don't succeed*
*When you get what you want, but not what you need*
*When you feel so tired, but you can't sleep*
*Stuck in reverse*
"Fix You" (b) ~ Coldplay

As a relatively young woman when diagnosed, Abby felt very unsure about her future. Her relationship with her body felt unsafe and unfamiliar, and she was often overwhelmed with fear, pain, isolation, fatigue, and depression. Being surrounded by women who had survived their diagnosis and treatment felt comforting and inspiring. Not only had they survived, they were strong, fit, dynamic, loving, successful, and thriving. There were scientists, veterinarians, farmers, teachers, mothers, and so many other paths represented among her teammates, and it showed her that she might get a chance to age. "These people were living fully despite challenges, and I wanted that.

Watching them helped me realize I might get to be a fierce athlete and competitor in my 60s or 70s. I also hadn't realized how much I'd missed being on a team, being coached, and competing. All winter we trained, thrilled at the prospect of going to France the following summer."

Abby finished her infusions in November and all winter felt the drugs leaving her system. "I was feeling really fit again, and starting to think about my future. The pandemic hit and made the world topsy-turvy, but I was working out more than ever, walking with friends daily, and enjoying the time at home and slower pace of life. My jobs at the airport and as a massage therapist ground to a halt, and I was patching stuff together, like delivering groceries for Instacart. I was even pursuing pregnancy after the requisite 7-month washout of the drugs that would cause birth defects. I went in for my 6-month check up with my surgeon, as I was over a year out of my surgery, and she told me that I was covered for annual MRIs because my breast cancer type was particularly aggressive, and I was so young."

# Heads Up, Always

Shock, disbelief, anger, fear. "Unimaginably, the MRI revealed two small tumors near my original incision, and after two MRI biopsies I was told that it was the same as my original cancer: triple positive invasive ductal carcinoma. Either my cancer was still there and hadn't fully responded to treatment, or it had returned. Terrible news. After receiving the recommended and aggressive treatment my survival chances were good; I had only an 8-10% chance of my cancer returning within 5 years. It had only been 6 months, so I was now an outlier in the worst way."

Like many others diagnosed with aggressive breast cancer, Abby's oncologist told her that the standard of care would now be a mastectomy. "With or without reconstruction, the 'tumor board' recommended that I also do more chemotherapy to try to kill any cells that may have escaped the breast tissue. It was a new targeted chemo drug, and they weren't sure how many rounds I should do as I didn't really fit the parameters of the trials they'd done. So the next few months were filled with imaging, second opinions in Boston, meeting with breast and plastic surgeons, insurance hurdles, researching clinical trials, and asking every woman I knew who had been through breast cancer treatment what they had done and what they would recommend. The thread through all of it was a sense of hopelessness and doom. Why me?"

When Abby went into her complex microvascular surgery in August 2020 (it ended up lasting twelve hours) that would require a twelve-week recovery, DHVT kicked into gear with a sustained and heartfelt support campaign: "Members organized a massive burrito bash fundraiser for me, started a meal train, blanketed me with cards, gifts and words of encouragement, and became my support system. I was no longer alone on this journey, as I had felt the first time around. Sisters called to see how I was doing, and comforted me as I cried and raged at my situation and the unknowns." A couple of months later, Abby would start another ten-month chemotherapy regimen, and her spirit was not nearly as strong this time around: "I didn't care about my research, my nutrition, my fasting before treatments, or any of the stuff I'd done the first time around. I sunk into a deep depression, and couldn't see beyond treatment to the other side. Through the pandemic and chemotherapy I was still working sporadically, massaging, and even keeping up my shifts as a baggage handler at the airport."

During the summer of 2021, the coronavirus made it very difficult for the Dragonheart teams to practice or compete because people couldn't be in such close proximity to each other, and many of its members were immune-compromised, like Abby herself. "I was wrapping up chemotherapy and 3 years of active treatment and wondering what was next. I felt equally grateful to be alive and unsure of what was to come. If I had a year to live, what would I be doing? How would I spend my time, and with whom? I felt like I was a different person, with different priorities, and that nothing was the same. Finishing treatment offered a new terror, of feeling like I wasn't doing anything to treat the cancer. A deep and debilitating grief set it, and I realized that a huge part of my treatment was just beginning: the mental and emotional part. When you're push push pushing, going through treatment, only looking forward to the next infusion or procedure, there's no time to process any of it, or even feel it. The shock and trauma were just sinking in, and I had a lot of healing to do."

*Lights will guide you home*
*And ignite your bones*
*And I will try to fix you*
*And high up above, or down below*
*When you're too in love to let it go*
*But if you never try, you'll never know*
*Just what you're worth*
"Fix You" (c) ~ Coldplay

# Grace Amazing

There are many symbols for grace as well as there are multiple meanings. The ocean is one of its largest symbols, with shallow and deep currents permeating its never ending motion. It may be unpredictable, but the motion of the ocean is a wonderful representation of the emotions tied to grace. Also seen as a symbol of stability, it is boundless, a place where one can easily be lost, and can therefore be seen to represent the unlimited span of our essence, and the way we can navigate our journey through life.

"The polarities of movement and stillness inform my life." For the last fifteen months since finishing chemotherapy, exercise has been Abby's savior. "The more I move the closer I am to sane and I am so grateful to get to work mostly on my feet. Breast cancer complicated my relationship with my body (even more): I did everything right, took such good care of myself, and I still got sick. We were allies! At times, it's been difficult to celebrate my body, unable to touch it, or even look at it. This is changing, and with a lot of grace, as medications and surgeries have made it look a certain way that is largely out of my control. My self-care is on fleek, and I love my body for its function and strength. Trauma is stored in the body, and it has taken me a while to get over the shock and fear, as well as the cutting and poking."

# Wholeheartedly Authentic

*You've gotta dance like there's nobody watching, love like you'll never be hurt, sing like there's nobody listening, and live like it's heaven on earth.*
~ William W. Purkey, writer, educator, researcher.

The past couple of years marked a return to hope and perspective, energy plus vitality that Abby cherishes, knowing she is the captain of her own destiny. Her self-nurturing attitude is inspiring as is her mindful approach to promote physical, emotional, and mental awareness. Deliberate actions for sanity. "I found myself dancing in my room at night to Maggie Rogers, or taking an evening bike ride through the hood, singing at the top of my lungs, feeling like a teenager—filled with joy and a sense of freedom. These are not small things."

*Oh, I couldn't stop it*
*Tried to figure it out*
*But everything kept moving*
*And the noise got too loud*
*With everyone around me saying*
*"You should be so happy now*
*"Light On"* ~ Maggie Rogers

Above and beyond, just keep at it, friend. Paddling, pedaling, and dancing.

# Your Thoughts Here
## On Taking Care Of Yourself and Caring For Those Next to You ~ And Beyond

# Every Day (I Thank You)

## 5

## For Harnessing the Higher Spheres of Music, Art, Science and Knowledge

*I sing because the moment exists and my life is complete.*
*I am not happy nor sad: I am a poet.*
*Brother of the ephemeral, I do not feel joy nor agony.*
*I cross nights and days in the wind.*
*Whether I break down or build*
*up, whether I stay or disperse,*
*—I don't know, I don't know. I don't*
*know if I stay or walk away*
*I do know that I sing. And the song is everything.*
*It has the eternal blood of a rhythmic wing.*
*And I know one day I will be silent:*
*Nothing more.*
"Motive" ~ Cecilia Meireles, poet

SHE COULD SEE BEYOND THE STARS, when it came to realizing her students' potential. Juliette Nadia Boulanger, French music teacher and conductor, was probably one of the most influential music teachers of the 20th century. Also a composer, she was the first woman to conduct many major orchestras in North America and Europe.

"Arguably, some say, the most influential teacher since Socrates." Beyond teaching at world famous musical institutions, Boulanger also taught a wide number of pupils privately. Her roster of music students reads like the ultimate 20th Century Hall of Fame. Just to name a few: Leonard Bernstein. Aaron Copland. Quincy Jones. Astor Piazzolla. Burt Bacharach. Michel Legrand. Philip Glass. Egberto Gismonti. Donald Byrd. Geirr Tveitt. John Eliot Gardiner. Daniel Barenboim. Elliott Carter. Nadia was a close friend of Igor Stravinsky. "George Gershwin wanted to study with her but was rejected because she was afraid that rigorous classical study would ruin his jazz-influenced style."

> *"That four bar passage during which the melody is restated emphatically while the harmony shifts… followed by a rimshot and a rest and then it's the head again. I live for that."*
> ~ David Becket, music sommelier

"All these musical giants, so different yet so groundbreaking in their own ways, studied with Boulanger. She gave them a rigorous grounding in academic musical analysis, yet somehow enabled each of them to find their own distinct language: perhaps the very definition of what makes a great teacher. She had a singular way of encouraging and eliciting each student's own

voice – even if they were not yet aware of what that voice might be. Boulanger's name remains largely unknown outside niche classical music circles, despite the astonishing impact she had on the soundtrack to all our lives, not just in the realm of classical but in jazz, tango, funk and hip-hop. Truly a cheer to the woman who contributed so much, with so little fanfare, to the history of 20th and 21st Century music."
~ Øystein Bru Frantzen, musician

It is an irrefutable fact that the visual, literary and performing arts do convey important insight into the way we conceive and understand the world as it is. Simply stated, it is widely acknowledged that art gives a significant degree of meaning to our lives. It has been like this for millennia. Art, literature, and music in particular, can elicit new beliefs and even new knowledge about ourselves so deep that it borders on the realm of transcendence.

From a mindfulness sharing perspective, art may give us knowledge about our human emotions and surroundings; it allows us to see life from different angles, and it makes us feel alive. It may also highlight the importance of our community and give us a deeper sense of "self." The arts shape the identities of individuals and cultures by exposing their true voices and sensibilities. Art can take the form of rituals, it might even incorporate religious symbolism, and sometimes it embodies the history of a given culture or community. And, more importantly, it has been used as a tool for cultural exchange, education, and expression.

Considering the contradictory and somewhat absurd nature of our existence—we can achieve great things with kindness and love, but we can also commit terrible acts; we can create beautiful art to stand the test of time and yet cause unimaginable pain; every day we taste the benign indifference of the universe in the face of human suffering, the pointless monotony of human labor, and the finality of death—why should we care about art from a knowledge standpoint?

Scientific studies have proven that art appreciation improves our quality of life and makes us feel good. When we create art, we elevate our mood by activating reward pathways in the brain, reducing stress, and lowering anxiety levels; we improve our ability to problem solve, and open our minds to new ideas. One of the things that has been alleged to be the purpose of art is its cognitive function: art as a means to the acquisition of truth. Our truth. Art has even been called the avenue to the highest knowledge available to humans and to a kind of knowledge virtually impossible to attain by any other means.

*Before children speak, they sing. Before they write, they paint. As soon as they stand, they dance. Art is the basis of human expression.*
~ Anonymous author

# Music as an Intro to Spirituality

Charlie Haden was one of those special creatures who embodied the connection between earthly and transcendence. A legend in jazz music, he started as a singer on his family's country radio show when he was just two years old. After losing his singing voice to polio as a teenager, he found a new voice by picking up the bass. That decision launched a career that spanned in jazz, country and gospel music for decades.

A lover of music as a language and beyond, while Haden did not identify himself with a specific religious orientation, he was profoundly interested in spirituality, especially in association with music. He felt it was his duty, and the duty of the artist, to bring beauty to the world and make it a better place. As a teacher, Charlie Haden encouraged his students to find their own unique musical voice and bring it to their instrument. Haden also urged his students to be present in the moment, emphasizing, "there's no yesterday or tomorrow, there's only right now." To reach this state and ultimately discover one's spiritual self, Haden advocated for humility and respect for beauty, gratitude for the ability to make music, and a commitment to giving back to the world through music.

He believed music taught him this process of exchange, which he, in turn, taught his students. Haden saw music as a medium that imparted incredibly valuable life lessons. He stated, "I learned at a very young age that music teaches you about life. When you're in the midst of improvisation, there is no yesterday and no tomorrow—there is just the moment that you are in. In that beautiful moment, you experience your true insignificance to the rest of the universe. It is then, and only then, that you can experience your true significance."

By fostering this mindset, Charlie Haden believed that artists could transcend the mundane and tap into a profound, universal connection through their craft.

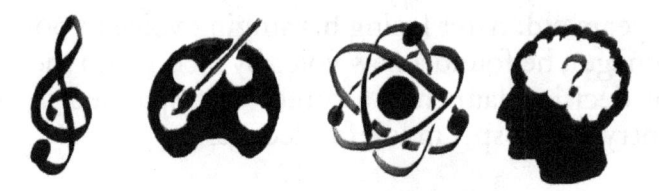

# Leonardo's Desk

Just like Johann Sebastian Bach is revered in the universe of music, it's hard to think of anyone's influence being more emblematic than Da Vinci's when it comes to being the true embodiment of art, science, knowledge, and manifestation. He serves as a role model applying the scientific method to every aspect of life, including art and music. Although he is best known for his dramatic and expressive artwork, Leonardo also conducted countless carefully thought out experiments and created futuristic inventions that were groundbreaking for the time.

The Renaissance Man, lefthanded, supposedly gay, essentially an outsider for the standards of his time, is "a genius and a potent symbol of the 'universal man' because of the breadth of his interests in the arts, science and technology." Jonathan Pevsner in his *"The Mind of Leonardo Da Vinci"* cites his superior curiosity at disciplines from "chemistry (he discovered acetone) to astronomy (he discovered the *lumen cinereum*, the ashy light of the moon) to math (he discovered the center of gravity of a pyramid)."

Leonardo's art and the myriad of his final elements of manifestation, though easily recognizable, is not the focus of this reflection. Instead, the core of this observation is centered in his deep engagement with the world; his pledge inspired his compassion for people, animals, and the environment. Renaissance humanism, the guiding idea of Leonardo's time, valued human dignity and education, while seeking humanity's natural place within the universe.

And here is the point of bringing this mega-luminary to this consideration: the artistic, curious mind as a conduit for sanity, purpose, and growth. Being curious about everything and curious just for curiosity's sake, not simply because it's useful, is the defining trait of Leonardo. It's how he pushed and taught himself to be a genius.

We'll never emulate Einstein's mathematical ability; or Copernicus' astronomical creation of a new model of the Universe positioning the Sun at its center; or yet, Beethoven who was arguably the greatest composer who ever lived. But we can all try to learn from, and copy, Leonardo's curiosity, his multi-dimensional widest and deepest legacy.

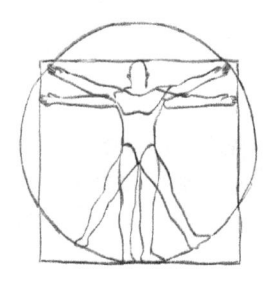

# Stykos's Refuge

Truly a curious character, the words that follow are drawn from this singular artist's web page: "Kristina Stykos wrote her first poem 'Walking Home on a Snowy Evening' as a fourth grader and performed her first original song 'On a Moonlit Summer Night' in the pavilion at Girl Scout camp. Working under the pseudonym Gardenessa for almost a couple decades, she's become known for her artful landscape design and top-notch flower gardening. But she's probably better known as a musician who runs her own recording studio, writing songs and singing late into the night ... or disappearing into the woods on a ramble. *Ridgerunner: One hundred poems and photographs from rural Vermont* is her first book of poetry."

Americana-style, wisdom, experience, and whim permeate this artist's path: "With her debut collection of poetry, Kristina Stykos emerges as a vibrant fully mature voice, writing lovely short stories and poems that resonate on many levels, as the best of stories and poems do. With soul and soil, ribbed with humor and delivering metaphor with a deft touch, *Ridgerunner* offers thoughtful moments etched as water over stone, to be enjoyed and returned to for the measure of what it is to be human upon this earth." ~ Jeffrey Lent

There are sensible reasons in my mind to draw analogies between the great Cecilia Meireles and the refreshing work of Kristina Stykos. Perhaps unseemingly and despite nationality, generational, and geographical aspects which separate these two wizards of the written word, both have silence and solitude in common. And both, musically gifted and intensely personal, at some point in their lives, began cultivating their own spiritual journeys where life and poetry would join together.

# Inspiring Parallel

Born in Rio de Janeiro, Cecilia Meireles dismisses a major introduction. Writer and educator, she is known mainly as a poet; a canonical name of Brazilian Modernism (1922-1945), she is one of the great female poets in the Portuguese language. "Motive", the opening lyrics of this chapter, a scriptural rune to me, is one of her remarkable poetic works. Cecilia Meireles, ahead of her time, is widely considered the best female poet in her native country, though she combated the word *poetess* because of gender discrimination.

One gets hooked by Kristina's poetry and writing talents. Says Ruth Porter, "When you read them carefully, the meaning ripples out, like rings in a pond when you throw a stone into the waterway." Just as well as her way of showing gratitude for one of her birthday wishes on a social media post that is as unique as it is honest and sharp-witted. Her means to express her outspokenly optimistic and seemingly extroverted soul shows how strong she evokes respect and affection from most likely everyone she comes into contact with. Here's how the post goes:

"THANK YOU, friends in kind, in mind, friends of friends, bots, and trolls! THANK YOU patrons, matrons, unrequited acquaintances who fill my cup with artistic fodder. THANK YOU by name, by level of fame, or ill repute or because we still harbor some ancient dispute. I praise what we shot, or shoot for, this urge to merge & be one, with zeros and naughts, in bits, & bytes, in cheese & chocolate, or by loving that's real, showing up at your door, with my troubles. THANK YOU for wanting to expunge & criticize, or dig what I utter, or be puzzled by how weird the world looks, thru my eyes. My year now, is started at the darkest of times, under brightening stars, & the sharpening cold, and the silencing snow and by loss, and by honor. THANK YOU to all you strong doers, & fixers, & dreamers; those abandoned at outposts, or left behind on cliffs, where the clicking flakes make drifts, and the rapping arctic howl sculpts an uneasy sleep, marked by hour, upon hour, of waking up alone. THANK YOU to the lonely malcontents, to the glib hiders of trauma, to those who still rise to the keys, to sing, & say, & soothe, and shower us, with their unburdening, & restless power. THANKS BE GIVEN EACH DAY, for this temporary shelter, and for the solace of our motley [on & off-line] human tribe, as we revive. For hearts can't stop, nor be slain, only gifted to the next, more perfect future, beyond our present pain."

Kristina Stykos consciously leads her interesting and meaningful life far from the frenzied throng. She is keenly aware of the mischievous and problematical world we live in, and deliberately elects a secluded lifestyle in rural Vermont as her safe harbor. Her poems from the bucolic Green Mountain State uncover "a joy shining through cracked prisms of love, loss and letting go," exploring from the ground up, what it is to be human. Also devoting her time working as a landscape gardener, while trying to "eke out a living as a musician," Stykos' "persistent voice is as singular as it is unsentimental, musing on a hardscrabble existence made transcendent by the nearly indescribable beauty of her wild and remote surroundings."

Elusive and yet transparent, musician, poet, producer, nature lover, Stykos uses language that is "conversational and easy to grasp, her poems are at once elegant and dynamic, taking us directly into the heart of her daily routines. Whether it's pruning a gangly rose bush, eating lunch on a truck tailgate, or taking a chance on a muddy and forgotten dirt road, she makes it clear that there is always more to understand and contemplate about this gnarly paradox we call life."

The lyrics of her song "River of Light" reveal the quality of her soul aligned with her free spirit:

"The wind will push you on, It knows where you belong, It's what you've been given, That makes you so driven, The road is your bed, You won't see them again, They can't change what you did, And the days go missing;

It doesn't matter now, When I hit the ground or how, The skin of the land is as soft as a hand, On this highway of snow, I know where to go, We'll meet there tonight, And cross the river of light."

*Understand well as I may, my comprehension can only be an infinitesimal fraction of all I want to understand.*
~ Ada Lovelace, mathematician, writer

# Factual and Verse, Where Do They Meet?

"One can't live poetically all the time. Life is a struggle between prose and poetry. Prose is boring, what you have to put up with. Poetry is that state of beautification, of communion, of joy, which gives love to the other, collective friendship, work of art. Each of us must seek to cultivate the poetic side of life because that is living. The other is just survival."

Known for his work on complexity and "complex thought," and for his scholarly contributions to such diverse fields as media studies, politics, sociology, visual anthropology, ecology, education, and systems biology, French philosopher Edgar Morin makes it easy for us to grasp the importance of balancing the concrete world and the conjectural world.

We all need prose-poetry in our lives, rather than one *or* the other. It's like adapting our living with the use of poetic devices such as 'fragmentation, compression, repetition, rhyme, metaphor, and figures of speech,' while preserving our sense of reality and grounded focus.

# Allegorical Truths

Eric Dorfman's article on the Carnegie Museum of Natural History web page—*Art, Science and The Intersection of Knowledge* is an eloquent representation of the confluence between these three critical elements which function as a tripod for our foundation as humans.

In Roman mythology, Vertumnus is the god of seasons, change and plant growth, as well as gardens and fruit trees. Dorfman portrays his admiration for the painting of the same name from Italian painter Giuseppe Arcimboldo produced in Milan c. 1590. Arcimboldo's most famous work, it depicts the Holy Roman Emperor Rudolf II as Vertumnus, the Roman god of the seasons, transformation and abundance.

"I've always loved this painting. Vertumnus looks serenely at the viewer, a slight smile making you think he knows something you'd like to. It's a clever work of Mannerism, seamlessly weaving a complex array of perfectly rendered fruits and other plants into the portrait of a human face full of character. The portrait is of the Holy Roman Emperor Rudolf II, a contemporary of Elizabeth I, William Shakespeare and the flowering of one of the important periods in Western culture."

Giuseppe Arcimboldo makes a flattering gesture by linking Rudolf to Vertumnus where the Emperor is allegorically depicted as "a godlike figure, responsible for eliciting positive change in his empire." Dorfman is drawn to the sense of fun portrayed in the painting—a juxtaposition of plants, grains and fruits that amuse the writer for its effectiveness and engaging effect.

"By marrying art and science (in this case, plant anatomy), Arcimboldo attempts to describe the world and, in some way, helps us understand his version of it through the oblique mechanism of allegory."

Dorfman delineates the need to understand the world around us as "one of our most primal needs" and the impetus we carry to share that understanding. "We are motivated to understand because we—humans in general—are (justifiably) afraid of the unknown. In fact, the craving for order and predictability is a trait that may have had its origins in our most ancient roots as a survival skill in our earliest ancestors. The early Hominids, like any other animal, would have been vulnerable to the dangers of changing environmental conditions. Being able to recognize and react appropriately kept them alive and that impetus is today equally resonant to business people as to hikers."

Viewed from the lenses of a scientist, and Dorfman is one of them, many scientists are either arts practitioners or have deep appreciation for the arts:

"Even disregarding the ways art and science might be superficially similar, it's also worth thinking about how they can also be integrated. Considerable creativity is needed to make scientific breakthroughs, and art is just as often an expression (or the product) of scientific knowledge. The science behind singing opera, mixing paint colors, baking, fashion design or creating perspective in a drawing, all have strong scientific underpinnings. In fact, getting science down to the point where it is second nature is the mark of a true master."

# STEM, STEAM

There is great consensus and awareness of the relevance of STEM (science, technology, engineering, and math) when it comes to knowledge and understanding between these interconnected areas of study. "It has been in use sufficiently long for educators to see outcomes and practices unfold in schools across the nation." The icing on the cake is that more recently, however, "some educators have proposed adding an 'A' (for arts) to the STEM curriculum. In doing so, they have sparked a national debate about whether the arts have a place in STEM education."

This is still cause for pause in the academic world. As Dorfman recognizes the great potential for integration, he poses the important question: "How can we move into a realm of true interdisciplinarity, which represents a nexus between the arts and sciences? One avenue I find promising is STEAM education, which explores these concepts as an integrated whole, rather than as silos to be conquered separately."

As examples of integration, Dorfman supports that artists must often understand accounting if they are running and managing their own business, as well as the materials with which their artworks are composed, and the requirements of humidity and temperature within which the pieces must be stored. Similarly, "practitioners who use science and math to create innovations also use design-thinking to help conceptualize their work.

Their communication incites enthusiasm in the funding community in order to secure support for their initiatives. They also work collaboratively with colleagues and investors to improve and expand ideas, and then speak eloquently about progress and discoveries to an engaged public."

# Art, Science and Knowledge to Help Save the Blue Dot

*I don't understand.*
*It is so vast that it surpasses all understanding.*
*Understanding is always limited.*
*But not understanding may have no borders.*
*I feel like I'm much more complete when I don't understand.*
*Not understanding, the way I speak, is a gift.*
*Not understanding, but not as simple-minded.*
*The good thing is to be intelligent and not understand.*
*It's a strange blessing, like being crazy without being insane.*
*It's a meek disinterest, it's a sweet stupidity.*
*But every now and then the restlessness comes:*
*- I want to understand a little.*
*Not too much: but at least understand that I don't understand*
~ Clarice Lispector, novelist, short-story writer

The planet yells for solutions to the environment that get pushed back by resisting forces (there will be more thorough environmental considerations in another chapter of this book). However, it is in this chapter that the debate is brought up in a meaningful introductory way. Here are some of Dorfman's reflections on the topic:

"The litany of environmental catastrophes is too long to recount and, for which, the concept of the Anthropocene (the shortly-to-be-named Age of Humanity) in some way serves as a convenient focal point. Even if you choose not to buy into the fact that our climate is changing due to human activity, it's impossible to deny the estimated 87,000 tons of garbage in the World Ocean, vanishing coral reefs, global declines of amphibians, bees and many other groups. Although you can't deny it, do you have to care?"

The answer lies in one's consciousness. Caring will make the difference with actionable consequences, and the least we can do is to give it a try.

> *He who knows only his own side of*
> *the case knows little of that.*
> ~ John Stuart Mill,
> philosopher, economist, civil servant

Da Vinci's integrative work between art, science and technology had vanished and become all but forgotten to civilization for almost 200 years after his departure from existence, "through a combination of poor planning, carelessness and profiteering." Michael White, in this biography *Leonardo: The First Scientist*, speculates on modern society and poses an intriguing question:

"Had this not been the case, we can only wonder what would have happened to the history of science, and from that the development of technology, if Leonardo's work had been known about and read widely soon after his death.

Where would we be today?"

# The World Inside the Words

*Socrates said, "The misuse of language induces evil in the soul." He wasn't talking about grammar. To misuse language is to use it the way politicians and advertisers do, for profit, without taking responsibility for what the words mean. Language used as a means to get power or make money goes wrong: it lies. Language used as an end in itself, to sing a poem or tell a story, goes right, goes towards the truth. A writer is a person who cares what words mean, what they say, how they say it. Writers know words are their way towards truth and freedom, and so they use them with care, with thought, with fear, with delight. By using words well they strengthen their souls. Story-tellers and poets spend their lives learning that skill and art of using words well. And their words make the souls of their readers stronger, brighter, deeper.*
~ Ursula K. Le Guin, sci-fi and nonfiction author

Where clues inspire us to make our lives better, and the push for curiosity gets diffused in ideas to silently move us to newer and greater heights, here's a mindful quote from novelist and essayist Siri Hustvedt:

"The more I read, the more I change. The more varied my reading is, the more I am able to perceive the world from thousands of different perspectives. In me reside the voices of others, many of them dead long ago. The dead speak, scream, whisper, express themselves through the music of their poetry and prose. Reading is a creative way of listening that modifies the reader. Books are consciously remembered through images and words, but they are also present in the strange and changing spaces of our unconscious. Others who, for whatever reason, do not have the strength to change our lives, tend to forget completely. Yet, those who remain, become part of us, part of that mysterious mechanism of the human mind capable of turning the tiny symbols written on a page into a vivid reality."

# Silently Closing

Pablo Neruda's unconventional wisdom is for the engaged, human-centered fellows not quite concerned about political correctness. Controversially oriented when supporting the world causes of his time, he was a prolific writer and passionate about the *"poemas de amor"*, or love poems. Here's an excerpt of one of his works:

*Slowly dies
who's slave of habits,
following every day the same paths,
who doesn't change gear,
who doesn't risk
and who doesn't change the color of their clothes,
who doesn't speak with unknown people.*

*Slowly dies
who avoid a passion,
who prefers black and white
and the dots over the I's
instead of a mix of emotions,
the very ones who make your eyes spark,
those that make a smile out of a yawn,
those that make your heart beat
over mistakes and feelings.*

*Slowly dies
who doesn't travel,
who doesn't flee,
who doesn't listen to music,
who doesn't find mercy in themselves.
Let's avoid death at small doses
by having in mind that being alive requires an effort
way higher*

*than simply the act of breathing.*
"Slowly Dies" ~ Pablo Neruda, poet

Your Thoughts Here
On Harnessing the Higher Spheres
of Music, Art, Science and Knowledge

# Every Day (I Thank You)

## 6

### For Choosing Your Leaders Wisely

*If you can bear to hear the truth you've spoken*
*Twisted and misconstrued by some smug fool*
*Or watch your life's work torn apart and broken down*
*And still stoop to build again with worn out tools.*
*If you can draw a crowd and keep your virtue*
*Or walk with Kings and keep the common touch*
*If neither enemies nor loving friends can hurt you*
*If everybody counts with you but none too much.*
*If you can fill the journey of a minute*
*With sixty seconds worth of wonder and delight*
*Then the Earth is yours and everything that's in it*
*But more than that I know You'll be alright*
*You'll be alright. Cause you've got the*
*fight you've got the insight*
"If" ~ Joni Mitchell, songwriter

FOR THOSE FORTUNATE ENOUGH to be allowed to consider choosing who to represent them in the spheres of power, just stop and think. Let's call democracy what it is: Sovereignty. A blessing? Yes. But it's also an experiment. It all started when...

Today, Americans—and not an insignificant number of peoples and democracies around the world—face an existential crisis of their constitutional systems. We can certainly all name someone we believe to be a good, or even great, leader, even if some names might invite disagreement if you ask a reasonably diverse selection of people. Alas, the reverse is equally true.

As we screen for particular individuals—be they local, regional, national, international or global, politician or mogul—whether they're in it for others, not for themselves; whether they lean on genuine people and experts to offer wise counsel; whether they learn from their own experiences and also from others'; whether they understand that honesty matters; whether they try to lead not only their supporters but all; whether they can ease, inspire, and help people focus during difficult times; whether or not some or all these assumptions factor in how we choose our leaders, our civil challenge is to get a clear vision of what we want from our kingpins and cherry-pick ones who incorporate those qualities.

One cannot stand for democracy, stand for the rule of law and simultaneously postulate anti-democratic ideology; one cannot embrace liberty and yet project authoritarian, pro-insurrection, pro-overthrowing government principles, and yet state that they are pro-freedom and pro-people at the same time. These are deep contradictions.

True leadership revolves around a basic foundation: one who willingly and spontaneously puts the needs, growth, and wellbeing of followers in the first place, adopting a serve-first mindset and prioritizing their community above themselves. Authentic leaders lead by example, fostering trust and encouraging strong relationships with individuals and teams. And most importantly, and here this cannot be emphasized enough, ensuring that all reach their full potential while achieving their objectives.

For a moment, let's stick with the workplace in mind. We all work somewhere, for someone, and for something, which serves the purpose of expanding our growth and wellbeing as professionals and individuals. Choosing a leader, not a job, is one of the most important things we can do for our careers.

This sounds easier said than done, understandably. John Maxwell, renowned author in leadership development says, "Everything rises and falls on leadership." This means that one's rise or fall, career-wise, can be based on their own self-leadership and the leadership of those they associate with. If we think about this for a moment, isn't it great to work for a great leader? One who identifies and leverages our strengths and potential in a way that gives us courage and confidence to try new things and quickly learn from our mistakes?

# Politics, Music and Leadership

"All leaders, to a certain degree, do the same thing. Whether you're talking about an executive, manager, sports coach, or schoolteacher, leadership is about guiding and impacting outcomes, enabling groups of people to work together to accomplish what they couldn't do working individually. In this sense, leadership is something you do, not something you are. Some people in formal leadership positions are poor leaders, and many people exercising leadership have no formal authority. It is their actions, not their words, that inspire trust and energy." The excerpt above is a fraction of an article on the theme by McKinsey & Company, a business consulting firm, and gives us a concise but clear idea of the dimension of leadership.

When reflecting about leadership other than in the realm of the workplace, I often think about politicians. Especially those with power to greatly influence the destiny of others beyond small communities. Here, I refer to their sway on the masses. Not necessarily with judgment in mind, although many of them give us reasons to let that thought flow through our systems. The reflection here, which you may find unusual, is on whether music is a true part of their existence. Really? What's the relevance?, you may ask. Ok, music is subjective and you may not see the connection here—but stay with me on this one. The inquiry in my mind is whether music, for public figures in power and in a position to change the lives of common citizens, is a sought-after pursuit to play a role in keeping their sanity in place. And I don't mean background music. Much less the connection between music and politics, particularly political expression in songs such as music portraying anti-establishment or protest themes, including anti-war songs.

Or yet, music representing pro-establishment ideas, for example, in national anthems, patriotic songs, and political campaigns. What I mean is music that makes you, as an individual, stop and truly listen to it. Appreciate it. Learn from it. Grow with it. Music that helps shape your character, your appreciation for the living creatures; music that values nature and makes us focus on the present and look into the future; music that brings about our curiosity beyond the senses. Music that incites imagination toward a more peaceful coexistence between peoples and cultures. Music that enhances the quality of everyday life, contributing to sustainability by promoting joy and happiness. Music that impacts our well-being, and aims at a balanced lifestyle. Music that has the power to create a sense of meaning and belonging, providing a soundtrack to life's important moments, and making the ordinary extraordinary.

> *Watch out for music. It should come with a health warning. It can be dangerous, it can make you feel so alive, so connected to the people all around you, and connected to what you really are inside. And it can make you think the world should, and could, be a much better place. And, occasionally, it can make you very, very happy.*
> ~ Peter Gabriel, songwriter

It's worth considering that the relationship between music and politics has existed for centuries, sometimes harmoniously, and other times not as much. It's also true that music can be damaging and just as well destructive when created, manipulated and distorted for unscrupulous purposes.

An example in history can be found in Richard Wagner's music, a German composer who lived in the 19th century. Hitler frequently had Wagner's music performed at party rallies and functions. It was not only Wagner's music that inspired Hitler, but also his political views. Wagner wrote a violently antisemitic booklet in the 1850s called *Das Judebthum in die Musik* (Judaism in Music) insisting the Jews poisoned public taste in the arts. He created the Bayreuth festival, which in the 1930s and 1940s was used by the Nazi party as a propaganda tool against the Jews.

When reflecting on whether this or that leader is being real and not bogus, candid and not a pretender, it comes to mind whether that individual ever pauses to truly reflect on their state of being before committing spurious acts, such as deceiving, being artfully insidious, and acting as slanderers. A quick pause for reflection here helps illustrates the thinking:

*I've been around the world*
*Had my pick of any girl*
*You'd think I'd be happy*
*But I'm not*
*Ev'rybody knows my name*
*But it's just a crazy game*
*Oh, it's lonely at the top*

*Listen to the band, they're playing just for me*
*Listen to the people paying just for me*
*All the applause-all the parades*
*And all the money I have made*
*Oh, it's lonely at the top*

*Listen all you fools out there*

*Go on and love me-I don't care*
*Oh, it's lonely at the top*
*Oh, it's lonely at the top*
"Lonely at The Top"
~ Randy Newman, composer, songwriter


Some of the recent political campaigns around the globe have used music for 'inspiration.' Exiguous actors have utilized music from popular artists from different genres, many times without their consent, to appeal to people's senses with the clear intent of misrepresentation: In that sense, some politicians resort to popular culture references risking appropriating elements of a particular culture or subculture without fully understanding their significance or context. This can lead to garble, stereotyping, or trivializing important cultural symbols, potentially offending or alienating certain groups. Sometimes subtly, sometimes in a wide open manner.

*"Choose your leaders*
*with wisdom and forethought.*

*To be led by a coward*
*is to be controlled*
*by all that the coward fears.*

*To be led by a fool*
*is to be led*
*by the opportunists*
*who control the fool.*

*To be led by a thief*
*is to offer up*
*your most precious treasures*
*to be stolen.*

*To be led by a liar
is to ask
to be told lies.*

*To be led by a tyrant
is to sell yourself
and those you love
into slavery".*
"Parable of the Talents"
~ Octavia E. Butler, science-fiction writer

# Leaders Must Be Scrutinized

Instinct tells us to challenge leaders constantly and consistently. It starts as a mental exercise and typically in silence. Look them in the eye, literally and figuratively. Ask them tough questions. Take their words and ideas seriously—for words and ideas have meaning. Then address them. Keep them honest. Make them feel they need to earn our trust. Put on healthy but steady pressure. Don't lose sight and don't let them distance themselves from their purpose. Ask them why they want to lead. What is their purpose for sustainable leadership? Who do they admire as leaders? Where do they draw inspiration to forge their path to leadership? Do they support self-determination of the peoples and of the individual? Do they have a personal connection to the issues they advocate for? Which are their values? Western liberal values or autocratic illiberal ones? Do they think climate change is real? If so, what actions within their sphere of influence should they take to mitigate its effects? What kind of legacy do they want to leave for the next generations to come?

> *I don't agree with those who plunge headlong into the middle of the flood and who, accepting a turbulent life, struggle daily in great spirit with difficult circumstances. The wise person will endure that, but won't choose it—choosing to be at peace, rather than at war.*
> ~ Seneca, philosopher

Part of the reason we found ourselves in the current bizarre political scenario may have to do with us not truly capturing reality as it is but only fragments of it. By truly capturing, I mean seeing through it. It is important for all of us citizens, in the US or elsewhere, not to shrug off the existence and highly influential role of dubious, strategically illiterate, pseudo leaders. Not to just go about our lives and pretend we are living through normal times. We're not living through normal times. That doesn't mean getting our eyes off the ball when it comes to our own needs and responsibilities. We have to take care of our families and kids, and go to work. We have to pay our bills and buy groceries; but the cynical assumption that nothing really matters and nothing's really important does the opposite of addressing the pressing issues of today.

Ian Bremmer, a well-known political scientist and author, raises significant concerns about the impact of technology companies—and their leadership—on democracy and society. In a recent TED talk, he highlights how the advertising-driven models and information control algorithms employed by these companies are contributing to societal fragmentation and democratic erosion. Bremmer's argument focuses on the following key points:

Advertising-Driven Models: These models prioritize user engagement and data collection to maximize advertising revenue. This often leads to the proliferation of sensational and polarizing content, which can deepen societal divisions and create echo chambers where individuals are only exposed to information that reinforces their existing beliefs.

Information Control Algorithms: Used by tech companies to curate content and information, they are designed to keep users engaged. However, these algorithms can also control and manipulate the information that users see, leading to biased or incomplete perspectives. This control over information flow can influence public opinion and undermine informed democratic decision-making.

From a societal impact perspective, Bremmer argues that these business practices are damaging to society by fostering polarization and misinformation. The spread of fake news and disinformation can lead to confusion, mistrust, and hostility among different social groups, weakening the social fabric and making it more challenging to address common societal issues.

The erosion of a shared reality and informed public discourse poses a direct threat to democratic processes, therefore putting democracy at risk. When citizens lack access to reliable and diverse sources of information, their ability to participate meaningfully in democratic governance is compromised. This can lead to diminished accountability, weakened institutions, and the rise of authoritarian tendencies.

Yet, when it comes to the geopolitical influence of tech companies, Bremmer reminds us that we are not living in a multipolar world solely in the traditional geo-political sense but in a world where technology companies have become major players. These companies wield significant power and influence, often transcending national borders and governmental control. The decisions they make about whose interests they serve—whether their own, those of governments, or the public—have profound implications for global governance and stability.

Equally relevant, the growing influence of tech companies raises critical questions about ethics and regulation. There is an urgent need for robust regulatory frameworks to ensure that these companies act in the public interest, protect user privacy, and promote transparency and accountability.

Thanks to Bremmer's lucid mind, his synthesis underscores the urgent need for a reevaluation of the role of technology in society. He calls for greater awareness and proactive measures to mitigate the adverse effects of technology on democracy and social cohesion. This includes not only regulatory reforms and ethical guidelines for tech companies, but also efforts to promote digital literacy among the public to navigate the complex information landscape.

"It's the emerging digital order," says Bremer, "that will become the world's next superpower. And governments do not run the digital order, they are run by technology companies. Big Tech's power over the algorithms in Web2 determining what information we transmit and receive is staggering."

As pointed out in the prologue of this work, Aldous Huxley's *Brave New World*, published in 1932, warns us of the dangers of giving the state and economic agents control over new and powerful technologies. Surgical in his concluding analysis, Bremmer is not shy about his daunting worries: "Are technology companies going to be accountable as they release new and powerful artificial intelligence? What are they going to do with this unprecedented amount of data that they are collecting on us and our environment? And the one I think should concern us all right now the most: Will they persist with these advertising models driving so much revenue, that are turning citizens into products, and driving hate and misinformation, and ripping apart our society?"

Ian Bremmer's decisive challenge to the tech leaders: "Today, the United States has become the principal exporter of tools that destroy democracy. The technology leaders who create and control these tools, are they OK with that? Or are they going to do something about it? We need to know."

Good leadership, with meaningful exceptions, has been slipping through the cracks and that is a big part of how we got to the present times. Therefore, our function as individuals is to stay on and pick our fights. The ones that elevate our condition as citizens. Silently or not, actively or not, but stay on and endure the course. There's a reason why popular knowledge says "the obstacle is the path." The answer may be right there.

# When Small is Truly Beautiful

Inspiration is found in small but significant places, organizations and activities. Looking back to our recent past, there have been worse years in US history, and certainly worse years in world history. But most of us alive today have seen nothing like the years 2020 and 2021 and their unfolding events. Life changed around us with none being spared of its consequences. The outbreak of the COVID-19 pandemic affected every possible life on the planet and the most vulnerable were the first ones to experience the effects. When it comes to organizations, specifically in the Green Mountains, there are two that stand out as tests for resilience and purpose.

One in particular, the Vermont Council on World Affairs—VCWA—was dramatically exposed to the new unexpected, unwanted winds: its very existence was threatened. Its core mission and activity—international exchanges—were suspended or flat out canceled overnight for, well, reasons we all know.

Small in scale but yet focused on a macro vision, the very idea of raising awareness and understanding among peoples and places, countries and cultures, all of a sudden seemed far distant from its leaders, members and the overall communities engaged in projects then facing uncertainty and relegated to the backburner.

In cooperation with the public and private sectors, this is an outstanding example of a vision for the future within their communities.

The VCWA has been for the past 70 years an advocate and promoter of *awareness* and *understanding* of the world and its people utilizing public forums, hosting international visitors and working with educational institutions to develop programs for students, faculty, staff and community.

Let's pause for a moment on the meaning of *awareness* and *understanding*, as well as on the combination of both. While *awareness* can be defined as the perception of the fact of something, e.g., the awareness of the knowledge of creating the wheel and bringing it into form, *understanding* is a different thing altogether. The latter involves comprehension, perspective, context and wisdom. Combined, we may assume that our precursors gained *awareness* of the knowledge necessary to create the wheel, but they surely lacked the *understanding* of how that invention would revolutionize their way of life. In that sense, we lack understanding of the impact of our creations, but more specifically, we lack the understanding of some of the laws that surround us.

In an effort to bring analogy to the aforementioned, by facilitating meaningful cross-border connections and dialogues, by fostering awareness and understanding of the world and its people, the VCWA moves mountains. Steadfast in its mission to forge global interaction and cross-cultural connections, year after year, the VCWA leadership and its members build, for example, critical programs revolving around diplomacy and, today more than never, climate movement; to these meaningful topics, they bring together local, national and international experts to discuss the crucial role of diversity and equity in addressing the climate crisis. Need say more about the relevance of these initiatives?

Like the wheel and its influence in transforming the way humans have lived since millennia, the importance of engaging communities and ensuring climate solutions in the pursuit of a path for just and equitable coexistence with the environment is beyond the mere concept of urgency. It calls for the sensible minds to embrace the cause and turn bearings into second nature; it requires the natural acceptance that awareness and understanding go hand in hand with proper action.

Noble causes?
Highly-aimed?
Morally pressing?
Checked, checked, checked.

A unique organization, the Vermont Council on World Affairs was founded in 1952 by Warren Austin, a former US senator and the first US ambassador to the United Nations. Today, its high-powered staff have inherited its legacy and wisdom from longtime pioneers to continue to build upon its strong foundation. Programs such as diplomacy and global climate change "provide a platform for the exchange of knowledge between Vermont businesses, individuals, and international guests, fostering an understanding of global perspectives, world cultures, geopolitical issues, and the evolving US role in foreign policy," predicates one of the members on the closing of one more year of activities at the VCWA.

What's ahead for these initiatives?
What's the purpose?
Why now?

Today's world does not lack initiatives in diplomacy. What the VCWA is aiming for is awareness and understanding of complex issues, in lieu of futile efforts lacking real protagonists—a crucial aspect of global diplomacy and international relations.

What's the word? Exactly: leadership.

While there are numerous initiatives aimed at resolving conflicts, fostering peace, and promoting mutual understanding among nations, the effectiveness of these efforts often hinges on the engagement and commitment of key stakeholders. There is indeed a bounty of diplomatic efforts at various levels, including bilateral talks, multinational agreements, peacekeeping missions, and cultural exchange programs. These initiatives are essential for maintaining open channels of communication, addressing global challenges, and building partnerships. However, the mere existence of these initiatives doesn't guarantee success.

The real protagonists or influential actors, their hearts and minds, are the ones to be won over. Without naming these or those champions, they are the ones with the power and willingness to effect change. These can be national leaders, influential states, international organizations, or even non-state actors with significant influence over a particular issue. Their backing is crucial because they possess the resources, authority, and legitimacy to implement agreements and persuade others to follow suit.

From a current and long term vision perspective, as a micro-representation of significant interstate regional, local and national initiatives, the VCWA is making meaningful progress in addressing global challenges and will continue to expand its reach and impact. It relies on the support of its members and community, and will continue to build bridges between cultures, "bringing people together in innovative ways, and expanding access to global education and engagement," as proposed by its leadership. Committed to fostering intercultural understanding and cooperation, may it stay integral to its core and forward-looking approach, emphasizing growth, community involvement, and the importance of education in bridging cultural divides.

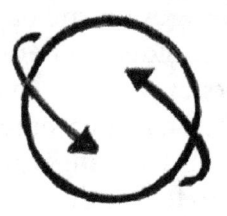

# From Early Stages, The Environment At Center Stage

Another beacon of true leadership development, enormously relevant to shape the future of things to come as it relates to sustainability, the Youth Conservation Corps (YCC) plays a significant part in promoting environmental stewardship, education, and personal development among young people. Youth Conservation Corps is designed to immerse participants in nature, where they can learn about ecosystems, conservation practices, and the importance of preserving natural resources for future generations. The role of YCC camps extends beyond just environmental education; they also foster leadership skills, teamwork, and a deep appreciation for the natural world. YYC helps build a generation of informed, skilled, and motivated individuals ready to take on the complex task of preserving and restoring our planet. In an increasingly environmentally depleted world, the importance of YCC camps cannot be overstated, as they lay the foundation for a more sustainable and resilient future.

Here are several key aspects of the role Youth Conservation Corps plays:

*Environmental Education and Awareness*

- Hands-On Learning: Corps members engage in hands-on activities such as planting trees, monitoring wildlife, and participating in water conservation projects. This direct involvement helps them understand the impact of human actions on the environment and the importance of sustainable practices.
- Ecosystem Understanding: Through guided hikes, wildlife observation, and scientific experiments,

participants gain a deeper understanding of how ecosystems function and the biodiversity within them.

*Personal Development*

- Leadership Skills: Many conservation camps include leadership training, where young people are given responsibilities and challenged to lead projects or groups. This helps develop their leadership and decision-making skills.
- Teamwork and Collaboration: Activities are often designed to be completed in groups, teaching members the value of teamwork, communication, and collaboration.
- Problem-Solving: Facing real-world conservation challenges, corps members learn to apply critical thinking and problem-solving skills to develop effective solutions.

*Fostering a Connection to Nature*

- Appreciation for the Outdoors: Spending time in nature helps young people develop a lasting appreciation for the outdoors and recreational activities like hiking, bird watching, and canoeing.
- Environmental Ethics: Camps instill a sense of environmental ethics, encouraging members to live sustainably and make environmentally conscious decisions in their daily lives.

*Community Impact*

- Service Projects: Many camps include service projects that benefit local communities or natural areas, teaching the importance of giving back and making a positive impact.

- Awareness and Advocacy: Educated and motivated young people are more likely to advocate for conservation efforts in their communities, spreading awareness about environmental issues.

*Long-Term Benefits*

- Career Inspiration: Exposure to conservation work can inspire participants to pursue careers in environmental science, wildlife management, forestry, and other related fields.
- Lifelong Stewardship: The experiences and lessons learned at youth conservation camps can foster a lifelong commitment to environmental stewardship and conservation.

The Youth Conservation Corps (YCC) is a national treasure. It is a youth employment program that engages young people in meaningful work experiences at national parks, forests, wildlife refuges, and fish hatcheries, while developing ethical mindsets toward environmental stewardship and civic responsibility. It contributes to a multifaceted role in educating and inspiring the next generation of environmental stewards.

# Leah's Journey

As the Executive Director of the Vermont Youth Conservation Corps, Leah Mital's path is marked by a profound connection to the natural world and a commitment to fostering a sense of community and belonging among young people. Her journey reflects a blend of personal exploration, educational pursuits, and a deep-seated belief in the power of youth engagement. Her childhood in New Mexico was defined by the rugged beauty of the Rockies, where she found solace and adventure among the ridges and canyons. This early exposure to nature not only provided a backdrop for her formative years but also instilled in her a lifelong love of the outdoors.

## Education and Vermont Connection

Leah's passion for nature and community led her to Vermont, where she attended Middlebury College. Here, Leah fell in love with the state's landscapes and the tight-knit community. Recognizing the potential for young people to connect with their environment and each other, Leah's belief, that youth seek a sense of belonging and are eager to contribute, began to crystallize.

## Vermont Commons School and Ecological Planning

The Vermont Commons School is based on engagement—"engagement in our school community, in academic classes, in the natural world, in our towns, our state, the country and the world at large." As one of the co-founders, this school is where Leah's dedication to education and the environment came together. In this innovative educational setting, she learned alongside students both in the classroom and in nature, the values that reinforced her belief in the natural world as both habitat and classroom. This hands-on, integrative approach to learning led Leah to pursue a master's degree in Ecological Planning at the University of Vermont (UVM), where she further honed her understanding of environmental stewardship and sustainable planning.

## Role at VYCC, Vision and Leadership

Each morning, as Leah opens her shades and contemplates the day's adventures, she embodies the spirit of VYCC's mission. Joining the organization feels like coming home, a place where her passion for the environment and dedication to youth development converge. At VYCC, Leah continues to foster a sense of place and purpose, ensuring that young people have the opportunity to build skills, contribute to their communities, and develop a deep connection to the natural world.

As Executive Director, Leah brings a vision rooted in her own experiences and educational background. She understands the transformative power of nature and community in young people's lives and is committed to expanding VYCC's impact. Her leadership is characterized by a blend of adventure, ecological awareness, and a strong belief in the potential of youth to drive positive change.

# A Teamwork Journey In The First Place

Leah Mital's journey to VYCC, along with a remarkable team of conscientious collaborators, is a testament to the power of nature, education, and community in shaping a fulfilling and impactful career. Her background—from the Rockies to Vermont, her educational pursuits, and her innovative work with the Vermont Commons School all contribute to her holistic approach to leading VYCC. "My job is, essentially, to foster guidance and ensure an organic interaction with members and students where VYCC continues to thrive as a place where young people can find belonging, build skills, and contribute to a more sustainable and connected world," summarizes Leah.

Here are a few reports of actions provided by the VYCC's members that substantiate some of its core activities and impact on the environment in particular areas:

Sustainable Trail Building and Students Engagement

"In September 2023, our first-ever day crew for young adults rebuilt a rotted turnpike, repaired surrounding drainage structures, and replaced old steps on Mount Philo's House Rock Trail in Charlotte. These structures will reduce erosion and protect the surrounding plants and soils from human impact. Running this crew in the fall allowed student volunteers from Winooski High School and participants of ReSOURCE's YouthBuild Program to gain skills and get excited about sustainable trail building."

Slowing The Flow of Water

"Concerned landowners' calls for action on erosion

and stormwater flow into the Missisquoi River led to a VYCC crew's work: building a terraced rain garden, planting hundreds of trees and live stakes, and constructing check dams in the gullies. Projects like this restore wetlands to their natural functions that protect land and communities downstream."

Farming in a Changing Climate

"Food & Farm Program staff are attuned to changing weather patterns and strategies to improve the farm's resilience to periods of saturating rain and drought. Our sloped farm is experiencing increased erosion during heavy rain events, especially on freshly formed beds where the soil has been significantly disturbed by tilling the soil with the tractor. This spring, the team is transitioning some fields from a tractor-based row cropping system to a human-scale, intensive market-gardening approach. New beds will be 100 feet long and 30 inches wide. Beds shaped this spring will be managed primarily with hand-labor. Drawing from published research and other farms' experience, we anticipate the new beds will result in reduced erosion, reduced use of diesel fuel, increased soil health, and an improved participant experience."

# Members' Words

Ian Ritter, a student at Mount Mansfield Union High School, completed a conservation crew in 2022 and returned in 2023. He reflects on the benefits of working as a group to complete projects:

"One surprise—I thought the adults were going to say 'Okay, here's what you have to do. You can only work this way. This is the only right way.' But when it comes to working on a project, there isn't just one right way about it. There are many ways to do it. Maybe some are better than others. They all have successes and disadvantages. Like, you could go for a strategy that makes a project faster but more risky or less detailed. Or, if you really want to finish every last detail, you can take more time to complete the project. How will it get done?' There are a lot of things to think about."

Grateful, Ian also shares his experience as a person with autism:

"The way I think projects should work is that everyone gets together and discusses, 'What needs to get done?' Before VYCC I was so isolated. There weren't many words I knew, and I couldn't explain myself very well. VYCC gives me a great opportunity to connect with others. I feel like I can just safely drop my figurative mask of being 'normal' and be who I want to be. Not enough people understand that every single person in this world is different. I'm glad that VYCC embraces that. When I think more deeply about people understanding each other, it makes me want to go into psychology. I want to understand more about how different groups of people think."

Petra Castaneda completed the 2023 Pro Forest Crew,

then took a teaching position at a Montessori school in Vermont. She is going to Belgium for a month this summer to gain skills in horticulture toward her ultimate career goal: childhood horticultural therapy.

"I came into VYCC having never picked up a chainsaw before. I didn't expect to learn so fast or get so comfortable so quickly; but with the hours we spent sawing, it became second nature after a while. It's an opportunity to not just be outdoors, but to have some influence over it. I discovered a lot of passion for conservation and chainsaw work. So, I feel torn because I want to start my career in childhood horticultural therapy, but I also found something at VYCC that I care about very, very much. Leaving VYCC, I got homesick for it. I still miss chainsaw work." Petra's testimonial is revealing:

"VYCC gave me more confidence. I learned a lot about my own limits and how much I can do, how I can stay calm under pressure. My Crew Leader told me a few times that she really appreciated that she could trust me when she had to step away. I took the initiative to make the crew more efficient and was always thinking about our timeframe. Long story short, I learned how to take initiative and how to be reliable."

Joining a conservation corps offers individuals a unique and transformative experience, driven by the desire to make a significant impact on environmental issues. Participants often arrive with a passionate heart, a bit of apprehension, and typically, limited prior experience with the projects they will undertake. "People join conservation corps to make a difference, to take action and put muscle into an issue they care about."

The work within a conservation corps is inherently challenging. It demands physical effort, resilience, and adaptability. However, it is precisely this combination of challenge, support from peers and mentors, and the meaningful nature of the work that leads to profound personal growth and skill development.

Need to say more about how young men and women can forge their path to true leadership?

Being an integral part of a conservation corps is more than just an opportunity to work on environmental projects; it is a journey of personal and collective growth. And without sound leadership, very little gets accomplished.

The combination of hard work, mutual support, and the sense of making a meaningful impact results in corps members leaving with not only a multitude of new skills but also a deeper sense of purpose and belonging.

At last, this transformative experience equips members with the confidence and competence to continue to enrich their own micro world and simultaneously make positive contributions to their communities and the environment.

If not the youth, then who?

# Your Thoughts Here
# On Choosing Your Leaders Wisely

# Every Day (I Thank You)

## 7

### For Embracing Your Planet the Same Way You Embrace Your Nation

*See the light as it shines on the sea? It's blinding
But no one knows how deep it goes
And it seems like it's calling out to me, so come find me
And let me know, what's beyond that
line, will I cross that line?
See the line where the sky meets the sea? It calls me
And no one knows how far it goes
If the wind in my sail on the sea stays behind me
One day I'll know how far I'll go.*
"How Far I'll Go" ~ Alessia Cara, songwriter

"LAST YEAR, I HAD A LIFE-CHANGING EXPERIENCE at 90 years old. I went to space, after decades of playing an iconic science-fiction character who was exploring the universe. I thought I would experience a deep connection with the immensity around us, a deep call for endless exploration.

"I was absolutely wrong. The strongest feeling, that dominated everything else by far, was the deepest grief that I had ever experienced.

"I understood, in the clearest possible way, that we were living on a tiny oasis of life, surrounded by an immensity of death. I didn't see infinite possibilities of worlds to explore, of adventures to have, or living creatures to connect with. I saw the deepest darkness I could have ever imagined, contrasting so starkly with the welcoming warmth of our nurturing home planet.

> *"This was an immensely powerful awakening for me. It filled me with sadness. I realized that we had spent decades, if not centuries, being obsessed with looking away, with looking outside. I did my share in popularizing the idea that space was the final frontier. But I had to get to space to understand that Earth is and will stay our only home. And that we have been ravaging it, relentlessly, making it uninhabitable."*
> ~ William Shatner, actor, after a suborbital tour flight. Mostly known as Star Trek's Captain Kirk

# We Don't Ask Him

"Our religion is all about thanking the Creator. That's what we do when we pray. We don't ask Him for things. We thank Him. We thank Him for the world and every animal and plant in it. We thank Him for everything that exists. We don't take it for granted that a tree is just there. We thank the Creator for that tree. If we don't thank Him, maybe the Creator'll take that tree away... We are made from Mother Earth and we go back to Mother Earth. We can't 'own' Mother Earth. We're just visiting here. We're the Creator's guests."

The above quote is by Leon Shenandoah,—former "Tadodaho" of the Grand Council of the Six Nations Iroquois Confederacy.

Steve Wall's book *To Become a Human Being* invites us to broaden our universe and rise to an expanded level of consciousness by living on the Earth as it was intended for us to live. He captures the essence of Native American wisdom, in the words of Tadodaho Chief Leon Shenandoah, high chief and revered spiritual leader among the Six Nations Iroquois Confederacy. "Our ancestors lived in physical and spiritual communion with Mother Earth."

The Native American way of life has kept its people close to their living roots. Shenandoah worked for the autonomous sovereignty of the Haudenosaunee Confederacy and Onondaga Nation as independent nations from the United States. Throughout his career, he refused many proposals by various businesses that he thought would weaken the sovereignty of the Haudenosaunee Confederacy or which broke the spirit of the Great Law of Peace. This included casinos, arms trafficking, and tobacco smuggling as well as the sale of fireworks, gasoline, and alcohol; casinos, in particular, he believed to be the latest scheme by the US Government to erode Indian society. He kept casinos off the Onondaga reservation, around Lafayette, NY and encouraged the leaders of the other Haudenosaunee tribes to do the same.

Shenandoah attended the United Nations General Assembly in 1985 and presented a speech calling for a global ceasefire and general worldwide peace. At the 1992 Earth Summit, in Rio de Janeiro, Shenandoah met with Indigenous Amazon leaders, burning tobacco, giving corn, and sharing a prayer with them. For his brothers of America south of the hemisphere, he shared advice on how to deal with white politicians, which led to the tribes demanding that Brazilian museums return their sacred religious artifacts. The tribes also lobbied for the creation of a new state dedicated to governing the indigenous peoples in Brazil.

Along with messages of peace and the calling for the global community to embrace environmental awareness, here are excerpts of Shenandoah's address at the United Nations:

"In the beginning, we were told that the human beings who walk about on earth have been provided with all things necessary for life. We were instructed to carry a love for one another and to show a great respect for all the beings of this Earth. We were shown that our life exists with the tree life, that our well-being depends on the well-being of the vegetable life, that we are close relations of the four legged beings. In our ways, spiritual consciousness is the highest form of politics… when people cease to respect and express gratitude for these many things, then all life will be destroyed, and human life on this planet will come to an end.

"These are our times and our responsibilities. Every human being has a sacred duty to protect the welfare of our mother earth from whom all life comes. In order to do this we must recognize the enemy—the one within us. We must begin with ourselves."

*You are a girl from the sun*
*You are queen of the sea world*
*Your light makes me sing*
*Earth, Earth you are so starry*

*Your blue mantle commands*
*breathing all creation*
*And after the rain wets*
*Rainbow comes to crown*

*The forest is your dress*
*And the clouds, your necklace*
*You are so beautiful, my Earth*
*Consecrated in your spinning*

*Navigator of solitudes*
*Taking us in space*
*Mothership and our home*
*Earth, Earth you are so delicate*
*Your men have no sense*
*So much love was forgotten*
*You offer your treasures*
*But no one appreciates you*

*Earth, Earth I am your child*
*Like plants and animals*
*Only to your ground I surrender*
*With love, I affirm your peace*

"Starry" (Estrelada)
~ Milton Nascimento, songwriter

# Key Influencers of the Environmental Cause

Like Shenandoah, years before and from the other side of the spectrum, Archibald Stansfeld Belaney, commonly known as Grey Owl, was a popular writer, public speaker and conservationist. Author of the relevant *The Man of the Last Frontier*, born an Englishman, in the latter years of his life he passed as half-Indian, claiming he was the son of a Scottish man and an Apache woman. He moved to Canada as a young man, establishing himself as a woodsman and trapper, before rising to prominence as an author and lecturer. His views on wilderness conservation, expressed in numerous articles, books, lectures and films, reached audiences beyond the borders of Canada, bringing attention to the negative impact of exploiting nature and the urgent need to develop respect for the natural world. He was particularly concerned about the plight of the beaver (Canada's national animal), which by the 1920s had been hunted almost to extinction.

Beloved and popular conservationist David Attenborough, the acclaimed man behind the wildly appreciated *Life on Earth* series among many other relevant documentaries, and his brother Richard, attended a lecture by Grey Owl in the 1930s and were significantly influenced by Grey Owl's advocacy of conservation. According to Richard, David was "bowled over by the man's determination to save the beaver, by his profound knowledge of the flora and fauna of the Canadian wilderness and by his warnings of ecological disaster should the delicate balance between them be destroyed." The idea that mankind was endangering nature by recklessly despoiling and plundering its riches was unheard of at the time, but it is one that would remain part of Sir David Attenborough's own credo for the rest of his life.

In the book *Consilience: The Unity of Knowledge*, the great biologist E. O. Wilson introduces his concept with the following words:

'The greatest enterprise of the mind has always been and always will be the attempted linkage of the sciences and humanities. The ongoing fragmentation of knowledge and resulting chaos in philosophy are not reflections of the real world but artifacts of scholarship." Webster's definition of the word 'consilience' is "the linking together of principles from different disciplines especially when forming a comprehensive theory." E. O. Wilson makes his mark on his own statement:

"These words resonate to me because it is in the unity of knowledge that I find the greatest hope for our future. Especially in the United States, for true environmental protection to take place, people have to care. When I was young, environmental protection meant setting aside breeding habitat for threatened species or banning the whale hunt. Now, single-species issues (which today are even more severe) have been eclipsed by issues that everybody has to care about. Air, water, arable land and other environmental goods and services."

*Silent Spring* is an environmental science book by Rachel Carson, American marine biologist, writer, and conservationist, whose influential work and other writings are credited with advancing the global environmental movement. Published on September 27, 1962, the book documented the environmental harm caused by the indiscriminate use of pesticides. Carson accused the chemical industry of spreading disinformation, and public officials of accepting the industry's marketing claims unquestioningly.

When the infamous DDT—Dichlorodiphenyltrichloroethane—became available for civilian use in 1945, there were only a few people who expressed second thoughts about this new miracle compound. One was nature writer Edwin Way Teale, who warned, "A spray as indiscriminate as DDT can upset the economy of nature as much as a revolution upsets social economy. Ninety percent of all insects are good, and if they are killed, things go out of kilter right away." Another was Carson, who wrote to *Reader's Digest* to propose an article about a series of tests on DDT being conducted not far from where she lived in Maryland. The magazine rejected the idea.

Taking several years to complete, Carson carefully described how DDT slipped through the food chain and gathered in the fatty tissues of animals, including human beings, causing cancer and genetic damage. To describe the severity of its use, a single application on a crop, she wrote, "killed insects for weeks and months—not only the targeted insects but countless more—and remained toxic in the environment even after it was diluted by rainwater." Carson's conclusion was that DDT and other pesticides had irreparably harmed animals and had contaminated the world's food supply.

The book's most uncanny and famous chapter, "A Fable for Tomorrow," depicted a nameless American town where all life—from fish to birds to apple blossoms to human children—had been 'silenced' by the insidious effects of DDT. It alarmed readers across America and, not surprisingly, brought a spree of indignation from the chemical industry. "If man were to faithfully follow the teachings of Miss Carson," complained an executive of the American Cyanamid Company, "we would return to the Dark Ages, and the insects and diseases and vermin would once again inherit the earth." Monsanto published and distributed thousands of copies of a brochure parodying *Silent Spring* entitled "The Desolate Year," relating the devastation and inconvenience of a world where famine, disease, and insects ran amok because chemical pesticides had been banned. Some of the attacks were more personal, questioning Carson's integrity and even her sanity.

Scientists more than often have the ability to expand our horizons in ways we are not always able to see. In that sense, they also offer us warnings. Rachel Carson's immense intelligence backed by scientific foundation pushed herself to prepare for the storm her findings would cause to the chemical industry. Anticipating its predictable reactionary outcome, she had compiled *Silent Spring* with no fewer than fifty-five pages of notes and a list of experts who had read and approved the manuscript. Many eminent scientists rose to her defense, and when President John F. Kennedy ordered the President's Science Advisory Committee to examine the issues the book raised, its report thoroughly vindicated both *Silent Spring* and its author. As a result, DDT came under much closer government supervision and was eventually banned.

A new public awareness that nature was vulnerable to human intervention is the critical legacy of Carson's work. In her consciousness, Carson had made a fundamental proposition: that technological progress may at times be so fundamentally in conflict with natural processes that it must be cut back lest deepening present and future unintended consequences. In that historic moment of the 1960s, a decade that started off as the dawn of a golden age to most Americans, conservation had never raised much public interest when few people really worried about the disappearance of wilderness. But the threats Carson had pointed out—the contamination of the food chain, cancer, genetic damage, the deaths of entire species—were simply too frightening to ignore. For the first time, the urgent need to regulate industry for the sake of protecting the environment became widely accepted. And, the rest is history: environmentalism was born.

Carson was well aware of the major implications of her revelations. Appearing on a CBS documentary about *Silent Spring* not too long before her death from breast cancer in 1964, she reflected: "Man's attitude toward nature is today critically important simply because we have now acquired a fateful power to alter and destroy nature. But man is a part of nature, and his war against nature is inevitably a war against himself. We are challenged as mankind has never been challenged before to prove our maturity and our mastery, not of nature, but of ourselves."

*Man is the most insane of species. He worships an invisible God and kills a visible Nature... without realizing that the Nature he kills is this invisible God he adores.*
~ Anonymous

# The Native, The Original

*Children of Native America Today* is an exceptional Children's Book by Yvonne Wakim Denis (non-related to this author) and Arlene Hirschfelder. Its valuable, warm, and engaging content portrays succinct and informative text and photographs highlighting the richness and diversity of Native lands, culture, and daily life of Native American children. Written primarily with the little ones in mind, it is a book in which everyone learns significantly about communities of the original peoples of North America. It is a factual publication, and quoting the words of Chief Joseph, Nee-Mee-Poo, from the Nez-Perce community of the Basin-Plateau in Washington State, "It does not require many words to speak the truth."

Buffy Sainte-Marie, OC (Order of Canada), singer-songwriter, musician, and social activist. has focused on issues facing Indigenous peoples of the United States and Canada. Sainte-Marie's singing and writing repertoire includes subjects of love, war, religion, and mysticism. In her foreword, Sainte-Marie is as gracious as she is direct on her view of the Indigenous reality:

"Many Native American children, through their families and communities, experience a special cultural richness. These kids understand that they live in a special relationship between the earth and the sky; that they are related to all other creatures; that their cultures are unique and precious. They also know many hard truths: that their native language is greatly endangered; that their ancestors experienced hatred and violence in their own country; that much of their greatness is unknown to most other people. But Native children, like all children, should also know that there is tremendous good work to be done in which they can share. They have a future."

*Hold your head up*
*Lift the top of your mind*
*Put your eyes on the Earth*
*Lift your heart to your own home planet*
*What do you see?*
*What is your attitude*
*Are you here to improve or damn it*
*Look right now and you will see*
*We're only here by the skin of our teeth as it is*
*So take heart and take care of your link with life*
"Carry It On" ~ Buffy Sainte-Marie

# A Path to Environmental Regeneration

It is in May 1992, during the United Nations conference on the environment and development, which took place in Rio de Janeiro, the Earth Summit, or Eco '92, that Kopenawa finally obtained legal recognition from the Brazilian government for a vast area of tropical forest reserved for the exclusive use of his people, the Terra Indigena Yanomami.

To this author's knowledge, there are no records of an encounter between Shenandoah and Kopenawa during the Earth Summit in 1992. But it is valid to imagine and assume that a relevant gathering between the leaders of the two nations might have happened at that world event and influenced actions that profoundly reverberate to this day.

> *The key to restoring the earth lies in respecting the natural law, observed by ancient and indigenous peoples.*
> ~ Hanne Strong, President of The Manitou Foundation & The Manitou Institute & Conservancy

August 9, 1994, marked the year the United Nations first recognized the International Day of the World's Indigenous Peoples. Elevating their deep wisdom acquired from millenia, it proclaims: "Indigenous peoples have the knowledge and practices needed for the global community to implement and scale-up climate action. From then on, it presented the unique opportunity to recognize the multifaceted role of indigenous knowledge and practices in stewarding the environment and combating climate change and its impacts."

Through generations of close interactions with the environment, indigenous peoples safeguard an estimated 80% of the world's remaining biodiversity. Together, the global community has an opportunity to reorient the way it interacts with nature and build resilience for all through collaborating with and learning from indigenous peoples, the stewards of nature.

"Indigenous communities are actively engaged in managing and caring for our communities. This sustainable management of biodiversity will be passed on to our young people, who will be doing this for a very long time," said Dr. Victoria Qutuuq Buschman, an Inuit knowledge holder from the Arctic, when speaking about the importance of engaging indigenous experts in climate policies and actions.

The significance and potential of indigenous practices have also been strongly recognized by the scientific community as key approaches to developing and implementing countries' national climate action plans (NDCs) and National Adaptation Plans (NAPs) under the Paris Agreement.

"Indigenous Peoples have been faced with adaptation challenges for centuries and have developed strategies for resilience in changing environments that can enrich and strengthen current and future adaptation efforts."

# Meaningful Practices

The article of the United Nations bulletin on Climate Change from August 2022 *How Indigenous Peoples Enrich Climate Action* highlights just a few but no less significant Indigenous Peoples practices and their impact to the environment:

As the world scales up climate action, tried and tested indigenous practices such as those exemplified below have an important role to play:

- Native tree plantation in Nepal which helps store carbon and promotes cultural values associated with forest stewardship.
- Community-managed natural forests (or village common forests) in Bangladesh which provide vital services to meet the daily needs of community members and help conserve local biodiversity.
- Active revitalization of traditional technologies connected to agriculture, aquaculture and natural resource management in the Pacific, which is a key strategy to mitigate climate change.
- Restoration of sustainable loko iʻa or fishpond system done by the Native Hawaiian community, which has the potential to produce thousands of pounds of sustainable protein annually, while mitigating coral bleaching, beach erosion, fish population overkills, and other imbalances in the marine ecosystem.
- These indigenous peoples' practices enrich and accelerate collective progress towards achieving the goals of the Paris Agreement.

# 'People of the Dawnland'

The Western Abenaki are among the Indigenous People of what is now called Vermont, New Hampshire, parts of New York, Maine, and northern Massachusetts, and part of Quebec in Canada. Today, there are four State Recognized Western Abenaki Tribes within Vermont and two First Nations Status Tribes of Canada.

For many millennia, the Western Abenaki people have maintained a reciprocal relationship with the land and water. They developed relational land practices that sustained the natural resources and allowed for biodiversity to flourish. The Abenaki are the first stewards of this land and its legacy of conservation. Abenaki communities across New England and Canada continue to affirm cultural traditions despite having faced hundreds of years of Indigenous erasure by state, national, and colonial governments.

"As human beings, we are part of Earth. We have a responsibility to it and all those plants and animals that depend on the land—including ourselves," says Dan Coutu, a member of Nulhegan Abenaki, one of the multiple Abenaki tribes in the region. It is fair to say that the Abenaki's connection to land cannot be described in the English language:

"They feel a kinship with it, and an obligation to protect its uniqueness and beauty for the generations to come," write Rosanne Greco and Chief Don Stevens in their *Clean And Green* article, *"Respect for Nature will be Our Spiritual Salvation"* (*The Other Paper*, November 2022). "Only now, witnessing the severe climate impacts from centuries of exploitation and extraction of the land for profit, are others beginning to understand what the

Abenaki have known for thousands of years."

Gus Speth, co-founder of the Natural Resources Defense Counsel (NRDC), a United States-based non-profit international environmental advocacy group, with its headquarters in New York City and offices in Washington DC, San Francisco, Los Angeles, Chicago, Bozeman, as well as New Delhi and Beijing, is direct on his view of the problem:

"I used to think the top environmental problems were biodiversity loss, ecosystem collapse and climate change. I thought that with 30 years of good science we could address those problems. But I was wrong. The top environmental problems are selfishness, greed and apathy, and to deal with those, we need a spiritual and cultural transformation—and we scientists don't know how to do that. We can talk about the problem, the technologies, but they don't address the root causes."

The NRDC's co-founder's profound statement highlights a crucial insight into the challenges of addressing environmental issues. It suggests unequivocally that the root causes of environmental degradation extend far beyond the realm of scientific and technological solutions. Instead, they are deeply embedded in human behavior and societal values, particularly arrogance and indifference around the issues. This perspective underscores the necessity for a significant shift in how societies value the environment, urging for a transformation that is beyond science's orthodoxy.

Such a transformation would entail a collective reevaluation of priorities, where the well-being of the planet and its ecosystems are placed at the forefront of global consciousness. It calls for education systems, religious and spiritual communities, governments, and individuals to foster a sense of responsibility toward the environment, encouraging actions that are sustainable, equitable, and respectful of all forms of life.

Addressing these deeply ingrained attitudes and behaviors poses a significant challenge, one that transcends the capabilities of science alone. It requires a multidisciplinary approach that includes philosophy, psychology, religion, art, and culture, aiming to inspire a change in hearts and minds toward more sustainable ways of living.

In essence, while scientific advancements are critical in providing the tools and knowledge needed to address environmental issues, they must be complemented by a broader societal shift toward empathy, compassion, and a collective sense of stewardship over the natural world. This holistic approach is essential for creating lasting solutions to the environmental crises facing the planet.

What will it take for us to come to terms and find common ground for a positive transformation of the environment?

# Word by Word, One Bead at A Time

*Placing one bead at a time, planting one seed at a time, and taking one step at a time... I know I can make a difference in each life I touch: one person at a time.*
~ Beverly Little Thunder, author, activist

From traditional Abenaki territory in the wetlands of the Green Mountains in Vermont, up comes the winds to lift the souls of female hearts. *One Bead at a Time* is an oral memoir that narrates the life and experiences of Beverly Little Thunder. A respected two-spirit Lakota Elder, Beverly Little Thunder originates from the Standing Rock reservation, which lies across the border between North and South Dakota, as part of what was known as the Great Sioux Nation. Through her memoir, Beverly Little Thunder shares her journey of living a life dedicated to serving Indigenous and non-Indigenous women across vast regions of the United States and Canada. Her story is not just a personal narrative but a powerful testament to her resilience, activism, and dedication to cultural preservation and education.

*"As women, we need to give back to the earth."*

The concept of "two-spirit" refers to a person who embodies both masculine and feminine spirits, a term that is used by some Indigenous North American communities to describe a traditional third-gender or other gender-variant ceremonial role in their cultures. Beverly Little Thunder's experiences as a two-spirit person provide profound insights into the challenges and triumphs of navigating life in both Indigenous and non-Indigenous spaces while carrying the wisdom and responsibilities of her Lakota heritage.

Her memoir delves into the significance of each bead in her life's story, metaphorically representing one bead at a time in the drapery of her experiences. This narrative approach underscores the importance of every moment, encounter, and lesson learned throughout her journey. It reflects the meticulous and thoughtful process of beadwork, a traditional craft in many Indigenous cultures that require patience, skill, and vision, paralleling the way Beverly has approached her life and work.

Kunsi Keya, the sanctuary established by Beverly Little Thunder and Pam Alexander, stands as a remarkable testament to the realization of a profound vision in the eastern Woodlands, a significant journey from Beverly's earlier life in the desert of California. This place embodies over three decades of dedication to creating a space where Indigenous practices and ceremonies are not only preserved but also adapted to be inclusive and supportive of all who identify as women, including those from the transgender, lesbian, bisexual, and queer communities. The inclusion of non-Indigenous women as part of the foundation and as helpers in various capacities signifies a groundbreaking approach to building community and fostering solidarity across different backgrounds.

At its core, Kunsi Keya is a living expression of Lakota women's ceremonies, emphasizing sacrifice, growth, peace, fulfillment, fun, and healing. Beverly Little Thunder's desire to share her story goes beyond personal narrative; painstakingly transcribed through several years of work by Sharron Proulx-Turner, herself a member of the Metis Nation of Alberta. It is an invitation to witness and participate in the continuation of a cultural legacy that has been shown to her by the Creator and her Elders. By opening up these ceremonies to a broader spectrum of participants, Beverly and her community are not only preserving precious traditional Indigenous practices but also evolving them to embrace a wider, more inclusive understanding of womanhood and community.

This approach to ceremony and community building reflects a significant shift toward inclusivity and healing that is deeply rooted in respect for traditional Indigenous teachings while also acknowledging the diversity and complexity of contemporary identities. Kunsi Keya, or Grandmother Turtle, through Beverly Little Thunder's vision, becomes a place where the boundaries between Indigenous and non-Indigenous, between genders and sexual orientations, are acknowledged but not seen as barriers to participation in sacred practices. Instead, these identities enrich the fabric of the community and the ceremonies, contributing to a deeper, more integral understanding of what it means to connect with one's spirituality and with each other.

> *"Ceremony has taught me a lot about forgiveness, about learning to forgive myself, and what that really means. It means more than just saying, I'm sorry. It means coming to peace within oneself and I have finally achieved that. It's a good place to be. It's a really good place to be."*

Living in such a space requires a commitment to collective well-being and a willingness to engage in the practical aspects of supporting one another.

Beverly Little Thunder's contributions extend beyond her immediate community, impacting the broader dialogue around Indigenous rights, gender, and spirituality. Her story is an educational resource that enlightens readers about the story of Kunsi Keya and Beverly Little Thunder's journey is a powerful reminder of the resilience of Indigenous cultures and the transformative potential of creating spaces where healing, acceptance, and growth are available to all who seek them. It is a testament to the enduring strength of following one's vision and the impact such a path can have on individuals and communities alike.

"Here on Kunsi Keya, on this land, our goal, mine and Pam's, is to create community. We would like to see the people move here and live on the land. That's a difficult thing to do because living here would mean being a part of the community and not many people understand what that means. It doesn't mean just coming together once a week for a meal and socializing. It means you get a load of wood, and we get a load of wood, and we come and help you stack yours, and you come and help us stack ours. If there's a snowstorm and you're getting low on wood, and we have more wood, you come to our house and we fix a meal together. We are snowed in together."

Meeting these two individuals was a privilege as it was an honor. Beverly and Pam's vision seeks to reimagine the essence of communal living, rooted in mutual support, shared responsibilities, and deep, interdependent relationships among its members, therefore challenging conventional notions of community and rather emphasizing the richness of Lakota traditions, the significance of two-spirit identities, the power of living a life committed to service and advocacy, and protection of the micro-environment for the sake of the broader wellbeing. Through her story, we are invited to reflect on and understand the complexities of Indigenous identity, the impact of colonialism, and the resilience of Indigenous peoples through the lens of a remarkable individual's life story.

# Sky Falling

"We are inhabitants of the forest. Our ancestors inhabited the sources of these rivers, long before the birth of my fathers, and even long before the white people's ancestors were born. In the past, we were really very numerous and our houses were vast. Then many of us died after the arrival of these outsiders, with their epidemic, fumes, and shotguns. We have been sad and known the anger of mourning too often. Sometimes we are scared that the white people will finish us off. Yet, despite all that, after having cried so much and put the ashes of our dead in oblivion, we live happily. We know that the dead go to rejoin the ghost of our elders on the sky's back, where game is abundant and feasts are endless. This is why our thoughts turn to calm despite all this mourning and these tears. We become able to hunt and work in our gardens again. We can travel through the forest and make friendship with the people of other houses. Once again, we laugh with our children, sing during our *reahu*, who feast, and make the *xapiri* spirits dance. We know that they remain by our side in the forest and they still hold the sky in place."

The aforementioned text describes what may have been the experience of any descendant of the Indigenous Peoples in any part of the world where the Original Peoples were affected by the actions of explorers. With a glimpse to history, the Conquistadors were the explorer-soldiers of the Spanish and Portuguese Empires of the 15th and 16th centuries during the 'Age of Discovery' , widely opening the floodgates for exploration. They were known to have sailed beyond Europe to the Americas, Oceania, Africa, and Asia, colonizing and opening trade routes. History books abundantly dissect the theme, 'educating' us around the 'great achievements' of that time. That time is long gone. Five centuries have passed since history began to seal the destiny of countless peoples around the world. Especially those who originally inhabited the 'conquered' regions.

The above quote is one of many reflections of Davi Kopenawa, registered in one of the important and contemporary literary works about the Indigenous People south of the equator, *The Falling Sky*. In the late 1980s, more than a thousand Yanomami perished in Brazil from illness and violence, resulting from the invasion of the territory by some 40,000 gold prospectors. This tragedy rekindled Davi Kopenawa's childhood memories of the decimation of his kin, leaving him distraught. Having struggled for several years in Brazil to obtain legal recognition for the territory, he began an international campaign to defend his people and the Amazon.

*The Falling Sky* gives us in its multitude a perspective of the huge efforts put in place during that terrorizing time for the Yanomami. But it also opens the doors for hope: "His unique experience with white people," Bruce Albert tells us, "his extraordinary firmness of character, and the legitimacy that came with his initiation as a shaman made him the most influential spokesperson for the Yanomami cause in Brazil and abroad. Over the course of the 1980s and 1990s he visited several European countries as well as the United States. In 1988, the United Nations awarded him the global 500 award for his contribution to defense of the environment."

Kopenawa's book is a unique and profound work that brings to the forefront the voice and perspective of a shaman and spokesperson for the Yanomami people of the Amazon rainforest. Through the collaboration with French anthropologist Bruce Albert, who spent several decades working with the Yanomami, the book provides not just an account of the environmental and social challenges faced by Kopenawa's people, but also serves as a profound philosophical and spiritual testament.

This work is significant because it bridges the gap between Indigenous wisdom and Western understanding, challenging the reader to consider the profound impacts of deforestation, gold mining, and cultural invasion on the Yanomami and the environment. The 'falling sky' metaphor is a powerful invocation of the existential threat that these practices pose, not just to the Yanomami, but to the global community, reflecting a deep concern for the future of life as we know it.

The book's contribution lies not only in highlighting the terror and disruption brought upon the Yanomami during periods of intense external aggression but also in its ability to kindle hope. Kopenawa's narrative, imbued with the rich spiritual and cultural traditions of his people, offers insights into a way of life that is in profound harmony with nature. It calls for a global reassessment of values and a deeper commitment to sustainable living that respects the rights and wisdom of Indigenous peoples.

David Kopenawa's *The Falling Sky* is more than just a document of struggle; it is an invitation to envision a future where humanity learns from the profound connection Indigenous cultures have with the earth. It argues for a world where environmental preservation and respect for diverse ways of being can lead to healing and renewal. Thus, it stands as a crucial text for anyone interested in environmental justice, Indigenous rights, and the search for solutions to the planet's most pressing problems.

# The Problem, As It Is

Fast forward to the year 2023.

"Illegal gold mining threatens the environment and human health in the Amazon," said shaman and Yanomami Indigenous leader Davi Kopenawa in a talk at Princeton Jan. 31. "And there are consequences for all of us, too, as mining in the Amazon rainforest diminishes one of the planet's largest natural carbon sinks and a bastion of biocultural diversity."

Yesterday's problems are still prevalent if not magnified. The Yanomami today are a group of 35,000 people living across 250 villages deep inside the Amazon Forest in northern Brazil and parts of southern Venezuela. Even after years of struggle against commercial encroachment, having won a major victory when the Brazilian government in 1992 preserved more than 37,000 square miles for the Yanomami to continue their way of life and stewardship of the forest's integrity, their struggle continues.

The myopic, retrograde federal government officials during their tenure from 2018 to 2022 promised to open the Amazon for commercial exploitation. Brazil's deforestation rate soared. According to the National Institute of Space Research, their four-year term saw 17,800 square miles of forest razed, an area approximately the size of Taiwan. That government made it clear that it was okay for developers/miners/poachers/entrepreneurs to ignore indigenous land rights and environmental laws with complete impunity. As a result, the Amazon biome at the end of that term neared what scientists described as ominous tipping points, where so many trees will have been cut that the rainforest can no longer keep its endless cycle of transporting water inland functioning efficiently.

"I'm in mourning," Kopenawa said at the beginning of his keynote address at Princeton University. "My people are dying." Brazil's new government that took office in January (2023), has promised to remedy the "absolutely urgent" situation, Kopenawa said.

Kopenawa later described the ways in which the struggles of the Yanomami have implications for humanity. "The whole world knows the importance of the Amazonian rainforest," he said. "We are living here, on this Earth. It's the only Earth we have for everybody."

# The Solution, As It Unfolds

Just like Kindness is one of the essential things that we as a group say is good but one that we collectively aren't good at, caring for the planet and its environment seems untenable and too distant for many of us to make a difference. The fact is, environmental problems can be complex and hard to resolve. The complexity arises because the components of the environment are so inextricably linked, added to their interactions that may be invariably separated by both time and distance.

The question that keeps growing in our minds is singular: Why do people not care about the environment? Firstly, the topic of the environment is notoriously difficult to understand. The science behind climate change is complicated and can be difficult to conceptualize. In addition, many people don't believe that climate change is something that will impact them during their lifetime.

The list of issues surrounding our environment is ample, and as a result of the root problems pointed out by the NRDC—Natural Resources Defense Council—we must face the three major issues that affect the majority of them overall: global warming and climate change; water pollution and ocean acidification; and loss of biodiversity. Undoubtedly, global warming is one of the biggest environmental problems of our lifetime: as greenhouse gas emissions blanket the Earth, they trap the sun's heat, leading to the warming of the atmosphere. Scientists attest that the last time carbon dioxide levels on our planet were as high as today was more than four million years ago. Month after record-breaking month, 2023 is on track to be the hottest year measured in human history. It has been a year of extraordinary drought, deadly rainfall, and searing heat waves. Extreme temperatures even reached underwater.

Whether we humans are aware of the gravity and consequential impact on the physical environment, facts do not lie: overpopulation, pollution, burning fossil fuels, and deforestation all have consequences. Changes like these have triggered climate change, soil erosion, poor air quality, and undrinkable water.

What can be done?

> *As a poet I hold the most archaic values on earth. They go back to the upper Paleolithic: the fertility of the soil, the magic of animals, the power-vision in solitude, the terrifying initiation and rebirth, the love and ecstasy of the dance, the common work of the tribe. I try to hold both history and wilderness in mind, that my poems may approach the true measure of things and stand against the unbalance and ignorance of our times.*
> ~ Gary Snyder, poet, essayist, lecturer, and environmental activist

The consequences of not taking care of the planet, which require a crucial mindset shift, are especially dire for climate and ecosystems, and the damage may accelerate and undermine how our societies function, worsen our lives and, perhaps most directly, harm our own well-being.

How can one help and be an agent for change?

# Changemaker

From a macrocosmic perspective to a microcosmic standpoint, there is little doubt that it is through education that one becomes capable of maintaining or modifying the appropriation of discourses of power. Especially as it relates to the environment and its myriad of variables.

Named Werá Jecupé by the shaman and chief Alcebíades Werá during the period in which he lived among the Guarani in the 1980s, countryman Kaká Werá is a child of Tapuia parents who migrated in the 1960s from the north of the Brazilian State of Minas Gerais to São Paulo, in the capital, to live near the last Guarani village in the southern region of the largest city in the country, where he was born in 1964. For thirteen years, yet still a teenager, Kaká Werá started a pilgrimage through several Guarani villages in the southeast and south of Brazil, going to Paraguay, seeking a deeper understanding of the Guarani culture. He retraced a route that historically became known as the "Search for the Land Without Evils." The same route had been taken between the 16th and 17th centuries, in which the Guarani spread across the southern and southeastern coast, fragmenting their ancestral wisdom along the way.

A writer, educator, therapist, social entrepreneur and lecturer, Kaká Werá is a forerunner of indigenous literature in Brazil, author of twelve books, including the award-winning ones: *A Terra dos Mil Povos* (The Land of a Thousand Peoples) and *Menino-Trovão* (Thunder-Boy), not yet translated into English. He founded the Arapoty Institute in 1994, developing projects in Brazil and France with a focus on valuing the traditional knowledge of indigenous peoples. Throughout his tireless work and career, he has been holding conferences in fourteen countries, including the United States, France, England, India, and parts of Africa.

While it is important to highlight that the Yanomami and the Guarani are relevant participants of the rich landscape of the Brazilian Original People, they represent a fraction of its historic compound. Before the arrival of Europeans in the year 1500, Brazil was home to at least 1,000 tribes with a total estimated population of 5-13 million people. There are about 305 tribes living in Brazil today, totaling around 1.7 million people, or 0.8% of Brazil's population.

# Galvanizing Trajectory

It is known that there are more than 380 ethnicities and hundreds of native languages in Brazil today. Nevertheless, and contrary to popular belief, Brazil's Indigenous People aren't confined to the Amazon Rainforest. Nearly half of them live in urban areas. Like in many countries where natives are stereotyped, on the surface and despite 500 years of an avalanche of historical facts, indigenous inhabitants are still perceived somewhat romantically, at best. It is a fact that the perpetuation of a romantic image does not help legitimizing the indigenous population in Brazil, as well as it does not contribute to a better understanding of their status as citizens.

"This is one of the central aspects of my personal questioning, of my relationship with the non-indigenous society, and of my indigenous relatives," says Werá. "When I went to the Guarani village in the beginning of the '80s, I was studying in a public school, called Manuel Borba Gato, which honored a great aggressor of the indigenous peoples. When I got to meet the community, its values, and its vision of the world and learned about the pressure that existed over the Guarani people by the fact that they were considered, in their own area, at that moment, and still today, at the periphery of the southern part of São Paulo, to be a hindrance, that experience mobilized me to interact with the non-indigenous society, and begin to present the other side of our ancestors, who they really were."

Werá is keen on his revealing experience:

"The students of the public schools learned that the indigenous used to like to swim, used to like to hunt; we learned about the indigenous of the past, as if they no longer existed. In the 1980s, it was said that there were 120,000 people of indigenous origin in Brazil and they were in the process of extinction, and that possibly before the 1990s they would cease to exist. It is then that I start my work to show that in fact, the reality of the indigenous peoples was very much present in the periphery of some of the largest Brazilian cities. It is then that I begin to work on what I like to call dismantling the catechization of the vision of the indigenous, which is frozen in time and space, and essentially in the past."

After supporting the Guarani in Aldeia Morro da Saudade to build the first center for the rescue and preservation of traditional culture, the Ambá Arandu Culture Center from 1989 to 1992, it is in 1994 that Kaká Werá founded the Arapoty Institute, aimed at disseminating the values and philosophy of Brazil's indigenous peoples and promoting sustainability and social entrepreneurship actions, through the appreciation of art, crafts, and the creation of an empowerment movement through indigenous literature, making indigenous citizens the protagonists of their own speech.

In partnership with the Phytoervas Foundation he published his first book: *Whenever We Said Goodbye* (*Oré Awé Roiru'a Ma*, in Guarani, *Todas as Vezes que Dissemos Adeus*, in Portuguese). Then, through the Peirópolis Foundation he developed several literary projects focusing on human values, having published *A Terra dos Mil Povos* and *As Fabulosas Fábulas de Iauaretê*, books considered highly recommended on several occasions by the Ministry of Culture and the National Children's Book Foundation.

Werá's knowledge of Brazil's ancestral culture led him to give lectures at the University of Oxford

(1997), Stanford University (2002), New York University (NYU) (2003), and UNESCO. It was during this period that Kaká Werá used literature as an instrument of (re)existence and dissemination of knowledge and values of indigenous peoples, being one of the precursors and encouragers of literary production by the representatives of these ancestral cultures, having also published TUPAN, *La Voix du Tonnerre* (TUPAN, Thunderous Voice) in French through the Fondation Danielle Mitterrand, and in German through the Anthroposophical Society.

In France, he was one of the founders of the Institut Arapoty France, responsible for organizing seminars, publications, courses focusing on ecology, cultural diversity, and philosophies of the ancestral peoples of Brazil.

Kaká Werá has been teaching for more than twenty-five years at the Holistic University of Peace (UNIPAZ), Santander, Colombia, whose rector is the anthropologist and psychologist Roberto Crema, who made him responsible for the indigenous chair at the University.

# True Universal Activism

The rich cultural traditions of indigenous communities in Brazil have come under threat from mainstream institutions that ignore or discredit their value. Kaká Werá works to bring indigenous cultures to the country's mainstream, strengthening self-esteem among natives and spreading crucial insights on environmental protection and cultural diversity.

Kaká Werá is also a fellow of Ashoka. Headquartered in Arlington, VA, Ashoka is a worldwide nonprofit organization which builds and cultivates a community of change, creating leaders who help transform institutions and culture encouraging changemaking for the good of society. Ashoka's mantra is that the world is defined by change and requires a new mindset. It envisions a world in which everyone is a changemaker; a world where all citizens are powerful and contribute to change in positive ways. It is with that principle in mind that Kaká Werá has founded a series of programs that use indigenous knowledge to address stubborn social issues from fresh perspectives. His flagship program is the "Aldeia do Saber Sagrado" (Sacred Knowledge Tribe) in the city of Itapecerica da Serra, near São Paulo city. This space offers training and activities for the youth and the elderly, serving thousands of adolescents, health professionals, and indigenous Brazilians each year. In it, children from public and private schools learn about indigenous history and culture, take classes in environmental education, and work in reforesting the devastated woods. Doctors, psychologists, and others interested in indigenous medicine attend courses on indigenous culture and learn the use of medicinal plants.

Through his umbrella organization, the Arapoty Institute, Kaká organizes volunteers to visit tribes in the region to help with emergency needs, provide health training, and identify potential leaders within each tribe. These leaders take part in training initiatives in the "Aldeia do Saber Sagrado" that prepare them to start new business ventures, to manage the production of arts and crafts, and generate income for the tribe. They also take on the responsibility of spreading the knowledge they gain at the "Aldeia do Saber Sagrado" throughout their communities.

Kaká works to spread and divulge the products and insights of indigenous culture beyond the borders of Brazil. He draws on the principles and infrastructure of movements for fair trade to establish new, lucrative markets for native products in Europe and farther. He has developed exchange programs that immerse European youths in the life of indigenous Brazilians, and put together international conferences that are rooted in indigenous cultures but organized around principles that transcend cultural boundaries.

A truly universal mind, Kaká Werá knows, like his ancestors did, what it is to think globally and to act locally; or in other words, to see the big picture by cultivating a global mindset. His hopeful, defining inspiration and disseminating work for the humanities and the environment is 100+ years late. And yet, 100+ years ahead of his time.

The Guarani could say something like this:

*Aguyje Aguyjevete ndéve. Upéicha toiko.*
Thank you. So be it.

# Your Thoughts Here
## On Embracing Your Planet
### the Same Way You Embrace Your Nation

# Every Day (I Thank You)

## 8

### For Going the Extra Mile Attempting to Capture What True Love Is

*Love alters not with his*
*Brief hours and weeks,*
*But bears it out even to*
*The edge of doom.*
*If this be error*
*And upon me proved,*
*I never writ,*
*nor no man ever loved*
"Sonnet 116"
~ W. Shakespeare, playright, poet, actor

WHAT IS THIS THING THAT WE THE PEOPLE keep pursuing, which we call love?

To begin with, we can all agree it's not a thing. As we reflect on love as a pursuit, a foundational meaning revolves on the sublime assumption that we are capable of striving to attain love with intention and purpose. Simply put, the elevated concept of love for the sake of loving, with no expectation of something in return: it's there when it comes to one's nurturing self-respect and dignity; it's there and prevalent in our relationships with our family and friends; it's also there in our relationships with coworkers; or yet, it's even there in our daily interactions with strangers.

Wouldn't that be wonderful?

We grow up learning to qualify the existence of love in our lives in many ways. One of them is based upon some public display of attachment built on desiring, clinging, needing and even lusting. Can we truly call these as true expressions of love?

Yes, we can. And cannot. Let's start with the romantic aspect of love that occupies our hearts and minds throughout our entire lives. Uh huh, our entire lives. From pre-adolescence through the fun (or not so much fun) teenager years, throughout adulthood—and beyond. As we stride for a clearer vision, let's use the example of an assisted living environment where many or most of their members have experienced and/or are going through some kind of separation from loved ones—past, present and future. As we spend a day observing folks come and go, it is not difficult to notice a multitude of forms of expression: from oblivion about the surroundings to interactive encounters, crossing looks of admiration, eyes dreaming of companionship, hands holding in the corridors and even imagining intimate caring for one another behind closed doors. These are all aspects of our longing for love manifestation at any given time of our existence.

It is true that we spend our time carrying the belief that love is mostly an outcome of nurturing romantic relationships. It is also true that we know that love is not limited only by romance and that it exists in many other aspects of our lives, too.

# Peeling Off The Surface

Here is a passage from *The Power of Love: What Does it Take for Love to Last a Lifetime,* by Oscho, inspiring twentieth century philosopher and spiritual teacher:

"One of the most important life events is falling in love, yet we never learn about it in school. Societies and religions force us into models and thought-forms that are often in opposition to an organic model of love, which is instead institutionalized by marriage, religious affiliations, and nationalism. This results in love that is, for most people, a painful challenge in one form or another throughout life."

We tend to forget that there are so many ways to experience love and to be loved in return. So, why not pursue all manifestations of love as opposed to waiting for it to manifest in our lives mostly in the form of romanticism?

As we evolve from the perception that vulnerability is not synonymous to weakness, it rather implies having the courage to be oneself and to accept others exactly as they are, and where they are in their lives— physically, emotionally and mentally. Perhaps a major challenge we encounter is that it requires one to be authentic, which starts with our own selves. It's like removing the layers built upon us, especially during our early years as teens and young adults, which sometimes obstruct us from seeing the truth as it is. To get to that, it may require a good level of emotional intimacy that many of us are not yet equipped with. But once we walk the first steps and overcome our anxieties, concerns and fears, we can begin building more profound and meaningful connections.

As we dive into the meaning of vulnerability, we are exposed to opportunities to practice being vulnerable in every encounter, such as telling someone you like them, or admitting having used wrong judgment, or recognizing a mistake at work, or yet asking someone for help.

From the *Power of Love*, here's another keen excerpt:

"The capacity to be alone is the capacity to love. It may look paradoxical to you, but it is not. It is an existential truth: only those people who are capable of being alone are capable of love, of sharing, of going into the deepest core of the other person—without possessing the other, without becoming dependent on the other, without reducing the other to a thing, and without becoming addicted to the other. They allow the other absolute freedom, because they know that if the other leaves, they will be as happy as they are now. Their happiness cannot be taken by the other, because it is not given by the other."

One's interpretation of being capable of being alone may differ as we're all at different levels of conscience. It's imperative that we feel good in our own skin before we open up to others. Therefore, moving away from fear plays a decisive role here. Fear of rejection and authenticity comes from our fear of vulnerability. Am I going to get hurt? Am I going to hurt them? Because of this fear, we spend more time hiding the truth than letting it out and, as a result, our relationships suffer and we endure hardships. But, it's important to note that even in our difficulties, there are moments of grace if we see vulnerability as the safest place to be; thus, allowing ourselves space for truthfulness and authenticity.

Finding power in our ability to be vulnerable and practice it in all of our relationships can change our lives for the better. As we open our minds and expand our universe, we may experience loving as it is, and add more value and meaning to our existence.

> *Do you like me?*
> *Well, I hope you do*
> *'Cause if you like me*
> *Then, I think I'm gonna have to like you, too*
> *If you tell me, I'll tell you too*
> *And we'll say the things*
> *And do the things that lovers do*
> *We'll keep it to ourselves*
> *We won'ta hurt no one*
> *Then, we'll say goodbye*
> *And go back home*
> *When the day is done*
> "Day is done" ~ John Prine, songwriter

"One day you will find a soul that was also looking for yours. Someone who, while walking the roads of life, also missed someone who still didn't know the name or appearance, but that their soul already knew.

"Because the most grandiose encounters somehow already happened through life.

"But the encounter alone is not enough if there is no maturity to sustain it. It takes a good deal of inner growth on both sides for an encounter to become a mutual walk. Because the encounter is just the beginning, it is the challenges along the way that will show the purpose of a union and how far along the path two people can walk. Just as there are people who only arrive to teach and leave, there are those who come to stay and grow together.

"People connected with you will always find you along the way. Meanwhile, take care of yourself, of your development, of your soul, of your heart. Learn to enjoy your own company, to value yourself, to love yourself regardless of someone else's love. Don't just wait and don't make your life a wait. Do not abandon yourself in the hands of someone believing that this person will take care of you. Wonderful people will find you and yet the responsibility to make yourself happy is yours.

"Because nobody comes to complete, people arrive to expand. No one will carry you on the walk, but you can walk by their side. And if both are prepared, they will reach a common goal.

"The more you take care of yourself, the more you attract people compatible with what you emanate and the deeper and more beautiful your encounters and the course of the journey are." ~ Alexandro Gruber, writer

# Looking For Answers, Finding More Questions

*Follow your destiny, water your plants, love your roses, the rest is the shade of other people's trees*
~ Fernando Pessoa, poet and writer

Love, in its many lights and shades, is broached, through Fernando Pessoa's perspective, by logic and paradox. A poet who communicates through creating a transcendental atmosphere with just simple words, he can also reveal his complexity and depth of thought. Curious and concerned with bringing philosophy to his writings, many aspects of his intellect are depicted in his multifaceted personality through the heteronyms he created to represent the diversity of his literary works.

In *The Book of Disquiet,* Pessoa portrays love through different lenses. His acute view of the problem is one that goes beyond the relationship between two individuals reciprocally, but most importantly an individual experience irrespective and independent of anyone. Love, from Pessoa's perspective, is a struggle with oneself and does not necessarily involve a counterpart. In his mind, if there's a significant individual in reference, it is because he or she fits the concepts of someone truly meaningful. "We never love anyone. What we love is the idea we have of someone. It's our own concept—our own selves—that we love." Put differently, in a state of loving, we can't clearly see who the other person really is and therefore don't go far beyond what we see inside other than our own inner projection. It's like conceiving and interpreting someone and falling in love with this interpretation.

Pessoa goes on to say that "The relation between one soul and another, expressed through such uncertain and variable things as shared words and proffered gestures, are deceptively complex. The very act of meeting each other is a non-meeting. Two people say 'I love you' or mutually think it and feel it and each has in mind a different idea, a different life, perhaps even a different color or fragrance, in the abstract sum of impressions that constitute the soul's activity." In his paradoxical frame of mind, Pessoa considers romantic love a path of disenchantment, which initially does not bring much hope for the enamored. Using an analogy, he compares a suit made by the soul or imagination and offered to those we deem fit when lives are crossed. But to one's disappointment, every suit, since only being temporary, won't last long and soon the suit of the ideal we have formed will be unmasked, thus the real completion of the person we dressed will be revealed. Though pessimistic as it may seem, he provides light after the tunnel:

"Romantic love is thus a path to disillusion, unless this disillusion, accepted from the start, decides to vary the ideal constantly, constantly sewing new suits in the soul's workshops so as to constantly renew the appearance of the person they clothe."

Clearly, time and space are factored in Fernando Pessoa's concept of love and its complexities. He knew the value of living in the present, therefore rejecting the past and future was a constant exercise of his soul to endure and remain himself, aware of his own temporality.

# 'The Love of Your Fate'

> *The longer I live, the more deeply I learn that love*
> *– whether we call it friendship, family, or romance – is*
> *the work of mirroring and magnifying each other's light.*
> ~ James Baldwin, writer, civil rights activist

Describing love is like describing the air around us. We can't see it, we can't touch it, we can't smell it, we can't taste it. We just feel it and breathe it. And, of course, we can't live without it for too long. But there's one thing we can do: as a constant act of giving and receiving, we can take control of how intensely we inhale and exhale it and use our sovereign will to let it manifest. Voluntarily. Intentionally. Decisively. Consciously. Abundantly. Graciously. Unreservedly.

There's life for love beyond romance and that's likely where the opportunity for true learning resides. Just like the excerpt that follows where Joseph Campbell's *Reflections on the Art of Living* gives us his testimonial of embracing the unknown: "Nietzsche was the one who did the job for me. At a certain moment in his life, the idea came to him of what he called 'the love of your fate.' Whatever your fate is, whatever the hell happens, you say, 'This is what I need.' It may look like a wreck, but go at it as though it were an opportunity, a challenge. If you bring love to that moment—not discouragement—you will find the strength is there. Any disaster you can survive is an improvement in your character, your stature, and your life. What a privilege! This is when the spontaneity of your own nature will have a chance to flow.

Then, when looking back at your life, you will see

that the moments which seemed to be great failures followed by wreckage were the incidents that shaped the life you have now. You'll see that this is really true. Nothing can happen to you that is not positive. Even though it looks and feels at the moment like a negative crisis, it is not. The crisis throws you back, and when you are required to exhibit strength, it comes."
~ Joseph Campbell, writer, professor

# A Boy From Madras

This is a brief story of a boy born at the end of the 19th century in the small town of Madanapalle, in the State of Madras, India, known today as the State of Tamil Nadu. Born in a Telugu-speaking Brahmin family, his father was employed as an official of the British colonial administration. The boy was ten when his mother died. His parents had a total of eleven children, of whom six survived childhood.

His name, Jiddu Krishnamurti. Having contracted malaria and suffered recurrent bouts of the disease over many years, he was a sensitive and sickly child, often taken as detached and absent, and for being intellectually disabled; besides, he would experience being beaten regularly at school by his teachers and at home by his father. From his early childhood years, aware of the connection between our inner world of thoughts and emotions and the outer world, he felt a bond with nature that was to stay with him for the rest of his life.

Krishnamurti's father retired and sought employment at the headquarters of the Theosophical Society, the organizational body of Theosophy, an esoteric movement founded by Helena Blavatsky in New York City in 1875. He was eventually hired by the Society as a clerk, moving there with his family in January 1909. The father and two boys were at first assigned to live in a small cottage that was located just outside the society's compound.

## 'I Will Do Whatever You Want'

Perceived by one of the leaders of the Society as emanating "the most wonderful aura they had ever seen, without a particle of selfishness in it," this leader was convinced that the boy would become a spiritual teacher and a great orator; the likely "vehicle for the Lord Maitreya" in Theosophical doctrine, an advanced spiritual entity periodically appearing on Earth as a World Teacher to guide the evolution of humankind.

"There was an element of subservience, obedience. The boy was vague, uncertain, wooly; he didn't seem to care what was happening. He was like a vessel with a large hole in it, whatever was put in, went through, nothing remained," according to Papul Jayakar, biographer, cultural activist and writer, in post-independence India. "No thought entered his mind. He was watching and listening and nothing else."

# World Teacher

Krishnamurti was purposefully nurtured by the Theosophical Society. "A small number of trusted members undertook the task of educating, protecting, and generally preparing Krishnamurti as the 'vehicle' of the expected World Teacher. In spite of his history of problems with schoolwork and concerns about his capacities and physical condition, the fourteen-year-old was able to speak and write competently in English within six months. It is during this period that Krishnamurti developed a strong bond with Annie Besant, one of the Society's main leaders, and came to view her as a surrogate mother. His father, who had initially acquiesced to Besant's legal guardianship of Krishnamurti, was pushed into the background by the swirl of attention around his son. In 1912 he sued Besant to annul the guardianship agreement. After a protracted legal battle, Besant took custody of Krishnamurti and his brother Nitya. As a result of this separation from family and home, Krishnamurti and his brother (whose relationship had always been very close) became more dependent on each other."

Biographer Mary Lutyens' quote above adds to the following: "In 1911, the Theosophical Society established the Order of the Star in the East (OSE) to prepare the world for the expected appearance of the World Teacher. Krishnamurti was named as its head, with senior Theosophists assigned various other positions. Membership was open to anybody who accepted the doctrine of the *Coming of the World Teacher*. Controversy soon erupted, both within the Theosophical Society and outside it, in Hindu circles and the Indian press."

A public image was cultivated by the Theosophists, attempting to characterize Krishnamurti with "a well-polished exterior, a sobriety of purpose, a cosmopolitan outlook and an otherworldly, almost beatific detachment in his demeanor," according to biographer Robert Vernon. However, as time progressed, the Theosophists noticed a change in him—one they might have kept from the public eye. "Krishnamurti showed signs of adolescent rebellion and emotional instability, chafing at the regime imposed on him, visibly uncomfortable with the publicity surrounding him, and occasionally expressing doubts about the future prescribed for him."

Between 1911 and the start of World War I in 1914, "the brothers visited several other European countries, always accompanied by Theosophist chaperones."

At the end of the horrific war, Krishnamurti embarked on a series of lectures, meetings and discussions around the world, related to his duties as the Head of the OSE, accompanied by Nitya, by then the Organizing Secretary of the Order. Yet, according to Mary Lutyens, Krishnamurti also continued writing. "The content of his talks and writings revolved around the work of the Order and of its members in preparation for the Coming. He was initially described as a halting, hesitant, and repetitive speaker, but his delivery and confidence improved, and he gradually took command of the meetings."

# Falling in Love and Life-Changing Experience

Mary Lutyens observes that in 1921 Krishnamurti fell in love with Helen Knothe, a seventeen-year-old American whose family was associated with the Theosophists. "The experience was tempered by the realization that his work and expected life-mission precluded what would otherwise be considered normal relationships and by the mid-1920s the two of them had drifted apart."

After a trip from Australia to the US, it was in 1922 in Ojai, California that Krishnamurti went through an intense "life-changing experience," according to Papul Jayakar. "This has been variously characterized as a spiritual awakening, a psychological transformation, and a physical reconditioning. The initial events happened in two distinct phases: first a three-day spiritual experience, and two weeks later, a longer-lasting condition that Krishnamurti and those around him referred to as the process." This condition recurred, his biographers tell us, at frequent intervals and with varying intensity for the rest of his life.

"The process at Ojai, whatever its cause or validity, was a cataclysmic milestone for Krishnamurti. Up until this time his spiritual progress, checkered though it might have been, had been planned with solemn deliberation by Theosophy's grandees. ... Something new had now occurred for which Jiddu's training had not entirely prepared him. ... A burden was lifted from his conscience and he took his first step towards becoming an individual. ... In terms of his future role as a teacher, the process was his bedrock. ... It had come to him alone and had not been planted in him by his mentors

... it provided Krishnamurti with the soil in which his newfound spirit of confidence and independence could take root," says Vernon.

Krishnamurti's growing discomfort with adulation and internal Theosophical politics further alienated the man that, to his own judgment, had gradually become more distant from the directions imposed on him by the straightjacket ruling of the organization. The Coming, as it was believed to take place, was imminent and widely rumored to be approaching.

Consecutively, Krishnamurti's brother Nitya's delicate health deteriorated quickly, culminating with his passing on 13 November 1925, at age twenty-seven, in Ojai from complications of influenza and tuberculosis. Though his health was in poor condition, his death was unexpected, and it fundamentally shook Krishnamurti's belief in Theosophy and in the leaders of the Theosophical Society. He had received their assurances regarding Nitya's health, and had come to believe that "Nitya was essential for [his] life-mission and therefore he would not be allowed to die," a belief shared by Annie Besant and Krishnamurti's circle, writes Lutyens.

"His belief in the Masters and the hierarchy had undergone a total revolution," wrote Jayakar. "Moreover, Nitya had been the last surviving link to his family and childhood. ... The only person to whom he could talk openly, his best friend and companion." According to eyewitness accounts, the news "broke him completely."

# 'Truth is a Pathless Land'

Krishnamurti's new vision and consciousness continued to develop over the next few years. "New concepts appeared in his talks, discussions, and correspondence, together with an evolving vocabulary that was progressively free of Theosophical terminology," wrote Lutyens. His new direction reached a boiling point in 1929, when he admonished attempts by the Society's leadership to continue with the Order of the Star.

The outcome came after two years of careful consideration which led him to dissolve the Order during the annual Star Camp at Ommen, in the Netherlands, on 3 August 1929.

In his own words, here's the highlight of his speech:

"I maintain that Truth is a pathless land, and you cannot approach it by any path whatsoever, by any religion, by any sect. That is my point of view, and I adhere to that absolutely and unconditionally. Truth, being limitless, unconditioned, unapproachable by any path whatsoever, cannot be organized; nor should any organization be formed to lead or coerce people along a particular path. If you understand that, then you will see how impossible it is to organize a belief. A belief is purely an individual matter, and you cannot and must not organize it. If you do, it becomes dead, crystalized; it becomes a creed, a sect, a religion, to be imposed on others. This is what everyone throughout the world is attempting to do. Truth is narrowed down and made a plaything for those who are weak, for those who are momentarily discontented. Truth cannot be brought down; rather, the individual must make the effort to ascend it. You cannot bring the mountain to the valley. If you would attain to the mountaintop you must pass through the valley, climb the steeps, unafraid of the dangerous precipices. You must climb toward the Truth, it cannot be 'stepped down' or organized for you. Interest in ideas is mainly sustained by organizations, but organizations only awaken interest from without. Interest, which is not born out of love of Truth for its own sake, but aroused by an organization, is of no value. The organization becomes a framework into which its members can conveniently fit. They no longer strive after Truth for the mountaintop, but rather carve for themselves a convenient niche in which they put themselves, or let the organization place them, and consider that the organization will thereby lead them to Truth."

# What Love Is Not, What It Might Be

*Love is an endless mystery, since
there is nothing to explain it.*
~ Rabindranath Tagore, poet,
philosopher and polymath

Krishnamurti kept moving around the world, leaving an immense wealth of knowledge, helping people to get unconditioned, striving to liberate the individual to become free. This was a man who has worked the hardest in the whole of history for man's freedom, for man's dignity and integrity. Probably one of the highest intelligences of the 20th century, he was never quite thoroughly understood.

Fifty years went by after dissolving the organization he was expected to lead, and seven years before his death at ninety, in 1979, Saanen, Switzerland, Krishnamurti tells us with great simplicity of his own finding about love:

"Love is not desire. It is a great thing to find out this for oneself. And if love is not desire then what is love? Love is not mere attachment to your baby, love is not attachment in any form; love is not jealousy, ambition, fulfillment or becoming; love is not desire or pleasure. The fulfillment of desire, which is pleasure, is not love. So I have found out what love is. It is none of these things. Have I understood these elements and am I free of them? Or I just say, 'I understand intellectually, I understand verbally, but help me to go deeper'? I can't; you have to do it yourself."

He gives us some hints, though. He warns us that love is not necessarily intrinsic into our veins, and that we must admit that in order to free ourselves from our own imposed restrictions. For many of us, a self-discovery path may take an entire existence to realize the intricacies. When asked why the simple truth taught by religions that we must love our fellow man is so difficult to carry out, he lays out his understanding based on his own experience:

"Why is it that we are incapable of loving? What does it mean to love your fellow man? Is it a commandment, or is it a simple fact that if I do not love you and you do not love me, there can only be hate, violence, and destruction? What prevents us from seeing the very simple fact that this world is ours, that this earth is yours and mine to live upon, undivided by nationalities, by frontiers, to live upon happily, productively, with delight, with affection and compassion? Why is it that we do not see this? I can give you lots of explanations, and you can give me lots more, but mere explanations will never eradicate the fact that we do not love our neighbor."

Jiddu Krishnamurti refers to true, authentic love. Love that transcends, especially considering our own fellow neighbors. His interlocutor seems to get to a breakthrough, which leads us to great pause for reflection:

"I am beginning to see what you mean," one says. "We are not simple; we don't discover anything for ourselves but just repeat what we have been told. Even when we revolt we form new conclusions, which again have to be broken down. We really don't know what love is, but merely have opinions about it. Is that it?"

To which Krishnamurti replies:

"Don't you think so? Surely, to know love, Truth, God,

there must be no opinions, no beliefs, no speculations with regard to it. If you have an opinion about a fact, the opinion becomes important, not the fact. If you want to know the truth or the falseness of the fact, then you must not live in the word, in the intellect. You may have a lot of knowledge and information about the facts, but the actual facts are entirely different. Put away the book, the description, the tradition, the authority, and take the journey of self-discovery. Love, and don't be caught in opinions and ideas about what love is or should be. When you love, everything will come right. Love has its own action. Love, and you will know the blessings of it. Keep away from the authority who tells you what love is and what it is not. No authority knows; and he who knows cannot tell. Love, and there is understanding."

*Ain't got a soapbox I can stand upon*
*But God gave me a stage, a guitar and a song*
*My daddy told me, "Son, don't you get involved in*
*Politics, religions or other people's quotes"*
*I'll paint the picture, let me set the scene*
*I know when I have children they*
*will know what it means*
*And I pass on these things my family's given to me*
*Just love and understanding, positivity*
*We could change this whole world with a piano*
*Add a bass, some guitar, grab a beat and away we go*
*I'm just a boy with a one-man show*
*No university, no degree, but lord knows*
*Everybody's talking 'bout exponential growth*
*And the stock market crashing in their portfolios*
*While I'll be sitting here with a song that I wrote*
*Love can change the world in a moment*
*But what do I know?*
*The revolution's coming, it's a minute away*

*I saw people marching in the streets today*
*You know we are made up of love and hate*
*But both of them are balanced on a razor blade*
*I'll paint the picture, let me set the scene*
*I know, I'm all for people following their dreams*
*Just remember life is more than fittin' in your jeans*
*It's love and understanding, positivity*
*Love could change the world in a moment*
*But what do I know?*
"What Do I Know?"
~ Ed Sheeran, songwriter


Closing thoughts: with the topic of love being so personal and intimate, one would agree that its complexity, as well as its simplicity, is immeasurable. It has dominated our hearts and minds for the entire history of mankind and it will continue to do so as long as there's a spark dangling over our most probable highest aim: spiritual freedom.

# Spinoza's Word of Advice

*Stop going into those dark, cold temples that you built yourself and saying they are my house. My house is in the mountains, in the woods, rivers, lakes, beaches. That's where I live and there I express my love for you.*
~ Baruch de Spinoza, philosopher

When Einstein gave lectures at US universities, the recurring question that students asked him most was: "Do you believe in God?" And he always answered: "I believe in the God of Spinoza."

Spinoza, with his unorthodox views, shares what he believes God would say to us:

"Stop praying. What I want you to do is go out into the world and enjoy your life. I want you to sing, have fun and enjoy everything I've made for you.

"Stop blaming me for your miserable life; I never told you there was anything wrong with you or that you were a sinner, or that your sexuality was a bad thing. Sex is a gift I have given you and with which you can express your love, your ecstasy, your joy. So don't blame me for everything they made you believe.

"Stop reading alleged sacred scriptures that have nothing to do with me. If you can't read me in a sunrise, in a landscape, in the look of your friends, in your son's eyes... you will find me in no book!

"Stop asking me, 'Will you tell me how to do my job?' Stop being so scared of me. I do not judge you or criticize you, nor get angry, or bothered. I am pure love.

"Stop asking for forgiveness, there's nothing to forgive. If I made you... I filled you with passions, limitations, pleasures, feelings, needs, inconsistencies... free will. How can I blame you if you respond to something I put in you? How can I punish you for being the way you are, if I'm the one who made you? Do you think I could create a place to burn all my children who behave badly for the rest of eternity? What kind of god would do that?

"Respect your peers and don't do what you don't want for yourself. All I ask is that you pay attention in your life, that alertness is your guide.

"My beloved, this life is not a test, not a step on the way, not a rehearsal, nor a prelude to paradise. This life is the only thing here and now and it is all you need.

"I have set you absolutely free, no prizes or punishments, no sins or virtues, no one carries a marker, no one keeps a record.

"You are absolutely free to create in your life. Heaven or hell.

"I can't tell you if there's anything after this life but I can give you a tip. Live as if there is not. As if this is your only chance to enjoy, to love, to exist.

"So, if there's nothing after, then you will have enjoyed the opportunity I gave you. And if there is, rest assured that I won't ask if you behaved right or wrong, I'll ask, 'Did you like it? Did you have fun? What did you enjoy the most? What did you learn?'...

"Stop believing in me; believing is assuming, guessing, imagining. I don't want you to believe in me, I want you to believe in you. I want you to feel me in you when you kiss your beloved, when you tuck in your little girl, when you caress your dog, when you bathe in the sea.

"Stop praising me, what kind of egomaniac God do you think I am?

"I'm bored being praised. I'm tired of being thanked. Feeling grateful? Prove it by taking care of yourself, your health, your relationships, the world. Express your joy! That's the way to praise me.

"Stop complicating things and repeating as a parakeet what you've been taught about me.

"The only thing for sure is that you are here, that you are alive, that this world is full of wonders.

"What do you need more miracles for?

"So many explanations?

> *"Don't look for me outside, you won't find me. Find me inside... there where your heart beats."*
> ~ Baruch de Spinoza, philosopher

# Your Thoughts Here
# On Going the Extra Mile Attempting to Capture What True Love Is

# Every Day (I Thank You)

## 9

For Navigating the Nuances of Life
and Death, War and Peace, Old and New,
Rich and Poor, Black and White, Male
and Female, Yin and Yang, and
Everything in Between

*The further on I go, oh the less I know*
*Friend or foe, there's only us*
*The further on I go,*
*I can find only us breathing*
*Only us sleeping*
*Only us dreaming*
*Only us*
*"Only Us"*
~ Peter Gabriel, songwriter, musician

IT IS PRESUMABLY TRUE THAT AS A SPECIES, dwellers of the blue water planet, eight billion souls and counting, each one of us, in one way or another, is striving for a better life for ourselves and for our loved ones. From the remote village where the Yaifo tribe resides, a very infrequently visited place among the most secluded people in Papua New Guinea, to the denizens of the beautiful and picturesque village of Gimmelwald, Switzerland, to the inhabitants of Tristan da Cunha, known to be the farthest ill-inhabited island in the world with 238 islanders, located some 2,787 km from Cape Town, South Africa, all the way to the Orangi Town in Karachi, Pakistan, where 2.4 million people live crammed in one of the largest slums on the planet, we are all looking for ways to make our survival more than a mere cradle to grave experience.

> *Men work together whether they work together or apart.*
> ~ Robert Frost, poet

In his article on *Medium*, "The Paradox of Human Nature: Why We Are All Walking Contradictions", entrepreneur, executive coach, author, and designer Alejandro Betancourt warns us of the contradictory nature of the human genus:

"Part of what makes us so contradictory is that we are constantly changing. We are not the people we were a year ago or even yesterday. We are always in flux and evolving. Our actions in the past do not reflect our efforts in the present or future. This is both a good and a bad thing. It's good because it means we can change for the better. It's bad because it means we also have the potential to change for the worse."

Betancourt highlights our contradictory nature associated with our capacity for self-deception: "We often deceive ourselves about our true motivations and intentions. We tell ourselves that we're doing something for one reason, but in reality, we're doing it for another. We act daily in ways that contradict our stated values and beliefs. We say one thing but do another. We make plans that we never follow."

It is fair to say that we tend to find reasons to justify our self-deception by looking out and pointing the finger at the outer world. The exercise of blaming others or the world outside us is a futile, if not naive waste of time. Why? Because our hearts and minds hold the key to treasure for our liberation and, in unison, conversely carry the pathway to our confinement.

Pursuing clarity when it comes to admittance of our own contradictions is rather an exercise of observation of our own thoughts, desires and actions. Yes, the outer world plays a role but it only becomes the protagonist as long as we give the world undue attention. We know the contradictions are there, and fighting them may not be the best course of action.

Admitting that we are "walking contradictions" implies that we gravitate from one flip of the coin to another. Fortunately, here is where nuance resides. As odd as it may sound, it is in fact not a bad place to be; quite the contrary.

Nuancing, the practice of reading between the lines, is the subtle difference in expression, meaning, and response to the opposites. It is there that we find our consciousness, it is in that realm that we meet awareness. Nuancing—in the way we look at our lives, in the way we think, act and react—is not only fundamental to our success, it is crucial to our survival.

How do we find the path within ourselves that allows us to navigate between the extremes, and desirably grow out of our contradictory nature?

David Berliner, a professor of anthropology at Université Libre de Bruxelles, with research in social memory and cultural transmission, on his article at Aeon, "How our contradictions make us human and inspire creativity", sees the theme of contradiction from a curious perspective:

"Humans live peacefully with contradictions precisely because of their capacity to compartmentalize. And when contradictory statements, actions or emotions jump out of their contextual box, we are very good, perhaps too good, at finding justifications to soothe cognitive dissonance. An environmentalist friend of mine, to whom I pointed out that smoking is not an ecological act, used to reply: 'I know, David, but I smoke rolled cigarettes!' as if rolled cigarettes are less toxic than industrial ones and don't depend on the destructive industry of tobacco exploitation—which he, of course, condemns."

# When the Means Justify the End. Or, Is It the Other Way Around?

*If I can stop one heart from breaking,*
*I shall not live in vain;*
*If I can ease one life the aching,*
*Or cool one pain,*
*Or help one fainting robin unto his nest again,*
*I shall not live in vain.*
~ Emily Dickinson, poet

Citing one of the greatest contradictions of our nature, and consequently one that markedly influences our existence in profound ways, there is one in particular that demands careful consideration: the ill-natured capacity of a human being to destroy another human creature; more specifically, to take another human being's life. It sounds eerie and it is, but the intent here is to deliberate on a critical aspect of our own strain. Whether this be an individual or collective act, self-inflicted, domestic, or on a larger scale, as shocking and unnatural as it is, this should not come as a surprise when we look at ourselves from our humankind perspective. We know who we are, what we are capable of, from the eons of time. But it is, always, shocking and surprising. Why is that?

If we recognize in ourselves the aim for self-realization, for striving for a better life, or call it the pursuit of happiness, why is it that we haven't grappled with a solution for a significant decrease in violence among our own species? To make things more complex, the occurrence of violence as a radical, strange, and erratic act comes across our conscious psyche as part of our daily lives and, for most of us, it is a reality that surfaces when we are young. As such, we grow up as observers of a phenomenon that over time gets normalized in our collective mind. As it is always devastating to learn of such quotidian and incessant events, we live our lives from dawn to dusk, numb and powerless, thinking of how it would be different if our aptitude for living happily, productively, with delight, if affection and compassion were prioritized and more effectively applicable for, and experienced by, all or most mortal beings.

Beyond the parallels between us and the animal realm, there's much to be considered to explain what's involved in our decision making process when it comes to 'an eye for an eye' attitude. On *The Roots of Human Aggression*, R. Douglas Fields observes: "From a psychological perspective, human aggression can be sparked by a seemingly endless range of provocations and motives, but from the viewpoint of neuroscience, only a few specific neural circuits in the brain are responsible for this behavior. Identifying them and understanding how they function is still a work in progress, but undertaking this task is critically important. The capability for violent aggression engraved in our brain by eons of tooth-and-nail struggle for survival too often malfunctions in response to disease, drugs or psychiatric impairments and can lead to tragic consequences."

The exploration of the neural underpinnings of human aggression is a crucial frontier in neuroscience. Understanding the specific brain circuits involved in aggressive behavior not only illuminates how such actions are mediated but also opens avenues for addressing pathological aggression, which can result from various dysfunctions within these circuits.

While neural circuits and neurotransmitters provide

the biological substrate for aggression, environmental and psychological factors play a significant role in modulating these responses. Stress, social provocation, and exposure to violence, no matter what the medium is, can all influence the likelihood of aggressive behavior by impacting the neural circuits involved. Additionally, learning and experience can shape how these brain systems respond to potential provocations.

# Why In The World? What Were You Thinking, Pal?

Neuroscientists are working hard to understand the intricacies of the brain systems but there are always new elements to be added to the entangled webs of our own demeanor as creatures.

Here's a story that defies comprehension and will be recorded in the memory of the Burlington, Vermont community for eons to come:

Thanksgiving Day in its truest meaning is when we take the time to appreciate life and the people around us. It's when we pause to acknowledge that life is a gift, and for that we should be thankful. It was one of those joyful times–November, 2023, that three young adults, closely related to one another, decided to take a trip and spend time with loved ones in Burlington, Vermont, a place that they and their families believed to be safe. These young adults, as normal as they seemed to family, friends and for the majority of common citizens, were not perceived as such by one single individual at a given time, space and place—one lone soul who, in an instant, due to his deep ignorance, sick and disturbed mind, by an unjustifiable act of aggression, ruined his life and profoundly affected the lives of the three young men forever.

The shooting of the three Palestinian-American college students, Hisham Awartani, Tasheen Ali Ahmad and Kinnan Abdalhamid, all at age twenty, came in the midst of the unspeakable Israel-Hamas conflict, for reasons unknown or not clear. The emboldened perpetrator was arrested and charged with three counts of second-degree attempted murder in connection with the shooting. Ironically, he had previously worked as a farmer, Ivy-league researcher, and ski instructor, according to his résumé—"He thought the world is a mess," his mother told a news channel. He had previously struggled with depression and had celebrated Thanksgiving with his family just days earlier, his mother told the news in an exclusive interview. "He has had a lot of struggles in his life but he is such a kind and loving person," said his mother. "I am just shocked by the whole thing."

*Even the longest lived of our species spends but a blink of time in the span of human history. How dare anyone cause harm to another soul, curtail their life or life's potential, when our lives are so short to begin with?*
~ Isabel Wilkerson, journalist and author

While Tasheen and Kinnan had non-life threatening injuries and were released earlier from the hospital, Hisham was more deeply affected by the horrific act. A student of mathematics and archaeology at Brown University, Hisham is a graduate of the Ramallah Friends School, a Quaker-run K-12 school in the West Bank. "My husband didn't want Hisham to come back for Christmas," says Awartani's mother Elizabeth Price. "He thought our son would be safer [in the U.S.] than in Palestine." Anxiously waiting while still in Ramallah with her husband Ali Awartani where the family resides, just before crossing the skies to see her son, she heard from the doctors the devastating prognosis that it's unlikely he'd be able to use his legs again. "He's confronting a life of disability, a potentially irreversible change to his life and what it means for his future."

Like mothers do, her love for her son naturally extends

to her son's friends, who shared a sheer brotherly relationship: "I think it's important for these boys to be seen as fully fledged people," Price says. "They are the brightest of the brightest. They would have discussions of mathematics and history. These are boys who grew up in my house. I consider all three of them my children. I am so glad I'm going to see them and care for them."

Though not at the time considered to be a hate crime, it was considered a 'hateful act.' The fact is that it does not alter the tragic consequences. For the victims and shooter, for their families, for the citizens of Burlington, and for Vermont as a whole, where bigotry is not commonly manifested, it is a tragedy that traveled across the nation and throughout the globe where the conflict now surpasses the collective imaginings of how terrifying life can get.

And if terrifying is not enough, catastrophic may be a word of choice to define the historic Hamas attack on Israel on October 7th 2023, and the subsequent war in that part of the world. Barbaric, indescribable actions mirroring one another exceeding ethical and legal limits, and where humanity rapidly fails, this is a horror story with potentially enormous present and future reverberations yet to be endured.

Will the truth about this appalling, sad, and untimely world episode ever be known?

> *We all know, through centuries, what the causes of war are: nationalism, economic separation, different kinds of societies, my country and your country, my prejudice against your prejudice, my love of my country and your love of country, my leader and your leader, and so on.*

*We have known this for millennia, and we are still at it.
So I say: what has happened to human beings?*

*They know the danger of
nationalism but they still wave the flag.*
~ Jiddu Krishnamurti,
philosopher, speaker, writer

# When the Vessel Feels Like a Dinghy, Unanchored

*Adrift, America in 100 Charts* is *The New York Times* Best Sellers author Scott Galloway's attempt to portray life in this vast land we inhabit, depicting a nation he considers astray from its original purpose. He provides an eye-opening examination of the period from the end of World War II to the present day to explain just how America arrived at these crossroads. Multiple crises such as Jim Crow, WWII, and the Stock Market Crash of 2008, added to the magnifying power of technology, a deep-rooted white patriarchy, and the socio-economic effects of COVID, gave form and substance to our recent disturbances. The book is an effort to make sense of a large spectrum of critical issues, and offers Galloway's unique view on where we're headed and who we might become:

"We lack neither wind nor sail, we have no shortage of captains or gear, yet our mighty ship flounders in a sea of partisanship, corruption, and selfishness."

Galloway's metaphor vividly captures the challenges facing many societies today, including ours. Despite having beyond abundant resources, capable leadership, and the necessary tools and infrastructure, progress is often stalled by divisive politics, corruption, and individual self-interest. These forces act as treacherous currents and fierce storms, impeding the collective journey toward a more equitable, just, and prosperous future. The author has no mercy when it comes to pointing out, in hard numbers, realities that routinely surround us as individuals and communities. Skeptical and yet quasi-hopeful, he is moved by his love for his country. Among those realities, one chapter in particular sticks out to explain some of the violence and its ultimate effects.

Not intended to be a free pass, but women rarely carry an elusive inclination for aggression and clearly have a more balanced and pacific demeanor compared to men. On the other extreme, validates the author, "mass murder is a uniquely male crime." Again, not surprisingly, there's a pattern here. The numbers are quite revealing as it relates to the demographics:

Antisocial, 30%; Diagnosed mental and health condition, 32%; White non-Hispanic, 51%; History of financial instability, 54%; Under 35, 68%; Male, the staggering rate of 92%.

The report comes from the US Secret service: "Bored (young) men without any pathway to economic security or a meaningful relationship aren't just dangerous to themselves, they're dangerous to society," Galloway postulates. The author adds to the understanding of the same pattern: "As a species, we need physical and social contact, and we crave deep, meaningful bonds. Men who fail to attach to a partner, career, or community grow bitter and seek volatility and unrest. The loss of economic pathways for young people is no less serious for women, but it appears to be less dangerous. When young women feel shame and rage, they don't turn to semiautomatic weapons."

Galloway knows that America is a microcosm, albeit a sizable one, of what happens in the world at large regarding men's predisposition for violence. Galloway sees the female tone and her usual genuine kindness as decisive contributors to making a difference and changing that dynamic.

In conclusion, this perspective highlights the belief

that women's inherent qualities—such as empathy, nurturing, and a collaborative approach—can play a crucial role in addressing and mitigating aggression and violence, both on the verge of a public health crisis. By fostering these traits in societal interactions and leadership, there is potential for creating more harmonious and peaceful communities, both within America and globally. Yes, the world is a mess in so many ways but still the right venue for the female sensitivity model to prevail. A reminder of the nuances and possibilities.

# The Rubber Hits the Road

*If blood will flow when flesh and steel are one*
*Drying in the color of the evening sun*
*Tomorrow's rain will wash the stains away*
*But something in our minds will always stay*
*Perhaps this final act was meant*
*To clinch a lifetime's argument*
*That nothing comes from violence and nothing ever could*
*For all those born beneath an angry star*
*Lest we forget how fragile we are*
*On and on the rain will fall*
*Like tears from a star, like tears from a star*
*On and on the rain will say*
*How fragile we are, how fragile we are*
"Fragile" ~ Sting, songwriter

*War and Peace*, by Leo Tolstoy, is a monumental work of historical fiction that chronicles the impact of the Napoleonic wars on a diverse group of Russian aristocrats. It explores themes of love, family, loyalty, and the futility of war. *War and Peace* shows us that no matter how deeply we hurt, and how bleak the future may appear, there is always a way back to life through love, if only we will allow ourselves to experience it.

In one of the most prominent moral messages reflected in Tolstoy's masterpiece, on the purpose of life, the author wonders about life's meaning and the pursuit of happiness. Sounds familiar, right? He argues that the aspiration for material wealth and power, as an example, is not necessarily the way to find happiness and fulfillment.

*War itself is, of course, a form of madness. It's hardly a civilized pursuit. It's amazing how we spend so much time inventing devices to kill each other and so little time working on how to achieve peace"*
~ Walter Cronkite, Journalist

*War and Peace* was published in the 19th century, a little over 150 years ago. In today's world, there are a lot of reasons to believe Tolstoy was on the mark about his views of happiness, just as there are reasons to shrug about that argument. Life is difficult even when there's abundance, one may say, let alone if we need to fight every day for survival and barely make ends meet. Therefore, it's hard going against the idea that the pursuit to happiness or success—the ever sought after dream of consumption—by definition, the achievement of desired visions and planned goals—is not a valid pursuit. It's just not smart to transgress that idea and we shouldn't. The problem though is that, in today's world, with the help of our tech toys and the meta corporations of the world, aligned with misinformation and the repugnant disinformation, it is ingrained in our values that achieving a certain social status revolves almost exclusively around what's described as a prosperous individual that "could also have gained fame for its favorable  outcome." Or, as the typical trivial dictionary describes success being "attaining wealth, prosperity and/or fame."

As attractive as it may seem, is that a sustainable proposition? Especially, taking into consideration the individuals that are still in the process of building their characters and simultaneously trying to understand how to situate themselves in the world, like the young fellows?

*What is success? To laugh often and much; to win the respect of intelligent people and the affection of children; to earn the appreciation of honest critics and endure the betrayal of false friends; to appreciate the beauty; to find the best in others; to leave the world a bit better, whether by a healthy child, a garden patch or a redeemed social condition; to know even one life has breathed easier because you have lived. This is to have succeeded!"*
~ Ralph Waldo Emerson, essayist, lecturer, philosopher, abolitionist and poet

There is a global interconnectedness in all domains of life, in everything we do, which influences our relationship with others and with our own selves in ways we are still learning how to interpret. Our ability to understand and function in an increasingly fast, complex, multicultural, international, yet integrated environment is pivotal to achieving prosperity in our endeavors. Success, like everything in life, the more we see it through multifaceted aspects, the better our chances to attain it in multifaceted ways. Therefore, limiting oneself, or limiting an individual's flourishing with goals like gaining wealth, power and fame, primarily, only reduces the same individual to become a potentially disappointed, if not frustrated, partial being instead. Mechanical at best, when not turned narrow-minded, intolerant, isolated, inequitable, and less sensitive to their fellow men and women, if the focus is exclusively on the material side of things. For clarity, there's nothing wrong with being wealthy or famous. Especially when there's talent, dedication, luck, and hard work involved. But there's life beyond that, and exploring the possibilities is what makes our existence worth the hassle.

*The plain fact is that the planet does not need more successful people. But it does desperately need more peacemakers, healers, restorers, storytellers, and lovers of every kind. It needs people who live well in their places. It needs people of moral courage willing to join the fight to make the world habitable and humane. And these qualities have little to do with success as we have defined it.*
~ David W. Orr, Professor of
Environmental Studies and Politics

幸

# Why Not Now?

*Seeking serenity seems to me a more reasonable ambition than seeking happiness. And perhaps serenity is a form of happiness.*
~ Jorge Luis Borges, author

Theory becomes reality when we live our lives in the present moment, which is arguably where happiness dwells. Right in the middle, suspended between past and future, like a bell curve. Fact or fiction, a good analogy to address the theme is bringing a significant aspect of our duality: our ever swinging pendulum between the old and the new in our natural order. What is the new if not the passing of the old? And what is the old if not the new in its maturity? In order for renewal to take place, both the old and the new must go; that's a logical statement and one that we experience every day from the time darkness gives way to daylight until another cycle restarts.

You may guess where I'm going here. Life and death, the latter being the almost always depressing topic to talk about, may play a key role if we look at it objectively in the pursuit for living more fully. Are you kidding?, one may say. Not really. Thinking—and talking— about a theme that makes us feel nervous or uncomfortable, such as mortality, is a good way to actually become serene with them. If the idea of death is something that grosses us out, prompting ourselves to think about it a little more consciously can help make the topic feel less chilling, while also increasing our quality of life. And that's the point here.

*Accepting the fact that the body is going to go, but the personality doesn't have to go, and that thing which is*

*the hardest to admit is that character doesn't have to go.*
~ Flossie Lewis, teacher

Thinking about our own mortality—and the fact that we won't be around forever—can propel us to live every day to its fullest. When we know we have limited time, we find ourselves making good use of the time we do have, by checking items off our lifetime goals, or off that bucket list if you prefer. It takes us to a place where we can deliberate and exercise our conscious decision to spend time doing activities we find most meaningful.

*When we are young, it's the illusion of perfection that we fall in love with. As we age, it's the humanness that we fall in love with- the poignant stories of overcoming, the depthful vulnerability of aging, the struggles that grew us in karmic stature, the way a soul shaped itself to accommodate its circumstances. With less energy to hold up our armor, we are revealed and, in the revealing, we call out to each other's hearts....Where we once saw imperfect scars, we now see evidence of a life fully lived.*
~ Jeff Brown, writer

# Empathy is King

*Snowflake?*
*Yes, I've heard this term. I think sociopaths*
*use it to discredit the notion of empathy.*
~ John Cleese, actor,
comedian, screenwriter, producer

As we pour the empathy paint onto our canvas, when we think about death, especially our own, we allow ourselves the opportunity to open the door for us to relate to our fellow men and women in more significant ways. How so? Commonly perceived as putting ourselves in someone else's shoes, empathy provides the opportunity for us to imagine how we would feel. Empathy alone is no substitute for experience, that's true. But remembering that we're ALL here for a short (and hopefully good) time, not necessarily a long time, can catalyze us to be a little kinder and more empathetic towards our loved ones, as well as to strangers.

We can find ourselves in a place where we become more patient and understanding, and can often feel inclined to slow things down when spending time with the people we love. As a couple of minor but meaningful examples, switching off our phones when hanging out with friends, or organizing more frequent, hours-long family gatherings may go a long way. More so than that, though, acknowledging and accepting our own temporality can encourage us to reconcile broken relationships and overcome past dramas that once were given too much attention or even undue relevance.

# Meet Melinda and Rick

*I have decided that aging is a time in one's life when our youthfulness gracefully transforms into unconditional love and infinite acceptance. It is a time when we can truly become who we were meant to be all along and it is a tremendous gift.*
~ Melinda Moulton, author, activist

Within the tapestry of every family and community, there are individuals who stand out, carving indelible marks on the hearts and minds of their kin, circle of friends, and collaborators. These legendary figures aren't always necessarily known by the world at large, but within the intimate circles of family and community life, their impact is profound and enduring. Whether through their exceptional accomplishments, talents, their unique personalities, or their unparalleled capacity for love and kindness, they become central figures in our narratives, shaping our perceptions and influencing generations.

Referring to these legendary figures isn't merely recounting tales of individuals; it's about capturing the essence of what makes them so memorable and significant. These family and community legends, through their actions, words, or mere presence, contribute to our understanding of what it means to be part of a particular group or society. They set standards, embody values, and often become the benchmarks against which future generations are measured.

The enduring story of Melinda and Rick Moulton is a testament to the depth and resilience of true love for one another and to the love and empathy they manifest to the community they are a major part of. From their personal perspective, meeting through friends and experiencing love at first sight, their journey together began in the early 1970s. Encapsulating the era's spirit as 'old hippies,' they initially eschewed marriage for a bond they felt was stronger in their hearts than any document could symbolize.

The decision to move to Vermont during the Vietnam era by individuals or couples who were actively protesting the war is a fascinating illustration of the complexities and tensions of that period in American history. For many, Vermont represented not just a serene and idyllic retreat from the tumult of urban centers or the direct actions of protest, but also a strategic position close to the Canadian border. This geographical advantage offered a potential escape route should the need arise to avoid draft conscription or escape legal repercussions stemming from their activism.

"Trouble could come at any time and we wanted to make sure we had an option in the eventuality of having to flee the country via the northern border," Melinda tells me.

The war was finally over and a new era loomed for the two soulmates in the Green Mountain State. And, the rest is history. Their eventual decision to marry, fifteen years into their relationship, with a surprise wedding sprung on unsuspecting guests at a ski party, highlights their unconventional approach to life and love. Their stories, embellished or not, over time, became a vital part of gatherings, shared again and again, each retelling adding another layer to their mythos. These narratives still serve not only as weaving elements for their own foundation as partners but as a means of transmitting their values, history, and culture from one generation to the next. The legendary status of these individuals is not just a reflection of their deeds or character but of the collective regard in which they are held by their community members.

More than their legacy to the local and regional landscape when it comes to filmmaking and producing award-winning documentaries, as well as developing multiple and landmark projects, respectively, it is their leadership excellence and exemplary volunteerism that stick in our minds. The inspiration drawn from these people is meaningful. Rick Moulton's career goes back to the 1960s as an independent filmmaker in which he has worked on numerous productions for the ski industry, further establishing his reputation dedicated to capturing the beauty and excitement of skiing. His contributions to the ski industry through his films have inspired and entertained countless viewers, showcasing the allure and adventure of skiing in various settings, so vital to the industry and to this State. As for Melinda, she forged her career as an environmental and socially conscious redevelopment professional in the 1980s. She has devoted decades of her life to creating a new model for development. Perhaps one of the most significant moments in her career was her jubilation at the inauguration of the first daily passenger train service between Burlington and New York City since 1953. It highlights an important milestone in public transportation and community advocacy. Her nearly four-decade-long campaign for this cause underscores the persistence and dedication required to bring about substantial infrastructural change, especially in an era where car travel has dominated American landscapes and policy priorities.

"I'm very, very pleased that in my lifetime I saw rail service come back to Burlington," said Melinda during the reactivation of that landmark in 2022.

The re-establishment of this train service not only marks a triumph of community and environmental advocacy, but also reflects a shift in transportation priorities toward more sustainable and interconnected modes of travel. Trains, as opposed to individual car travel, offer a greener alternative, reducing carbon footprints and potentially alleviating traffic congestion and air pollution, some of Melinda's substantial concerns.

This initiative's success, spearheaded by individuals like Melinda Moulton, serves as a reminder of the impact that dedicated advocacy and community support can have in shaping public policy and infrastructure for the better. It illustrates the power of persistent, grassroots efforts in overcoming decades of inertia and challenges to create more connected, sustainable, and vibrant communities.

While some victories are savored, other causes are regrettably put to the test. Melinda Moulton's life is emblematic of the interweaving of personal experience with broader societal issues, illustrating how individual stories can illuminate the stakes of collective challenges. Her passionate engagement with a variety of causes, from civil liberties to environmental sustainability to the safeguarding of democratic principles, reflects a deep commitment to advocating for a better future. Yet, it is the cause of women's reproductive rights that resonates with her on the most personal and profound level, a reflection of her own history and the tragic loss of her mother.

The untimely death of Moulton's mother when Melinda was a teenager, resulting from a botched hysterectomy, serves as a stark reminder of the dangers women face when their healthcare and bodily autonomy are not safeguarded. This personal tragedy has fueled Moulton's activism, driving her to advocate fiercely for women's rights to make informed and safe choices about their reproductive health.

Her mother's story, shared publicly, has become a powerful testament to the critical importance of preserving and protecting these rights.

The overturning of Roe v. Wade by the US Supreme Court represents, for Moulton and countless others, not only a step backward in the fight for equality and autonomy, but also raises concerns about the future of reproductive rights broadly. This decision, a significant setback, intensifies the urgency of Moulton's activism. It underscores the ongoing struggle against the imposition of control over women's bodies by patriarchal structures, and the critical need for vigilant defense of fundamental human rights.

Moulton's poignant reflection, "I got my train, and I lost my reproductive rights," captures the bitter irony of witnessing progress in one area of her life and advocacy, while facing devastating loss in another. This juxtaposition highlights the complex nature of progress and the need for continued advocacy and resilience in the face of setbacks. Moulton's story, and her unwavering commitment to women's reproductive choice, serves as a call to action, reminding us of the importance of standing firm in the defense of autonomy and dignity for all individuals.

But there's resilience. Living on a meadow in a stone house that they built themselves on the hills of Huntington, having raised two children, and navigating the complexities of life together, the Moultons' story is one of partnership, transparency, and mutual support. Their ability to maintain an open line of communication, where nothing is hidden and every concern is shared and addressed together, underscores the importance of honesty and teamwork in a lasting relationship.

Celebrating over five decades together, their love story continues to evolve, characterized by a deep understanding of each other's personalities and a shared commitment to facing life's challenges unitedly. Rick's serenity, in contrast to Melinda's dynamic energy, illustrates the balance they've found in each other, a balance that has undoubtedly contributed to the longevity of their relationship.

As they essentially look forward to quality time together, along with their children and their children's children, each and every day, the Moultons embody the belief that love, when nurtured with openness, respect, and shared dreams, can indeed grow stronger with time. Their story is a beautiful reminder of the power of love to sustain and heal, a message that resonates as strongly today as it did when they first met. Every day embodies love and affection, serving as a reaffirmation of their journey together and the enduring strength of their bond.

The vibrant lives of this galvanizing couple—now enjoying retirement, alive and kicking, with their rich backgrounds, herself in piano playing, writing, cliff diving, horse training, himself in skiing and giving voice to topics surrounding its promotion, understanding and development, and a shared love of the outdoors—embody a spirit of adventure and a refusal to be defined by age. Sound inspiring? Well, it is. Their buoyant life is a pledge to remaining active, engaged, and connected to the passions that have fueled their lives. With a lot of wisdom, testing the brakes but not slowing down is a metaphor for their approach to maturing—cautiously navigating the physical limitations that come with age, while continuing to embrace life fully.

# The Dilemma That Is Not

The intersection of material comfort, spirituality, and the contemplation of wealth and poverty presents a rich field for reflection and inquiry. Individuals who grow up in environments of relative material comfort and are also exposed to spiritual teachings, are uniquely positioned to engage deeply with questions about the nature of satisfaction, the responsibilities of privilege, and the true sources of happiness and fulfillment.

A number of questions naturally come up when considering this: Are wealth and material development important, or simply a distraction from spiritual development? Is it wrong for us to enjoy physical comfort and material prosperity? On the other hand, is the deliberate choice of living in poverty a recipe for attaining spirituality? Is there a common ground between these opposites?

If we glance throughout the history of faith, the aspects of wealth and spirituality have often appeared to be in conflict with one another. One of the most well known Christian verses supporting this notion is the aphorism that "it is easier for a camel to go through the eye of a needle, than for a rich man to enter into the kingdom of God."

This sentiment is similarly echoed by a number of other historic faiths in which material poverty is often described as a blessing rather than a curse. Again, it is said that Christ famously prophesized that the "meek" would be the ones to inherit the earth.

When looking at the teachings of the various religions, it may in fact appear that wealth is to be avoided, while poverty is to be embraced. However, while many of the so-called 'Messengers of God' have remarkably similar teachings on this subject, it is worth considering that the interpretation and application of such teachings may be revised given the demands of our current times.

In an attempt to bridge one end to another, development and self-realization, or call it the convergence between a meaningful existence and spirituality, in his article *"Culture, Spirituality, and Economic Development"*, William F. Ryan, S.J. contemplates the gap of "conventional Western discourse to ignore or dismiss the cultural, moral, and spiritual dimensions of human well-being as either irrelevant to development or so intractably subjective as to be unamenable to a 'practical paradigm."

Ryan goes on to say: "Yet—and it is a big yet—beyond a basic level of survival and security, for most people in most parts of the world, innermost attitudes and behavior towards change—individual or societal—are not motivated by economic or political interests. Many people in most cultures start at the other end of Maslow's scale: at the most personal level, they are moved by deep underlying moral and spiritual assumptions that reflect and explain reality and that support the values that guide their decisions about whether to change or not to change."

"For the most part", explains Ryan, "these assumptions and values are not expressed in conventional rational paradigms or in quantifiable terms, but in myth, ritual, and religion. These 'ontological needs' or priorities include such things as: love of other, one's commitment and responsibility to family, clan, and community; self-worth, one's sense of dignity, honor, and respect; sexuality and gender, roles and relationships—both individual and social; work, both as a means of sustenance and as a creative act; beauty and joy, as expressed in dance, music, art, poetry, and play; a sense of the sacred and the transcendental, spirituality and formal religion; loyalty to the tribe, nation, or other ethnic identity; love of place, a sense of belonging; reverence for life, matter, and spirit in nature, the origin of nature, and its relation to self; the unseen; ancestors; and life and death."

The perspective presented in the study highlights the profound impact of cosmological visions or worldviews on human decision-making and development. This approach suggests that these overarching narratives or belief systems serve as foundational frameworks, which guide individuals and communities in making significant choices that shape their interaction with the environment, their orientation toward time, their capacity for innovation, and their moral and ethical judgments.

By framing these choices within the context of cosmological visions, the study emphasizes the interconnectedness of cultural, environmental, and ethical considerations in shaping human actions and societal progress. This perspective encourages a deeper reflection on the underlying values and assumptions that inform our decisions and their long-term implications for development.

The dichotomies presented—such as transforming nature versus inhabiting it, being present-oriented versus future-oriented, and innovative versus passive—reflect different pathways and priorities that can lead to varied outcomes in terms of societal well-being, sustainability, and ethical integrity. The distinction between right versus wrong, or good versus evil, further underscores the moral dimensions of these choices, highlighting the role of ethical deliberation in guiding human actions toward constructive or destructive ends.

By exploring these themes, the study offers valuable insights into how cosmological visions or worldviews can serve as critical lenses through which societies navigate complex challenges and opportunities. It suggests that a broader, more nuanced understanding of these visions can inform more holistic and sustainable approaches to development, emphasizing the importance of aligning human choices with principles that promote harmony, innovation, and ethical integrity in the relationship between humanity and the natural world.

E. F. Schumacher, author of *Small is Beautiful: Economics as if People Mattered*, a well-known researcher and theorist who has written extensively on the principles of 'Buddhist Economics,' summarizes a similar perspective in an eloquent manner: "It is not wealth that stands in the way of liberation but the attachment to wealth; not the enjoyment of pleasurable things but the craving for them."

From yet another perspective, one of the central principles of the Baha'i Faith is that the world is currently in a state of disequilibrium, particularly in regards to wealth. To the Baha'is, one of the most urgent tasks is to devise ways to more justly and equitably distribute resources among all of humanity:

"We must not only be detached from wealth and material comforts, but also strive to help all of humanity meet their physical needs and reduce the deleterious effects of poverty."

Encapsulating the Baha'i teachings in a few points would go something like this: "There is nothing wrong with enjoying the benefits of this material existence. However, wealth can be one of the greatest hindrances to spiritual growth and, particularly for those of us blessed with material prosperity, we must be ever mindful of our tendency to become attached to luxuries and physical comfort. While there is nothing inherently wrong with wealth, the extreme inequalities of wealth and poverty are detrimental to the spiritual and social development of humanity."

There is no right or wrong answer to the topic of spirituality. The choice to pursue or not pursue spirituality is such a personal, individual decision, that the debate invariably turns sterile. However, although the apparent conditions for its seeking are there for everyone, irrespective of race, genre, or social or income status, it is a fact that without a balanced environment, in addition to a crafted and developed effort by the same individual, very little can be accomplished.

Another reminder that a fertile ground for growth, when available and/or by deliberate choosing, may go a long way.

*We were all humans until race disconnected us, religion separated us, politics divided us and wealth classified us.*
~ Anonymous

# Blackbird Singing

Several statements regarding both his inspiration for the song and its meaning had been given by the creator of this meaningful tune in 1968. In one of them, Paul McCartney has said that he was inspired by hearing the call of a blackbird one morning when the Beatles were studying Transcendental Meditation in Rishikesh, India and also writing it in Scotland as a response to the Little Rock Nine incident and the overall Civil Rights movement, wanting to write a song dedicated to people who had been affected by discrimination.

Following a show in Dallas, Texas in May 2002, McCartney discussed the song with DJ Chris Douridas: "I had been doing some [poetry readings] in the last year or so because I've got a poetry book out called *Blackbird Singing*, and when I would read 'Blackbird,' I would always try and think of some explanation to tell the people ... So, I was doing explanations, and I actually just remembered why I'd written 'Blackbird,' you know, that I'd been, I was in Scotland playing on my guitar, and I remembered this whole idea of 'you were only waiting for this moment to arise' was about, you know, the black people's struggle in the southern states, and I was using the symbolism of a blackbird. It's not really about a blackbird whose wings are broken, you know, it's a bit more symbolic."

It was not until 1954 that the United States Supreme Court ruled that segregated schools were illegal. The case, Brown v. The Board of Education has become iconic for Americans because it marked the formal beginning of the end of segregation.

The Smithsonian's National Museum of African American History and Culture has the record straight: "The

"Little Rock Nine," as the nine teens came to be known, were to be the first African American students to enter Little Rock's Central High School. Three years earlier, following the Supreme Court ruling, the Little Rock school board pledged to voluntarily desegregate its schools. This idea was explosive for the community and, like much of the South, it was fraught with anger and bitterness.

Arkansas governor Orval Faubus would deploy the Arkansas National Guard to Central High School, where the first black students were slated to attend. Mobs gathered outside the school. Some threatened to lynch the students. It was 1957. The intimidation would last until the national government federalized the Arkansas National Guard and deployed the 101st Airborne Division to forcibly desegregate Central High School.

From its inception, it would take four years for the desegregation ruling to take place, in the spring of 1958. Ernest Green became the first African American to graduate from Central High. Following years of an ordeal to implement the ruling, each day the nine teens were exhausted, taunted, and threatened by many of the white students as they took small steps into deeper, more turbulent waters.

Try to imagine the torrent of emotions that ran through those young men and women. Imagine the courage they had to muster each day. Try to picture the white students who jeered and harassed them. Imagine also what it would have been like to be a white student or teacher who supported the Little Rock Nine".

# A System Encroached

In the book *Caste: The Origins of Our Discontents*, journalist and author Isabel Wilkerson asserts that "the brutal Indian system of hierarchy illuminates more about American racial divides than the idea of race alone can." Wilkerson's extraordinary work defines eight pillars of caste based on her research and compilation of the ancient principles examined in parallels, overlapped, and brought in common between three major caste hierarchies. "These are the principles upon which a caste system is constructed, whether in America, India, or Nazi Germany, beliefs that were at one time or another, burrowed deep within the culture and collective subconscious of most every inhabitant in order for a caste system to function."

Wilkerson's narrative on the origin of the word caste is revealing: although perceived as synonymous with India, its roots do not come from that part of the world. It turns out that it comes from the Portuguese word casta, "a Renaissance-era word for race or breed" which took place from the European cultural, artistic, political and economic 'rebirth' following the Middle Ages. "The Portuguese, who were among the earliest European traders in South Asia, applied the term to the people of India upon observing the Hindu divisions," observes Wilkerson.

The caste debacle is not exclusive to the three highlighted countries as they are not alone in the experience of imposing a caste system onto their own people. Brazil, home to the largest African population outside Africa, with more than half of its citizens claiming African ancestry, was the largest historic Portuguese colony. Having received almost half of the twelve million Africans kidnapped and sent to the Americas for chattel enslavement, it was the last country in the Americas to abolish the practice in 1888. Following abolition, the government encouraged immigration from Europe throughout the 20th century, to "whiten" the population. "Brazil has a very hierarchical and stratified social structure, which is the legacy of what, for practical purposes, was a caste system, a racial caste system that combined slavery plus the aristocratic social structure that Brazil inherited from Portugal," says Kendall Thomas, a professor and scholar of comparative constitutional law and human rights at Columbia Law School.

Isabel Wilkerson stresses the tyrannical nature of the caste system and its distorted view with its inhuman consequences: "We are judged on the very things we cannot change: a chemical in the epidermis, the shape of one's facial features, the synopsis on our bodies of gender and ancestry—superficial differences that have nothing to do with who we are inside." And makes it clear to the observers that the understanding and ability to change dwells in ourselves:

"A caste system persists in part because we, each and every one of us, allow it to exist—in large and small ways, in our everyday actions, in how we elevate or demean, embrace or exclude, on the basis of the meaning attached to people's physical traits. If enough people buy into the lie of natural hierarchy, then it becomes the truth or is assumed to be."

*I don't write to burn down houses*
*but to light sparks in the eyes of those who read me*
*I don't write to satisfy the hunger of crowds*
*but I hope my words fill a void that helps you stand*
*I don't write to govern the people*

*I listen to what they say and use my
voice to spread their message
I don't write to get your approval
but to record my trajectory and that of so many
black women who have already been
silenced*
"My Condition" ~ Mel Duarte, poet

# Black-and-White Thinking is Absolute Thinking

Life is all about nuances. Every time we find ourselves thinking in absolutes, the chances of getting stuck in patterns and trapped inside our minds are exponential. History explains the past and changes the present if our interpretation of the past is seen through subtleties. We miss so much of life's grace and beauty when our attention is focused on either all or nothing. There's so much in between, and even middle ground is one aspect of it. Fostering a vision for the present and how things could be different if we change perspective is a choice that must be nurtured for sanity's sake, if nothing else.

Rebecca Joy Stanborough, MFA on her article at *Healthline* "How Black-and-White Thinking Hurts You (and What You Can Do to Change It)" alerts us to the perils of a partial and pulled apart thinking: "Dichotomous or polarized thinking, according to the American Psychological Association, is considered a distortion because it keeps us from seeing the world as it often is: complex, nuanced, and full of all the shades in between."

Stanborough's analysis is quite interesting: "Most of us engage in dichotomous thinking from time to time. In fact, some experts think this pattern may have its origins in human survival—our fight or flight response," the automatic physiological reaction to an event that is perceived as stressful or frightening.

Black-and-white thinking, says the author, hurts us in multiple ways: the use of words such as always, never, impossible, disaster, furious, ruined, and perfect are signs of our pendulum mind traveling fast: "Of course, these words aren't bad in themselves. However, if you notice that they keep coming up in your thoughts and conversations, it could be a signal that you've adopted a black and white perspective on something."

Two of the relevant ways our judgment is affected may sometimes impair our own development: in both our relationships and in our learning process. "Relationships happen between individuals, whether they see each other as family, friends, neighbors, co-workers, or something else entirely. And because people have ups and downs (to phrase it dichotomously), plus quirks and inconsistencies, conflicts inevitably arise. If we approach normal conflicts with dichotomous thinking, we'll probably draw the wrong conclusions about other people, and we'll miss opportunities to negotiate and compromise."

From a learning perspective, the author highlights that the binary measure of learning, the pass or fail system, does not allow for a meaningful growth experience; quite the contrary. "It's all too easy to fall into dichotomous thinking about your academic accomplishments." Conversely, "the growth mindset encourages students to recognize incremental progress toward mastery—to see themselves moving closer to being able to do what they have set out to do."

# Giant Steps Needed

Black and white thinking has nothing to do with color and race. But understanding the dynamics of thinking in extremes can help mitigate the ever-so-present effects of bias and prejudice. It can help deflect the ever-so-limited vision of a world around us ruling on what is good and what is bad (male is better than female, white is better than black, rich is better than poor, etc., etc., etc.). It is true that the last 500 years have allowed for great advances for humanity. But they have also been perverse in allowing distorted history to be recorded and with subsequent dire consequences.

*Caste: The Origins of Our Discontents* is eloquent in laying out such aberrations. Be them due to the effect of the myriad of traumatic conflicts which regrettably evolved and continue to evolve into wars, be them by the ever present greed, be them by the mental disorder infringed upon by the ignorance and incompetence of narcissistic rulers and their twisted systems, the fact is that an obtuse mindset can make things really difficult on a societal level when applied to the human experience.

Wilkerson's book, harsh on its analysis and yet inspiring on its substance, has the power to shift the beliefs that people hold in their lives and, in the process, to change their hearts forever. The conclusive notes of her literary work revolve around the clear perception of a world that predetermines what we will become, as if a place had already been assigned for us since birth, unless we consciously make a decision to make it our own. "It was up to each of us to accept or challenge the role we were cast into, to determine for ourselves and to make the world see that what is inside of us—our beliefs, how we love and express that love, the things that we can actually control—is more important than the outward traits we have no say in. That we are not what we look like but what we do with what we have, what we make of what we're given, how we treat others and our planet."

# Male, Female, East, West: The Cultural Quest

*When sweet eyes were painted by God on your face, He put the key to my knots in your myriad grace. Time tied round your waist the sash of your gilded attire, Reducing me and the cypress to the dust of a lone desire. To answer your call, the morning breeze began to blow, Bringing the bud to bloom and elating my heart of woe.*

*The Wheel of Fortune decreed in your bond my delight; Alas, the bird of my happy lot your hand holds tight. Cast not for my miserable heart a knot or a snare; My heart's musk has formed a vow with your hair. O breeze of union! You sought another heart to exult; I cherished futile fidelity to you; that was my fault.*

*"I shall go," I said, "In you, cruelty was all I found."*
*He smiled, "Go Hafiz! Who's tied you to the ground?"*
"Craving For You" ~ Hafiz, poet

Persian culture is ancient. It is among the most influential in the world. Iran (Persia), a part of the world that a lot of people don't quite understand, especially we the people in the US, is widely considered to be one of the cradles of civilization.

Due to its historic dominant geopolitical position in the world, it has heavily influenced peoples and cultures situated as far away as Southern Europe and Eastern Europe to the west; Central Asia to the north; the Arabian Peninsula to the south; and South Asia, East Asia, and Southeast Asia to the east. Not to be overlooked, Persian history has had a significant influence on the world through art, architecture, poetry, science and technology, medicine, philosophy, and engineering.

Persian literature, with poetry as its most significant aspect, comprises oral compositions and written texts in the Persian language and has some of the world's oldest literature. It spans over two and a half millennia. Its sources have been within Greater Iran including present-day Iran, Iraq, Afghanistan, the Caucasus, and Turkey, regions of Central Asia (such as Tajikistan), South Asia, and the Balkans where the Persian language has historically been either the native or official language.

# A Little Knowledge Goes a Long Way

Rick Steves is a well-known travel writer, author, activist, and television personality. His travel philosophy encourages people to explore less-touristy areas of destinations and to become immersed in the local people's way of life. In his every-so-often compelling travel blog, he traveled to Iran over a decade ago to better understand a country with whom we in this nation seem perennially on the verge of war. "I came home with a one-hour public television special *(Rick Steves Iran: Yesterday and Today)* that attempted to understand the Iranian psyche and humanize the Iranian people. I believe if you're going to bomb a place, you should know its people first. Even if military force is justified, it should hurt when you kill someone."

More than a decade ago, the dangers of going into war with Iran—an improbable but always plausible outlook beyond the always prevalent proxy wars—seemed to loom on the horizon. And in today's world, history is stubbornly showing that unnerving likelihood once again.

"Some things just don't change," says Rick Steves. The ongoing, open ended, indescribable conflict between Hamas and Israel, then a fraction of the pernicious reality of today's strife, puts the countries once again in confrontation.

To make things more complicated, Iran's support to Russia via the provision of armaments against Ukraine, the actions of Hezbollah in Southern Lebanon and the Houthi militants from Yemen in the Arabian Peninsula, added to the continuous pursuit to be a nuclear threat, just helped escalate that inconvenient prospect of contention.

Steves goes on: "Just like a decade ago, we are not prepared for that reality. As a nation, we don't adequately understand Iran. From my travels there, it's clear to me that Americans underestimate both Iran's baggage and its spine."

"'Baggage' shapes a country's response to future challenges. In the USA, our baggage includes the fight against socialism during the Cold War and the tragedy of 9/11. Iran's baggage has to do with incursions from the West. Examples include 1953, when the US and Britain deposed a popular Iranian prime minister (after he nationalized their oil) and replaced him with the Shah; and the 1980s, when—with US funding—Saddam Hussein and Iraq invaded Iran, leaving hundreds of thousands of dead soldiers on Iran's Western Front."

"Iran is a proud and powerful nation of (more than) 80 million people—long a leader in its corner of the world. When I was in Tehran filming my TV special, I went to the National Museum of Iran expecting to film art from the great Persian Empire (the 'Empire of Empires' ruled centuries before Christ by great leaders like Cyrus, Darius, and Xerxes). I found almost nothing. Apologetically, the curator explained, 'You'll need to go to London or Paris. Iran's patrimony is in the great museums of Europe.'" Steves is surgical on his analysis: "This is baggage."

Leading to the rise of the ayatollahs, the Iranian Revolution of 1979 deposed the US-friendly Shah Reza Pahlevi. Since then, this is seen in the USA as a terrible thing. "But traveling in Iran," says Steves, "I heard a different narrative: The revolution was a people's uprising in the context of the Cold War, as Iran's young generation wanted to be neither East nor West (independent from the USA or USSR realms).

"If you don't know Iran (as, I fear, is the case with our country's decision-makers), it would be easy to underestimate their spine. Filming there, I was impressed by the caliber and the goodness of the people on the street—and haunted by a feeling that we could easily radicalize them with a reckless foreign policy."

As reciprocity is fundamentally true, which only contributes to more dissent and exacerbated acrimony between the two nations.

Steves is not a career diplomat but he clearly advocates for diplomacy in and out his travels around the world. "I realize that Iran is a challenging puzzle to solve. It seems we will always be in conflict with Iran, and the answers will never come easy. But surely whatever we do should be built upon a foundation of understanding: We must get to know Iran on its own terms. We would be foolish not to recognize its baggage—and not to appreciate its spine."

# All for The Union

Rumi is undoubtedly the greatest Sufi mystic and poet. Highly appreciated in the West, he is a creature of the 13th century, son of old Persia, who wrote all his poems and stories in the Persian language. His teachings have widely influenced mystical thought and literature throughout the world.

Nobieh Kiani, international yoga instructor and author of *Dance of No Name: A Beautiful Journey Within*, writes about her interpretation of the poet's view of man and woman:

"In the stories of the Masnavi, one of the most influential works of Sufism, Rumi talks about the real power of a man, and he reminds us that if the power is in the physical strength, then the elephant is much stronger than a man! He reminds us that the real power is love and tenderness.

"He calls on to men and says:

> *"Don't claim in spring on stone some verdure grows*
> *Be soft like soil to raise a lovely rose—*
> *For years you've been a stony-hearted man*
> *Try being like the soil now if you can!"*

It is undeniable that women have a civilizing effect on men; perhaps Rumi's hints for us to give the proper attention to that aspect of our gender equation. This has been echoed in various forms throughout history, often suggesting that women influence men to behave in a more refined, cultured, or socially acceptable manner.

Kiani continues on: "Rumi's suggestion is to open the heart; if we become softhearted, we will find our true power (our love and tenderness)."

Rumi's words on women are to rephrase like this:

"Woman is a ray of God. She is not that earthly beloved: she is creative, not created."

Nobieh Kiani's interpretations are enlightening: "This basically means she is not your beloved (she doesn't belong to you). She is an uncreated ray of light directly from God. That is how Rumi describes the spiritual importance of women. Throughout world history, it has always been a fear to empower women. In many traditions and cultures, women have been limited to staying in the shadows, so they don't shine their lights too brightly into the world."

And Kiani pauses for an intriguing reflection: "Maybe it's been a fear of the power she has? Fear of when she connects to her true soul and wild nature. If a woman knows of her true power, she can't be tamed, and that's what most religions and cultures tried to suppress."

# A Moment of Truth

Throughout history, women in Iran have played numerous roles, and contributed in many ways, to Iranian society. Historically though, tradition maintained that women be confined to their homes to manage the household and raise children.

During the Pahlavi dynasty (1925-1979), there was a drastic social change toward women's desegregation, such as ban of the veil, right to vote, right to education, equal salaries for men and women, and the right to hold public office. Then came the Islamic Revolution in which women were active participants: major changes ensued.

Persia, renamed Iran in 1935, had been a monarchy ruled by emperors almost without interruption, from 1501 to the end of the Revolution, when it became an Islamic republic in 1979. Its constitution proclaims equality for men and women under Article 20, while mandating legal code adhering to Sharia law. Article 21 of the constitution as well as a few parliament-passed laws give women rights such as being allowed to drive, hold public office, and attend universities. One critical caveat is the exigence of wearing a veil in public—the hijab. Disobedience can be punished by law; and when in public, all hair and skin except the face and hands must be covered.

# The Law

Islamic principles govern the legal system in countries where Sharia law holds sway, such as Saudi Arabia, Iran, and Afghanistan. While it dictates various aspects of life, including personal conduct, family matters, criminal law and economic transactions, its implementation disproportionately impacts women's rights and freedoms in several countries.

Sharia law varies in interpretation across different countries, leading to unique legal systems with varying degrees of severity. In some countries, it has become a tool to perpetuate inequality and restrict women's freedoms.

In Iran, despite their active participation in education and the workforce, Iran's enforcement of Sharia law poses significant challenges for women.

As in Saudi Arabia, a male guardianship system governs women in Iran, requiring women to obtain permission to marry, divorce, get custody, inherit and even travel abroad. The legal age of marriage is thirteen, and girls can be married even younger if their male guardian deems it appropriate.

The enforcement of dress codes, particularly the mandatory hijab (headscarf), has been a contentious issue in Iran. Women who choose not to wear the hijab or wear it loosely risk facing fines, arrest, or even imprisonment, and those who advocate for greater gender equality often face harsh persecution.

For better understanding, it is relevant to look at the history of the hijab in Iran. According to Joshua Askew's viewpoint in *Explained: Why the hijab is crucial to Iran's Islamic rulers, by euronews.culture,* the traditional head covering has been worn by Muslim women for 'modesty' for centuries (the word for modesty is Haya, which in Arabic means 'natural or inherent shyness and a sense of modesty'). The use of the hijab has been practiced as a compulsion supported by law in Iran more emphatically after the 1979 revolution. In the 1920s, a few women started to appear unveiled. Under the Reza Shah period, it was discouraged and then banned in 1936 for five years.

Under his successor, Mohammad Reza Pahlavi, hijab was considered 'backward' and rarely worn by upper and middle-class people. Consequently, it became a symbol of opposition to the shah in the 1970s, and was worn by women (educated, middle and upper class) who previously would have been unveiled.

# The Short Life Of Mahsa Amini

*Let the weather dictate what we wear*
*Or let the occasion or the fair.*
*Not any government or god man*
*We don't need to be shoved any dress plan!*
*Let how we dress show our style;*
*Our behavior, our inclusive character*
*Women need as much freedom*
*Without any meddling barrister!*
*We are as strong as any man*
*As smart and intelligent too*
*The time has come yet again*
*To convey...*
*We are God's equal creation too!*
*"Women—Life—Freedom"*
*~ Sache Bel, author, poet*

In September 2022, the country and the world experienced the horrors of extremism, this time from within the state. Twenty-two-year-old Iranian activist Mahsa Amini died from injuries she sustained at the hands of Iranian forces, who arrested and tortured her—not for not wearing her hijab—but for wearing her hijab incorrectly.

Her absurd, untimely, and unjust death three days after her arrest by the morality police in Tehran, prompted the spread of large-scale protests in Iran, unprecedented in terms of both their geographic range and the diverse social backgrounds of the demonstrators. The movement extended to large and small cities outside Tehran, including Kurdish areas—where Amini came from—and youth from across the socioeconomic and educational spectrum took part. This resulted in authorities detaining tens of thousands and, even worse, deepening the pain by killing hundreds of Iranians, including children.

As the protests intensified, videos of women cutting their hair and burning their hijabs spread, acts which served as both an expression of anger directed toward the morality police responsible for Mahsa Amini's death, and a rejection of the policy of compulsory hijab more generally. However, the acts of hijab burning and hair cutting did not merely launch a rebellion against government-imposed dress codes, but also came to symbolize broader demands for fundamental political and economic reforms.

Since the death of Mahsa Amini, the hijab has once again become a political symbol, this time in opposition to the Islamic Republic. Defiance of the law by younger women has been called "too widespread to contain and too pervasive to reverse," writes Farnaz Fassihi in his "Their Hair Long and Flowing or in Ponytails, Women in Iran Flaunt Their Locks," in *The New York Times*. As of April 2023, however, the Islamic Republic has vowed to enforce the "divine decree" of the hijab.

As of 2024, Iranian women's steadfast refusal to comply with hijab laws has afforded them a small win: Iranian authorities announced an intention to review the hijab law and eliminate the "'morality police.'

Though physical punishments are now banned, Iranian women still deal with fresh plans to install surveillance technology to identify those without hijabs. Additionally, a law that came into effect in April 2024 fines women without a hijab up to thirty billion Iranian rials (USD 60,000) and revokes their driver's licenses, passports and internet access.

"The issue of the hijab," write the editors of *FairPlanet*, a global non-profit social enterprise and solutions media organization in Berlin, "is part of a broader conversation about women's rights and gender equality in Iran—resolving it necessitates comprehensive and sustained efforts, including a fundamental shift in the country's societal and political structures that currently reinforces gender-based discrimination. Meaningful change occurs by educating society, condemning acts of oppression and continuing to pressure those in power to respect human rights."

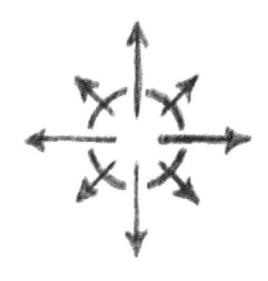

# Can This Pain Be Eased?

*Is that a dagger or a crucifix I see? You*
*hold so tightly in your hand*
*And all the while, the distance*
*grows between you and me*
*I do not understand*
*In the blood of Eden lie the woman and the man*
*With the man in the woman*
*And the woman in the man*
*I can hear a distant thunder*
*Of a million unheard souls*
*Watch each one reach for creature comfort*
*For the filling of their holes*
"In the Blood of Eden"
~ Peter Gabriel, songwriter

Persia is the cradle of Sufism, with little or no dispute about that. Sufism formed one of the cultures of resistance which has existed in the social fabric of Persia since antiquity. Such resistance continues to manifest itself today with many looking to Sufism as a model of cooperation between East and West, between traditional and modern.

It is worth mentioning that Sufism is considered as being the esoteric aspect of Islam. Simply put, the aim of Sufis is to gain direct knowledge of the eternal, in this life, as opposed to the exoteric, or traditionalist, aspect of Islam which focuses on achieving a state of blessedness after death by way of carrying out divinely prescribed works.

Rumi was one of the great spiritual masters and poetic geniuses of mankind. It is said that Sufism was created to follow his teachings. When revisiting Nobieh

Kiani's interpretations of a few of Rumi's teachings when it comes to how women are perceived, treated and limited on their forms of expression, Kiani has a clear dimension of the picture, as follows:

"Even in Sufism, there've been many restrictions on women so that they stay aside and don't become the center of attention. One example of this is the Sufi whirling—a form of physically active, dance-like meditation which originated among certain Sufi groups, and which prohibits women from performing it in public. Even now, only men can perform whirling in traditional Sufi celebrations, and women can only witness.

Kiani concludes with a firm, positive and profound outlook: "A true Sufi-hearted man (or any sage) knows that a part of him becomes feminine when he reaches God. He would never deny the immense power of the woman; he would embrace and acknowledge it. Maybe even use her power to unite our souls—to become closer to the essence of Godliness. God is feminine and masculine in the realm of love; there is no discrimination of genders.

"So my hope is for all women to know their true power—to embrace their goddess within. Let go of all the shame, blame, guilt, and limitations. I hope for a time when women can live in-touch with their beautiful femininity and true power, and celebrate life in its total freedom. I am calling all women to get in touch with their wild, authentic parts and have the courage to live it out of the veils of any religion, culture, or limiting beliefs."

Kiani's closing evocative words are emblematic of her understanding and vision of the possibilities: "...and for all the men to also get in touch with their true power of the heart. Only then can we all celebrate life in unity and ecstasy of liberated souls."

# The Yin and Yang in Ourselves

The striking beauty of the blue planet viewed from space is an incomparable image and one that's overwhelming to the senses. To picture and nurture a world with no national borders, divided only by deep waters, fills the soul with hope of a wholesome, integrated sphere. In contrast, on the ground, the reality of the same blue planet is objectively different from the idealization we experience in the mind: political borders, igniting nationalism, territorial silos, ethnocentrism fueled by intolerance.

Back to space, what is most astonishing about the iconic planet is its unity. There is harmony and consensus when visualizing its oneness. No political borders or divisions. No territorial silos. If that is not enough, the image is neither permanent nor transitory, but present. The greatest challenge we humans consistently face is the reconciliation of our planet's singleness. Achieving that sense of terrestrial integrity requires recognition and engagement of multiple, diverse perspectives, supportive opposites, solidarity in divisions, overcoming binaries, and transcending antagonism.

How do we do that?

It is said that there are two kinds of people in this world: those that build bridges and those who are finding their way over them.

The first group represents the creators, the builders, and the facilitators who actively work to connect ideas, people, or places. They are the ones who provide the means for others to cross over obstacles or gaps, literally or metaphorically. Bridge builders are visionaries and problem solvers, often working behind the scenes to make transitions and progress possible for others.

The second group of individuals are in the midst of navigating their paths, utilizing the bridges that have been built. They might be in a state of exploration, learning, or transition, seeking new opportunities, understanding, or connections. This journey is essential for personal growth and development, as it involves encountering and overcoming challenges, experiencing new perspectives, and ultimately, finding one's place or direction.

Both roles are crucial and interdependent. The builders provide the infrastructure, support, or solutions, while those navigating the bridges engage with these opportunities, enriching their lives and often inspiring new bridges to be built. Together, they create a dynamic process of growth, discovery, and community building.

The purpose of bridge building works as an analogy for imagination because it runs alongside the formation of an idea or object that takes people to new harbors. If we stop and think about it, many things we are achieving in our lives at this very moment are the result of the bridges we have built, and continue to build, and the bridges built for us, consciously or not, intentionally or by chance, substantially or visionarily.

The poem below offers the template to understand the framework and purpose of such actionable effort:

*An old man going a lone highway,*
*came at the evening cold and gray,*
*to a chasm vast and deep and wide.*
*The old man crossed in the twilight dim,*

*The sullen stream had no fear for him;*
*but he turned when safe on the other side*
*and built a bridge to span the tide.*
*"Old man," said a fellow pilgrim near,*
*"You are wasting your strength with*
*building here; your journey will end*
*with the ending day. You never again*
*will pass this way. You've crossed the*
*chasm, deep and wide, why build a*
*bridge at evening tide?"*
*The builder lifted his old gray head;*
*"Good friend in the path I have come,"*
*he said, "there followed after me today*
*a youth whose feet must pass this way.*
*This chasm that has been as naught to me,*
*to that fair-haired youth may a pitfall be.*
*He, too, must cross in the twilight dim.*
*Good friend, I am building this bridge for him!"*
"The Bridge Builder" ~ Anonymous

# Connecting Dots

What's the linkup between bridge building and Yin and Yang, the Chinese symbol based on the two opposing principles?

Using music conceptually, the notion of a bridge is the equivalent to transition. "The majority of songs contain some combination of a verse, chorus, and a bridge, combined into an overall song structure." *The Master Class* is a place to learn: "Songwriters often place their catchiest musical ideas in the chorus and their most evocative lyrical ideas in the verses. However, the bridge provides songwriters with the opportunity to insert a musical change of pace into a song." It's that place between two remarkable pieces that requires skillful art, inspiration, nuance, dedication, and hard work to link two harmonious parts in order for the melody to make sense to the ears. It is intended to provide contrast to the rest of the composition.

As an attribute, besides representing the idea of connection, a bridge offers the ability to overcome obstacles. It is also inherently symbolic of communication and union, whether it be between the esoteric heaven and the familiar earth or between two distinct realms. For this reason it can be seen as the connection between mystery and reality. It may also be the passage to existence, or merely a symbol for journey and intersection.

*Big Think* is a multimedia web portal, a site that publishes interviews and round table discussions with experts on a wide range of fields. Jonny Thomson, a staff writer at *Big Think*, writes about philosophy, theology, and psychology, and gives us his takes on the concept, explaining that we humans are not just one consistent entity. "The kindest person you know has a tiny recess of cruelty in them. The happiest person you have ever met will have their depressive moments. The gentlest person you can think of can be filled with rage by one particular thing. There is no purity of any kind; life is a messy cocktail of things."

The simplified description of the reality of things, of our own reality as humans, is the truth behind one of the most famous symbols in the world: the Yin and Yang. In Chinese cosmology, the universe creates itself out of a primary chaos of material energy, organized into the cycles of Yin and Yang and formed into nature, objects and lives. Yin is considered retractive, passive and receptive, while Yang is active, repelling and expansive; The concept is associated with the idea of the five phases or elements—metal, wood, water, fire, and earth—lending substance to the characteristic perception in a cyclical theory of becoming and dissolution, and an interdependence between the world of nature and human events.

In that sense, Yin and Yang alternate with one another and traverse bridges intermittently.

In his engaging book *Bridge Builders: Bringing People Together in a Polarized Age,* author and reporter Nathan Bomey had in mind to write how to bring people together despite their differences. And he was determined not to use divisive nonsense and phrases to describe our environment of toxic polarization from past years.

Bomey's idea is an important contribution to the dialogue on how to bring back a country that has been insisting on walking away from its original core: "… one nation, indivisible…". It is, directly and indirectly, a reflection to our individual lives and ways of perceiving things. The book profiles diverse leaders from throughout America who do not accept the status quo of what he calls "seemingly bottomless rage toward people who aren't like them," to explain the rationale behind his thinking: the embracing of a counterculture. He explains: "They do not accept buzzwords. They do not use labels. They choose nuance over caricature because they realize that boxing others in also boxes themselves out of the possibility of forging meaningful connections that can lead to genuine change."

The author is aware of our duality and inconsistency as men and women: "Bridge builders are not ignorant of ignorance. They understand that people are flawed. But they see others aspirationally, and they believe people are capable of change. They've seen it happen. And that's why they don't seek to shame or to humiliate. They believe that shame and humiliation are tools of destruction that typically drive both sides further apart. Instead, bridge builders use tools of construction: Inquiry. Listening. Acknowledgment. Edification. Conversation. Education."

Non-conformist in his views and yet conciliatory in his encompassing humanity, he makes sure he gets his message through: "That does not mean they accept hate. They do not. That does not mean they accept misinformation. They do not. That does not mean they believe in letting people off the hook. They do not. Bridge builders believe in accountability. They believe in challenging people's beliefs because you can't build a bridge without ensuring that the structure is anchored to a firm foundation of truth."

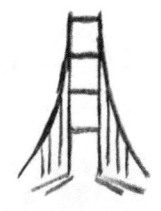

# Everything in Between

*For the longest time, it feels like I have been trying to make sense of life but now I see there is no sense to be made, only life to be lived. There is no set purpose to fulfill, there are no checklists to complete, just an ephemeral moment to breathe, to love, to be kind, to feel. Life is in all the simple, little things that we so often overlook. Uncomplicate your heart, be here, be present, embrace your own journey. There is so much beauty and wonder to be found right where you are.*
~ Anonymous

Marianne's story paints a picture of a young woman full of life and ambition, embarking on a journey filled with personal and professional fulfillment. At twenty-eight, living in the vibrant setting of Long Island, New York, in 1994, she had already carved out a niche for herself with a successful decorative painting business. To this day, her entrepreneurial venture not only showcased her creativity and passion for art but also her ability to turn that passion into a thriving career.

Recently married, Marianne's personal life was as flourishing as her professional one. Marriage represented a new chapter, filled with hopes, dreams, and the promise of shared adventures. Her partnership with Alex, set against the backdrop of their lovely home, brought stability and contentment. The inclusion of a little room dedicated to her art studio within their home was, and still is, a testament to her commitment to her craft, providing her with a sanctuary to create and innovate.

An avid runner, Marianne also understood the importance of health and well-being. Running, besides its mental and physical benefits, likely served as a source of inspiration, stress relief, and personal satisfaction. A discipline that required persistence, resilience, and a connection to the environment around her.

Marianne's life at this point was a blend of personal happiness, health, and professional success. Her story is a snapshot of a moment in time where everything seemed aligned, offering a foundation from which numerous possibilities could emerge. It's a narrative about making the most of life's opportunities, cherishing personal connections, and pursuing one's passions with dedication and joy.

Marianne shares, "The future was bright. One day, I was painting a client's ceiling with clouds and sky. As always, when painting a ceiling after many hours, my neck hurt. I came home, went for a run, took a shower hoping to ease my neck pain. My husband rubbed my stiff neck. As he was rubbing he noticed a lump on my right clavicle. He asked how long it had been there. I had not noticed. I returned to work the next day, not feeling great, body ache and a little nauseous. Could I be pregnant, I thought?" Her neck pain was getting unbearable: "I went for a massage and then I was able to see a local chiropractor where I got an x-ray. The Chiropractor didn't like what she saw and had me go down the block to a doctor who specializes in infectious disease. He had me go to a local lab to get blood work. 20 vials later I was able to go home. I remember the nurse at the lab saying, 'they are looking for something....' From a stiff neck? I thought."

Within a few days, Marianne got a call. "'You have Lymphoma...' was all I heard. I had no idea what that was. There was no internet to look up the word. All I had was an old medical book from 1946. I learned

Lymphoma was cancer of the lymphatic system. I was 28 and had stage II Hodgkin's Lymphoma." Marianne thought this was typically a young person's cancer. She looked for a new doctor and an oncologist. "When I went to the office with my Mom, all the patients were elderly. When the nurse called my name, they looked at my mom. During the consultation, the doctor told me I had a grapefruit size mass between my heart and my lungs."

Marianne's situation presented a deeply challenging and transformative period in her life. A prophylactic splenectomy, a surgical procedure to remove the spleen, is often recommended in various medical conditions to prevent potential life-threatening complications. However, this step, along with several rounds of radiation therapy, introduces significant risks and side effects, including the possibility of infertility. "I ran out of the office to my car. I cried and cried. How was I going to tell my new husband, not only that I have cancer, but we couldn't have kids? My mom got in the car and cried with me. I went home. I just recall my husband throwing a chair in anger and fear. We then went to fertility specialists. We were going to try to freeze my eggs, but ultimately there was no time. They wanted me to have surgery and radiation as soon as possible for fear of spreading."

Lymphoma is known to be the 'easy' cancer when caught quickly, but it can easily spread quickly through the lymphatic system attaching to other organs. "At this time, I went into my little art studio and drew large, rough, dirty and angry charcoals. I tore them off the wall and stuffed them in my closet, not to be seen."

As some cancer cells manage to survive despite initial treatments, cancer recurrence may happen and may include surgery, chemotherapy, radiation, or a combination of these. The nature of lymphoma, with its ability to spread through the lymphatic system, makes it particularly prone to such recurrences. Three years later, that's exactly what occurred:

"The doctors were convinced that what they saw in the CAT scan was just scar tissue." One of them encouraged her to get a biopsy. "The cancer was back! This time I had chemotherapy ABVD. My life stopped again. Having a child was definitely out of the question. I was 31."

Marianne met with a new team of oncologists, which would inevitably become her family. "I had several rounds of chemo. During this time, my artwork was large pensive portraits in pencil. Then, after two years, I was cleared of the disease. My Doctor said: 'Why don't you try to have a child?' We DID try. In 2000, My Leonardo was born. Happy and healthy. My miracle! A happy ending to my cancer journey... so I thought."

A new lump was found in 2014 in Marianne's breast, twenty years after the first lump had been found. "My gynecologist said it looked unimpressive, but he also said with my history I should get a mammogram and sonogram. I was able to get an appointment that afternoon. Within a day, I was diagnosed with breast cancer. And life was on hold once again. I was told I would need to have surgery and chemo. Apparently, the cancer was from the radiation I had 20 years earlier!"

What ensued was painful and almost inevitable: "I had a double mastectomy with reconstruction followed by four rounds of Cytoxen and Taxol and ten years of tamoxifen. Unfortunately, the implants caused five major infections which left me sick and septic and in the hospital for weeks at a time. Eventually, I had to have the infected implant removed and eventually removed the other implant. Now living flat with Aesthetic flat closure."

Marianne Duquette Cuozzo's art during this period of her life offers a deeply personal and symbolic exploration of her experiences with cancer, her body's changes, and her emotional journey. Through the use of whimsical and thought-provoking imagery, she communicated complex feelings about identity, loss, resilience, and hope. Her art became a visual narrative that transcended personal struggle to touch on universal themes of human experience.

The motif of women, often representing herself, intertwined with elements of nature such as trees, speaks to a connection with the natural world and perhaps a sense of growth, renewal, and the cycle of life. Trees are resilient, standing strong through the seasons, much like Marianne has endured through her cancer diagnosis and treatment.

The birds in her artwork, symbolizing her breasts, and the act of saying goodbye to them, directly references her experience with cancer and the physical alterations to her body. This imagery might represent loss—not just of a body part but of a sense of self and femininity that society often ties to physical attributes. Yet, the presence of birds also conveys a sense of freedom and liberation, perhaps suggesting a journey toward accepting change and finding new ways to define her identity.

The birdcages depicted in her work add another layer of meaning, symbolizing her sexuality and struggles.

The cage can represent confinement or restriction, reflecting the emotional and physical constraints imposed by her illness and its treatment. Her varying interactions with the birdcage—being next to it, on it, or in it—illustrate her fluctuating relationship with her own sexuality and femininity throughout her cancer journey.

One of the most poignant symbols in her art is the string with a heart on the end, representing hope. This motif underscores the resilience and optimism that have been central to Marianne's experience. Despite the challenges and the profound changes to her body and self-image, hope remains a constant, guiding her through the darkness and serving as a reminder of the possibility of healing and happiness.

Marianne Duquette Cuozzo's art serves not only as a therapeutic outlet for herself, but also as an inspiring testament to the power of creativity in facing life's most daunting challenges. Her work invites viewers to reflect on their own vulnerabilities and strengths, encouraging a deeper understanding of the human capacity for resilience and the enduring nature of hope.

# "Your Body is Not Your Masterpiece—Your Life Is"

*It's you I like,*
*It's not the things you wear,*
*It's not the way you do your hair,*
*But it's you I like.*
*The way you are right now,*
*The way down deep inside you.*
*Not the things that hide you,*
*Not your toys,*
*They're just beside you.*
*But it's you I like.*
*Every part of you.*
*Your skin, your eyes, your feelings*
*Whether old or new.*
*I hope that you'll remember,*
*Even when you're feeling blue.*
*That it's you I like,*
*It's you yourself*
*It's you.*
*It's you I like*
"It's You I Like"
~ Mr. Rogers, TV host,
author, producer

One of her friends shared a photo of Marianne, breastless, on social media and added author Glennon Doyle's words. The strange-photo-to-be-shared quickly gives way to a deeper understanding of one's experience of overcoming one of the major dilemmas of one's life: the facing of our inner being versus our outer appearance, the object of this reflection, the everything in between, and what we do or don't do with it:

"It is suggested to us a million times a day that our bodies are PROJECTS. They aren't. Our lives are. Our spirituality is. Our relationships are. Our work is.

"Stop spending all day obsessing, cursing, perfecting your body like it's all you've got to offer the world. Your body is not your art, it's your paintbrush. Whether your paintbrush is a tall paintbrush or a thin paintbrush or a stocky paintbrush or a scratched up paintbrush is completely irrelevant. What is relevant is that YOU HAVE A PAINTBRUSH which can be used to transfer your insides onto the canvas of your life—where others can see it and be inspired and comforted by it.

"Your body is not your offering. It's just a really amazing instrument which you can use to create your offering each day. Don't curse your paintbrush. Don't sit in a corner wishing you had a different paintbrush. You're wasting time. You've got the one you got. Be grateful, because without it you'd have nothing with which to paint your life's work. Your life's work is the love you give and receive—and your body is the instrument you use to accept and offer love on your soul's behalf. It's a system.

"We are encouraged to obsess over our instrument's shape—but our body's shape has no effect on its ability to accept and offer love for us. Just none. Maybe we continue to obsess because as long as we keep wringing our hands about our paintbrush shape, we don't have to get to work painting our lives. Stop fretting. The truth is that all paintbrush shapes work just fine—and anybody who tells you different is trying to sell you something. Don't buy. Just paint.

"No wait—first, stop what you are doing and say

THANK YOU to your body—right now. Say THANK YOU to your eyes for taking in the beauty of sunsets and storms and children blowing out birthday candles and say THANK YOU to your hands for writing love letters and opening doors and stirring soup and waving to strangers and say THANK YOU to your legs for walking you from danger to safety and climbing so many mountains for you.

"Then pick up your instrument and start painting this day beautiful and bold and wild and free and YOU. Paint this day beautiful, bold, wild & free."
~ Glennon Doyle, *Momastery*

Marianne's experience serves as a reminder of the strength found in vulnerability, the beauty in imperfection, and the liberating power of living authentically. Through her journey and the reflection it inspires, we are encouraged to look beyond the surface, to find bloom in resilience, and to redefine our perceptions of strength and beauty in a way that honors our true selves.

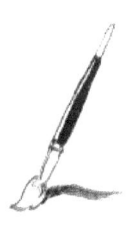

# Your Thoughts Here
## On Navigating the Nuances of Life and Death, War and Peace, Young and Old, Rich and Poor, Black and White, Light and Darkness, Male and Female, Yin and Yang, and Everything in Between

# Epilogue

*We are lyrical and musical creatures. Like the birds that plummet from the skies, and like the creatures that emerge from the bottom of the deep, we are more compatible with love, with a smile, with a flower*
~ Unknown author

The pursuit for seeing, understanding and accepting the world as it is, and yet exerting balance and actions for change, besides helping us situate ourselves at any historic moment, allows for a poetic expression that captures the complexity and multifaceted nature of perspectives and reality. When we make the extra effort to look at things from multiple aspects, it succinctly highlights how each story or situation is perceived from different viewpoints, each with its own version of events or understanding. It is as comforting as it is crucial to find out that beneath these layers of perception and interpretation lies the truth, often elusive and objective, waiting to be uncovered or agreed upon. This notion serves as a reminder of the importance of seeking out and understanding multiple frameworks of reference to get closer to the real essence of any story or event, especially our own.

One of the topics of this literary work is the allusion of humans elevated and projected to godlike status, whether for opportunistic motives or through exploitation and manipulation of nature and our fellow beings. It is a reflection of what happens in many parts of the world and one that ought to have no place in modern times. It is as complex an issue as it is timely to move beyond such practices and mindsets. As earthbound souls, we have the choice to recognize our connection with nature and each other, rather than asserting dominion over them. It is time to acknowledge and exert our responsibility to coexist more harmoniously with the planet and its inhabitants, leaving behind the hubris of considering ourselves as superior, exceptional beings, and in some situations, sometimes even bordering messianic daydreaming.

As we navigate in the sea of possibilities, we open ourselves to capturing a profound realization that many people come to at various points in their lives. It speaks to the essence of humility, of being fully present in the moment, of appreciating the simple joys, and of recognizing the intrinsic value of life beyond the pursuit of goals and achievements. This perspective invites a shift from seeking external validation or trying to impose a predefined structure on life, to embracing a more fluid, intuitive approach to living.

In acknowledging that life doesn't have to be about fulfilling a set purpose or ticking off items on a checklist all the time, we can choose to highlight the beauty of experiencing life as it unfolds, in all its intricacy and yet simplicity. This mindset fosters a deeper appreciation for the 'now,' the richness of human connections, and the small wonders that daily life offers. It's a call to uncomplicate one's heart and mind from the societal pressures and expectations that often weigh us down, allowing space for authenticity, growth, and peace.

This perspective doesn't negate the value of ideals or planning one's present and future; rather, it balances these with a grounded sense of being, encouraging individuals to find meaning and joy in the journey itself, not just the finish line. It reminds us that amidst life's inevitable challenges and uncertainties, there lies a continuous opportunity to find contentment, to give and receive love, and to engage with the world in a way that is true to one's self.

Embracing this viewpoint can lead to a more fulfilling, enriched life, where the emphasis shifts from what we are striving to achieve to who we are becoming in the process. It encourages a celebration of life in its entirety, with an openness to the myriad experiences it offers, fostering a sense of gratitude and wonder for the very act of living.

# Double-Edged

Once more, it is compelling to tap into Fernando Pessoa's vision. Writer, literary critic, translator, publisher, and philosopher, he is one of the most significant literary figures of the 20th century and one of the greatest poets in the Portuguese language. His words reflect his recognition of the ambivalence in our humanity. Truly a philosophical standing, the poet emphasizes neither to do good nor evil; he invites a contemplation of ethical humbleness and the realization of our limitations in fully understanding the impact of our actions.

"I have a very simple morality: not to do good or evil to anyone. Not to do evil, because it seems only fair that others enjoy the same right I demand for myself— not to be disturbed— and also because I think that the world doesn't need more than the natural evils it already has. All of us in this world are living on board a ship that is sailing from one unknown port to another, and we should treat each other with a traveler's cordiality. Not to do good, because I don't know what good is, nor even if I do it when I think I do." His reflection is profound: "How do I know what evils I produce if I teach or instruct? Not knowing, I refrain. And besides, I think that to help or clarify is, in a certain way, to commit the evil of interfering in the lives of others. Kindness depends on a whim of our mood, and we have no right to make others the victims of our whims, however humane or kind-hearted they may be."

His words are to be seen from his contextual reality but yet they apply widely. They encourage a respectful distance that honors the autonomy of others, suggesting that perhaps the most profound way we can share this journey is by acknowledging our shared vulnerabilities and extending to each other a "traveler's cordiality," as he beautifully puts it. This perspective offers a valuable lens through which to navigate the complexities of a principled life, reminding us of the importance of intention, the variability of outcomes, and the dignity of restraint.

↔

# Right in the Middle

*What we are today comes from our thoughts of yesterday, and our present thoughts build our life of tomorrow. Our life is the creation of our mind.* ~ Buddha

The Middle Path, a fundamental concept in Buddhist philosophy, represents a balanced approach to life that avoids the extremes of self-indulgence and self-humiliation. At the core of this path is the cultivation of equanimity, a mental state of stability and composure undisturbed by experience of, or exposure to, emotions, pain, or other phenomena that may cause others to lose their perspective. This principle is deeply rooted in the understanding of the nature of existence, as characterized by impermanence, suffering, and the notion of non-self.

Chances are that it is in the middle, that place where it is not always comfortable to be, where legitimate love dwells. It is a place where love chooses to manifest. It speaks to the vast, often intangible space that exists within the continuum of human experience, where realities contrast. It's a rhythmical way of acknowledging that love doesn't reside in the extremes of life's black-and-white moments but rather flourishes in the nuanced, complex areas that lie between. This space encompasses the everyday moments, the seemingly mundane interactions, and the quiet, overlooked gestures that, collectively, form the essence of love.

In this context, love is not just a peak experience or a dramatic gesture; it is found in the shared laughter over an inside joke, in the comfort of a silent room with a loved one, in the innocent look of a child, in the wise words of the elderly; the understanding glance exchanged in a moment of shared struggle, and the countless small acts of kindness and compassion that fill the gaps of our lives. It's in the middle that love weaves itself into the fabric of our daily existence, binding us together in its subtle yet profound presence.

# Cheers Every Day, One By One

The sentiment 'so it ends as it begins' evokes a cyclical perspective on experiences, events, or even the broader scope of existence. This viewpoint can be reflective of various philosophical, spiritual, and literary interpretations, suggesting that in many aspects of life, there is a return to the origin after a journey or a cycle of events. It surely is and it implies a sense of fulfillment, renewal, or rebirth, resonating with themes of continuity, the link between beginnings and endings, and the cyclic nature of time and existence. Whether in the context of a personal journey, the unfolding of historical events, or the cycle of nature, it encompasses the essence of closure intertwined with the promise of a new beginning.

Gratitude, the sheer theme of this book, is the return to the origin. It calls us to remember where we come from, to recognize the forces that sustain us, and to acknowledge our place within the broader network of life. It becomes a transformative force, guiding us back to our most fundamental connections with ourselves, each other, and the universe at large. Gratitude closes the loop in the cycle of giving and receiving, creating a continuous flow that strengthens relationships, builds communities, and fosters a sense of belonging and unity.

For all of that, I'm every day grateful for the significant role that intelligent and innovative individuals play in society, emphasizing their contribution to the positive and healthy transformation of others' lives. Grateful for the presence and importance of people with remarkable intellectual and empathetic capabilities, creativity, and problem-solving skills, who use their talents not focused on personal gain but rather to effect change, improve conditions, and inspire progress within their communities and beyond. These brainiacs and fond creatures are parents, caregivers, adopters, educators, poets, artists, musicians, scientists, entrepreneurs, activists, or anyone whose actions and ideas lead to meaningful improvements in the world around them. Their impact underscores the value of intellect, innovation, and altruism in addressing challenges and enhancing the well-being of others.

If you've come this far reading this book, chances are you are one of the many wizards willing to stir the pot.

# Giving Thanks

Gratitude to you, reader, for the energy and dedication you put into nurturing your life and the life of others with kindness, purpose, and joy. Your commitment to living with compassion and understanding creates a ripple effect of positivity that touches those around you. Your sense of purpose infuses each day with meaning and direction, guiding you toward your goals and dreams. And your ability and curiosity to find joy in the simplest moments illuminates the path ahead, reminding us all of the beauty that surrounds us. Thank you for being a beacon of light and inspiration in this world.

Every day, I am thankful for your deliberate choice to adopt a mindset of patience and no-harm. Your faith in approaching life with balanced patience allows for greater understanding, empathy, and resilience in the face of challenges. By choosing to act without causing harm, you contribute to a more compassionate and peaceful world, starting with your own. Your mindful approach to interactions and decisions fosters harmony and positivity, benefiting not only yourself but also those around you. Kudos to you for embodying these qualities and making a positive difference every day.

Thanks to you for making the extra effort every day to understand and support your fellow human beings. For your compassion and willingness to listen and create a safe, wider space for others to share their joys and struggles. Your support and encouragement uplift those around you, providing a sense of connection and community. Your zest to understanding different perspectives promotes harmony and mutual respect. Thank you for sharing your strengths and for reaching out to the forces that produce countenance to one another in our paths to realization.

Every day, I extend my gratitude to you for taking care of yourself and for magnifying that care to those around you, and beyond. Your allegiance to self-care sets a powerful example, reminding us all of the importance of nurturing our own physical, mental, and emotional well-being. By respecting and prioritizing your own health and happiness, you are better equipped to care for others with compassion and strength. Your deliberation spreads outwards, touching the lives of those in your immediate circle and extending to the broader community. Thank you for being a source of love, care, and support for those next to you, and for making an optimal impact on the world around and beyond yourself.

My thanks to you for harnessing the higher spheres of music, art, science, and knowledge. Your dedication to these realms of human endeavor enriches our lives and expands our understanding of the world. Through music, you evoke emotions and stir the soul. Through art, you capture beauty and provoke thought. Through science, you seek to unravel the mysteries of the universe. Through knowledge, you enlighten and inspire. Your contributions to these disciplines elevate humanity and help leave a lasting legacy of ingenuity, discovery, and wonder. Thank you for your curiosity, passion, and creativity, and for your pursuit of excellence in these higher spheres of manifestation.

Every day, I appreciate your honest and conscientious attempt to choose your leaders wisely. Your thoughtful consideration and discernment in selecting those who lead us shape the course of our communities and societies. By electing and supporting leaders who pursue emotional intelligence, and embody temperance, truth, integrity, compassion, maturity, thoughtfulness, and competence, you set a high standard for governance and inspire positive change. Your commitment to becoming a leader yourself, or for seeking out genuine leaders who prioritize the common good and work for the benefit of all is a reflection of your dedication to creating a better world. Thank you for your conscientiousness and for being an advocate for authentic, responsible, and effective leadership.

My immense gratitude goes to you for understanding the urgency of embracing our planet with the same care and devotion as you do your nation. Your stewardship of the Earth, our shared home, reflects a deep sense of responsibility and love for the natural world. By recognizing the interconnectedness of all living beings and ecosystems, you honor the fragile balance of the blue dot. Your efforts to protect the environment, conserve resources, and promote sustainability, contribute to a healthier and more harmonious world for present and future generations. Thank you for your dedication to caring for our big blue marble and for recognizing that our well-being and that of all living creatures is intricately linked to the health of the Earth.

Every day, I give thanks to you for going the extra mile in attempting to capture what true love is. Your pursuit of understanding and embodying love in its purest form is a testament to your compassion and dedication to others, and to yourself in the first place. Whether it's in your relationships, your acts of kindness, or your expressions of empathy, you strive to embody the essence of love in all that you do. Your willingness to go above and beyond to nurture and cherish those around you is a reflection of your fair, generous spirit and capacity for unconditional care. Thank you for your efforts to cultivate and share true love, for it is through your actions that the world becomes a brighter and more meaningful place.

Lastly, my profound gratitude to you for navigating the nuances of life and death, war and peace, old and new, rich and poor, black and white, male and female, yin and yang, and everything in between. Your ability and attempt to travel these complexities with grace, empathy, and understanding is a testament to your wisdom and strength. In a world filled with diverse perspectives and experiences, you embrace the richness of inclusion and seek to erect bridges with compassion and respect. Your openness to learning and growing from these contrasts enriches not only your own life but also the lives of those around you. Thank you for embodying harmony amidst diversity and for embracing the full spectrum of our human experience.

# Afterword

As a result of this somewhat introspective journey, I like to think that I wrap up this canon with a sense of completion. Notwithstanding, I wonder whether this has effectively been an accomplishment or if it's just a drop in the ocean. I must say that I've tried to apply a reasonable level of exploration and awareness sought in navigating some of the complex themes of our times. In a world often marred by conflicts, polarization, and a barrage of negativity, I cannot ignore but to look for glimmering lights, seek discernment, bridge divides, and foster a deeper connection to the multitude of inspiring human experiences as an essential aspect of my existence.

In this journey, I've tried to underscore the importance of not just witnessing or acknowledging the countless realities that exist beyond our own comfort zones but to actively engage with them. It is through such engagement that we can hope to emerge from the echo chambers that confine us, challenging ourselves to grow, empathize, and contribute to a more nuanced and comprehensive grasp of the world around us.

Therefore, my deepest respect for those who are the true protagonists of these journeys.

One of my friends, an accomplished author, when filled in on what this book was about, made the observation that this was quite an ambitious project to tackle. I was surprised with the comment and couldn't think of an immediate exchange. I must admit that in the breadth of topics covered I've tried to use a reflective and open-minded approach. It surely served me as a reminder that the pursuit of knowledge is, in itself, a valuable objective in my view, and one that enriches not only our own lives but potentially the lives of others we touch along the way.

The real impact of any journey often unfolds in the days, months, and years that follow, as the seeds of understanding that are planted begin to influence our contributions to the world around us. My wish is that in navigating some of the complexities of our global landscape, this may become a milestone and a springboard for one's continued exploration, dialogue, and connection. And with that, making use of the metaphor, perhaps bring the entire ocean in a drop. The journey of understanding is ongoing, and each step taken enriches not only the individual embarking on it but also the collective canvas of our telluric adventure.

There isn't

anything

more adventurous

than

the truth.

~ Anonymous

# Acknowledgements—I

*And the seasons, they go round and round*
*And the painted ponies go up and down*
*We're captive on the carousel of time*
*We can't return, we can only look*
*Behind, from where we came*
*And go round and round and round, in the circle game*
"Circle Game" ~ Joni Mitchell, songwriter

Every Day (I Thank You) was already ninety percent completed when the episode you will learn about in the next pages took place. Before you are filled in, as I approach the transitional part of my existence into the unknown, there's a question that keeps on coming to my mind.

What's up with the concept of "lifetime"?

With a little research that suggests a more philosophical notion, "lifetime" can be described as "extending beyond the mere duration of an individual's life, delving into the qualitative aspects of existence and the human experience." Philosophers and sages often explore lifetime not just in terms of length—and here is where we typically get stuck—but in the richness of experiences, the evolution of the self, ethical living, and the pursuit of meaning within the finite bounds of human existence. Thus, lifetime is not merely a span to be measured but a screen on which the human condition is expressed, explored, and understood. It encapsulates the existential drama of being human, confronting limits, making choices, seeking meaning, and ultimately shaping one's essence over the course of life.

Popular wisdom says, "Life is like a box of chocolates: it's full of surprises." It's not an exaggeration to state that most of us love, or at least, appreciate eating chocolate. Using the analogy, as we breeze through our lives, or, as we savor the box, we like most of it but don't always care for the whole selection and invariably have to 'deal with the hand that's given to us,' reflected in the package. There are always those things that happen to us, or those chocolates that we would gladly give away—or simply leave them in the box, untouched. Without throwing the unfinished carton out, we wait until an occasion manifests before we get rid of it and go for the next one; or, we take a little longer to finish up the pack and occasionally end up eating even those we are not too fond of. To put into our life context, not everything that happens to us we truly enjoy or think is necessary for us to go through. Yet, we have no control of that and embracing the unknown becomes a skill to be tapped into.

## Nearly A Perfect Storm

This is one of those life experiences, or to be fair to the image, one of those chocolates that I would rather not have to taste.

Silvia and I had planned to help my extended family in caring for my ninety-four-year-old mother in our home country, Brazil, in 2024. Starting in March, the first of a three-time planned overseas travel effort; besides spending quality time with my mom, the purpose was to alleviate my sisters of the constant care required by our loving elderly one, now for a couple of years unable to fully live by herself. It is at the end of our undertaking that my wife and I would have to experience an unexpected quandary that would completely change the course of our journey.

In the dawn hours of the day preceding our overnight return flight home, my wife found me staggering and mumbling, a very unusual circumstance for a usually healthy guy like myself. Nervously aware of a potential undesired outcome, she immediately reached out to my sister Liliana and her husband Marco for help. Located a block away from my mother's apartment in São Paulo, they quickly took me to the hospital, suspecting I could be having a stroke.

Arriving at the hospital, after the expected uneasy check-in process and following a battery of tests, they were told the diagnosis was most likely a combination of meningitis and encephalitis. This is a condition that's usually caused by a virus, bacterium, parasite, or other microorganism. Out of nowhere, it's the inflammation of the brain and spinal cord membranes with symptoms such as confusion, lack of coordination, fatigue, muscle weakness, speech issues, possible hallucinations, and loss of consciousness.

Contrary to Silvia's expectation of spending just a few hours in the healthcare unit for a speedy treatment and release, my first-ever hospitalization turned into a fifteen-day ordeal. Rushed into the ICU, the doctors instantly initiated the treatment and medication process. Apparently stable, it took about eighteen hours for the virus, not bacteria thank God, to take a turn for the worse and gain control over my system. Typical of such bouts, my wife suddenly witnessed my upper body contorting in what was revealed to be a serious seizure. As a consequence, my body's oxygen levels dropped dramatically. Next, was that moment of fighting for one's life: avoiding cerebral hypoxia—when one's brain doesn't get enough oxygen—the major concern. With the symptoms showing disorientation, difficulty in communication, and the culminating seizure, this was a medical emergency that could be fatal or cause life-long brain damage if not tackled with the proper skill, speed and earnestness.

Followed by frantic attempts to keep the oxygen levels to the minimum required degree before becoming irreversibly damaging, preoxygenation—pumping oxygen before intubation—was implemented so that the body's oxygen reserves could reduce the risk of hypoxia during intubation. This is a common practice in emergency situations, recommended for all victims of this affliction as ventilation and intubation difficulties can be unpredictable.

Induced to coma, that traumatic experience, especially for my wife, who was next to me non-stop at my hospital bed, would last about five days. For Silvia, this was the toughest part of the experience since she could not fathom what the outcome would be for me.

## A Storm Turned Into Catharsis

"Doc, I need to get out of here!" I told the physician in charge of the ICU.

"Dude, you almost died!", the doctor shook his head, exasperated. "The treatment needs completion before I can release you!"

As I slowly returned to my senses, the worst was over. After my wife's initial euphoria that I was okay, she had a thousand questions: "Do you know where you are? Do you know your name? What's your mom's address? How old are your kids? What's twelve times seven?

What's your gmail address?"

Answers checked off correctly, Silvia sighed with relief. Had it not been for Silvia's diligence and clear perception that things could go haywire, the outcome could have had tragic consequences.

Though the danger of brain damage had been ruled out, a new consequence of the seizure came about: a four-part fractured shoulder as a result of the violent body twist while still in the hospital bed. Boy, when it rains it pours. The shoulder surgery would have to wait till we got back home.

Not meant to happen, it was not my time to go to the other side yet. Was I ready? I'm not sure I have an answer to that. One thing I'm sure of: Silvia saved my life more than once throughout the whole experience.

To my loving wife, to the one who holds my heart, my most profound gratitude for your love, support and immeasurable dedication throughout the entire recovery process—and beyond.

At five thousand miles away during the event, my deep appreciation to my children, Catherine Bianca, Giana and Eric; to Matthew Cioni and our granddaughter Emilia Maureen, and to Brendan McCormick for their support to Silvia and for backing one another; as well, for living days of uncertainty with encouragement and resilience.

# Acknowledgements—II

My deepest gratitude goes to my sister Liliana, her husband Marco, and their son Rene; to my sister Cristina for singing healing tunes by my hospital bed, and for spending critical hours at the hospital supporting my wife. And to my sister Silvia Regina, who made the extra effort to visit me in the hospital on my last day before release. And, of course, to Jeritza, my mom, for her ever graceful omnipresence and positive loving nature.

Deep gratitude goes to my great friend since kindergarten, Homero Horta Aquilino, an angel, who happens to be—amazingly—a neurosurgeon, and gave Silvia incredible support during the excruciating days and hours, ensuring with his wisdom and knowledge that the care provided by the hospital was fully appropriate.

My most sincere thankfulness to friends, colleagues and family, nearby and at a distance, for their unbelievable support during and after hospitalization: Eric Hart and the NPI Team, Mindy Wilson, Eric Whalen, Mike Tremitiere and the Unifi Team; Octavio, Alice and Caio Barollo, Ruy Mondolfo, Sergio and Yvonne Lima, Jessica Lima, Luciano and Sofia Ferraz, Luiza Ferraz, Omar and Catarina Alexandro, Helena and Elisa Wakim Moreno, Ben Russell, Matt, Genie and Peyton Eagens, James and Patricia Meade, Laura and Alberto Colirri, Sergio and Denise Alencar, Ricardo and Marta Carvalho, Georgeanne Baker, Maryanne Larkin, Sarah Chamberlain, Kim Kilbon, Ricardo and Ivani Wakim, Sandra and Ricardo Trentini, Sergio, Lucia, Paulo and Bob Wakim, Marcelo, Rodrigo and Marina Hamam, Gloria and Nico Lorenzo, Nicholas,

Alessandra and Gonzalo, Alessia and Antonia, Roosevelt, Wilneide, Rogerio, Rafael and Ricardo Hamam, Sergio Gallo, Arnaldo Werblowsky, Carlos Alberto Den Hartog, Almir Thales Gramani Jr., Eduardo Rottman, Cassio de Azevedo Marques, Nelson Lerner Barth, Milton Millioni, Peter Strotbek, Jose Emilio de Moraes, Sergio Caribe, Ronaldo Filet Fernandes, Ricardo Anauate, Jose Carlos Castillo, Victor Nemi, Ron Lewis, Luiz Eugenio Rubbo, Jatyr de Souza Filho, Betty Navin, Dorene Quesnel and Sue Mehrtens. Last but not least, to the entire hospital teams—physicians, nurses and caregivers, both in São Paulo and Burlington—for their invaluable help and care.

This book would not have been possible without the extraordinary work of art, love, and vision of these individuals: Pat Metheny, and Michael Brecker (in memoriam), for their timeless musical gift. Jan Riordan, Karyn Ross, Theresa A. Wood, Nikkie Kent, Sascha Mayer, Lili Udell Fiori, Abby Kenney, Kristina Stykos, Leah Mital, Beverly Little Thunder, Kaká Werá, Jiddu Krishnamurti, Melinda and Rick Moulton and Marianne Duquette Cuozzo. And Bill Mares (in memoriam), for his friendship and inspiration. Your efforts and actions toward building a more meaningful world, together with your exquisite and moving life stories, are true contributing inspirations for the writing of this literary work.

All my gratitude.

# Bibliography

Victor L. Wooten. *The Spirit of Music*, Vintage Books 2021.

Aldous Huxley. *Brave New World*, Chatto & Windus 1932.

Aldous Huxley. *Island, Chatto & Windus*, Harper & Brothers 1962.

Houston Kraft. *Deep Kindness—A Revolutionary Guide for the Way We Think, Talk, and Act in Kindness*, Simon & Schuster 2020.

Eric Weiner. *The Socrates Express—In Search of Life Lessons from Dead Philosophers*. Avid Reader Press 2020.

Seneca. *On the Shortness of Life: Life Is Long if You Know How to Use It*. Penguin, 2005.

Marcus Aurelius. *Meditations (Gregory Hays)*. Modern Library, 2003.

Maria Popova. *The Stoic Key to Kindness*. The Marginalian, 2022.

Karyn Ross. *The Kind Leader: A Practical Guide to Eliminating Fear, Creating Trust, and Leading with Kindness*. CRC Press, 2021.

Andrew Swinand. *Why Kindness at Work Pays Off*. Harvard Business Review, 2023.

Jonas Ressem. *How to Use Self-Talk to Build a Better Mindset*. Medium, 2021.

Hannah Arendt. *The Origins of Totalitarianism*. Meridian Books, 1962.

Luke Mogelson. *The Storm is Here: An American Crucible*. Penguin, 2022.

Joe Broadmeadow. *American Impatience: Blessing and Curse*. JEBWizard Publishing, 2020.

Alexandra V. *The Russians 'Endless Patience' and Why it Matters When it Breaks*. Foreign Policy Rising, 2017.

Manfred F. R. Kets de Vries. *The Cabin Fever Syndrome: Managing the Coronavirus*. INSEAD Knowledge, 2020.

John Kelly. *On the highway of life, maybe we should all be student drivers*. Washington Post, 2022.

Tony Bingham and Marcia Conner. *The New Social Learning: A Guide to Transforming Organizations Through Social Media*. Berrett-Koehler, 2010.

Molly Remer. *Breastfeeding as a Spiritual Practice. Restoration Earth: An Interdisciplinary Journal for the Study of Nature & Civilization*, Author's Blog, 2012.

Lana Hallowes. *From Mongolia to Italy: How breastfeeding differs around the world*. Babyology, 2012.

Amy Bentley. *Inventing Baby Food: Taste, Health, and the Industrialization of the American Diet*. University of California Press, 2014.

Maureen Shaw. *Shame No More Series. America's sexualization of breasts is so pervasive even other women think public breastfeeding is gross*. Quartz, 2016.

Karlee Vincent. *Pump or Bust: A New Mama's Guide to Office Politics, Breast Health, and Pumping on the Road!* Praeclarus Press, 2023.

Jean Watson. *Nursing: The Philosophy and Science of Caring.* University Press of Colorado, 2008.

Lili Udell Fiore. *Lili's Caregiver's Guide.* Balboa Press, 2023.

Angelique Chan. *Asian countries do Aged Care differently.* The Conversation, University of Singapore, 2020.

Jonathan Pevsner. *The Mind of Leonardo Da Vinci.* Scientific American, 2019.

Kristina Stykos. *Ridgerunner: One hundred poems and photographs from rural Vermont.* ShiresPress, 2019.

Eric Dorfman. *Art, Science and The Intersection of Knowledge.* Carnegie Museum of Natural History, 2020.

Michael White. *Leonardo: The First Scientist.* St. Martin's Press, 2000.

Steve Wall. *To Become a Human Being: The Message of Tadodaho Chief Leon Shenandoah.* Hampton Roads Publishing, 2002.

Grey Owl . *The Men of the Last Frontier.* Reading Essentials, 2019.

Edward Osborne Wilson. *Consilience: The Unity of Knowledge.* Vintage, 1999.

Rachel Carlson. *Silent Spring.* Mariner Books Classics; Anniversary edition, 2022.

Yvonne Wakim Dennis, Arlene Hirschfelder. *Children of Native America Today Charlesbridge*, Reprint edition, 2014.

United Nations, *Climate Change. How Indigenous Peoples Enrich Climate Action*, 2022

Rosanne Greco and Chief Don Stevens. *Respect for Nature will be Our Spiritual Salvation*. The Other Paper, 2022.

Beverly Little Thunder. *One Bead at a Time*. Inanna Memoir Series, 2016.

Davi Kopenawa, Bruce Albert. *The Falling Sky: Words of a Yanomami Shaman*. Belknap Press: An Imprint of Harvard University Press; 2nd edition, 2023.

Kaká Werá. *A terra dos mil povos: História indígena do Brasil contada por um índio (Portuguese Edition)*. Editora Peirópolis, 2020.

Fernando Pessoa. *The Book of Disquiet*. Penguin Classics, 2002.

Joseph Campbell, Diane K. Osbon. *Reflections on the Art of Living: A Joseph Campbell Companion*. Harper Perennial; Reprint edition, 1995.

Jiddu Krishnamurti. *Total Freedom: The Essential Krishnamurti*. HarperOne; First Edition, 1996.

Steven Nadler. *Spinoza A Life*. Cambridge University Press; 2nd edition, 2022.

Alejandro Betancourt. *The Paradox of Human Nature: Why We Are All Walking Contradictions*. A Substack's

*Newsletter publication*, "Beyond Two Cents.", 2022.

David Berliner. *How our contradictions make us human and inspire creativity*. Aeon, 2016.

R. Douglas Fields. *The Roots of Human Aggression*. Scientific American, 2016.

Scott Galloway. *Adrift: America in 100 Charts*. Portfolio, 2022

Leo Tolstoy. *War and Peace*. Vintage Classics, 2008.

William F. Ryan. *Culture, Spirituality, and Economic Development*. Opening a Dialogue. IDRC, 1995.

E. F. Schumacher. *Small Is Beautiful: Economics as if People Mattered*. Harper Perennial Modern Thought, 2010.

Paul McCartney. *Blackbird Singing: Poems and Lyrics, 1965-1999*. W. W. Norton & Company, 2002

Isabel Wilkerson. *Caste: The Origins of Our Discontents*. Random House, 2020.

Rebecca Joy Stanborough. *How Black and White Thinking Hurts You (and What You Can Do to Change It)*. Healthline, 2020.

Nobieh Kiani. *Dance of No Name: A Beautiful Journey Within... the Art of Expressing Your True Self and Dance Your Authentic Being, a Wonderful Way to Celebrate Your Uniqueness*. Balboa Press, 2020.

Joshua Askew. *Explained: Why the Islamic headscarf is crucial in Iranian society*. Euronews.culture, 2023.

Farnaz Fassihi. *Their Hair Long and Flowing or in Ponytails, Women in Iran Flaunt Their Locks.* The New York Times, 2023.

Nathan Bomey. Bridge Builders: *Bringing People Together in a Polarized Age.* Polity, 2021.

Printed in the USA
CPSIA information can be obtained
at www.ICGtesting.com
CBHW021835091024
15572CB00015B/1045